Beginner's
JAPANESE

Beginner's
JAPANESE

Joanne R. Claypoole
edited by
Emiko Hara

HIPPOCRENE BOOKS
New York

For information, address:
HIPPOCRENE BOOKS, INC.
171 Madison Avenue
New York, NY 10016

ISBN 0-7818-0234-2

Printed in the United States of America.

ACKNOWLEDGEMENTS

There are many people I wish to thank for their invaluable input on this project. Thank you Emiko Hara, Eiko Imai, Tokuichiro Oku, and Nobutaka Oku for helping make the Japanese accurate and natural. Thank you Hallie Bandy for your encouragement, advice, and design ideas. Michele Moncrief, thank you for being so helpful and for putting the layout ideas into something real. Thanks Bob Arnold for your creative input and enthusiasm. Thank you so much to my mother, Kathy, and sister, Sally - I would have never started this had it not been for you. Most of all, thank you to my Heavenly Father, for things are possible through you.

I would like to dedicate this book to my Japanese instructor and friend, who has taught me much more than just language. This book is for you, Michiko Hirakawa, my "ichiban ii sensei."

TABLE OF CONTENTS

INTRODUCTION

"You want to study Japanese? Isn't that one of the most difficult languages to learn?" **NO**.

Believe it or not, learning Japanese is not as hard as you might think. While learning a language is an ongoing process, it generally takes the average Japanese person five to eight years to become fluent English, while only two to three years for an English-speaking individual to become proficient in Japanese.

PURPOSE OF THIS BOOK

This book is designed to equip the learner with a solid foundation of Japanese conversation. As with many languages, Japanese contains various levels of social language; this book will focus on language that is acceptable to all Japanese individuals.

This text provides the foundation for a strong grasp of Japanese conversation and grammar structure, and the skills to read Hiragana and Katakana, two of the Japanese phonetic alphabets.

BOOK STRUCTURE

DIALOGUES

Dialogues are written in Hiragana and Katakana, followed by Romaji, and translated into English. Try to read Hiragana and Katakana as often as possible. Practice dialogues with another partner, preferably a Japanese person. The dialogues are based on every-day conversations.

VOCABULARY

New vocabulary words are introduced in each dialogue, and are defined in each chapter. Additional words taught in the lesson are included. Memorize all vocabulary words and note the usage of each word in sentences.

COLUMNS

Special notes are located in columns on the right pages of each chapter. This section explains complex words, phrases, or articles. It also includes cultural information and other helpful tips.

GRAMMAR EXPLANATION

New grammar concepts will be explained in this area. Examples are given for clarification.

EXERCISES

In this section, you will practice drills to develop vocabulary and grammar skills. It is important to master this section before moving to the next lesson because the lessons build on each other.

SHORT DIALOGUES

Short dialogues are given for practice in every-day conversations, so you can easily adapt to a conversation when words or phrases are slightly changed.

SELF-TEST

This section is for you to test yourself and make sure you understand the words and concepts in the lesson. Answers are located after lesson 25.

DIFFERENCES BETWEEN JAPANESE AND ENGLISH

• Most Japanese books and newspapers read from top to bottom, right to left.

• The Japanese do not put spaces between words or characters.

• Verb conjugation is the same regardless of gender, number, or the person of subject. This reduces much difficulty in learning the language.

• Plurals are rarely used in Japanese.

• Japanese adjectives are changed to reflect past tense and negatives.

• There is no future tense in Japanese.

• Japanese people generally speak in a monotonous tone, rarely fluctuating their voices.

JAPANESE WRITING AND PRONUNCIATION

The Japanese have 3 methods of writing. They are *Hiragana, Katakana*, and *Kanji. Romaji*, Japanese characters translated into the English alphabet, was created by Americans shortly after World War 2.

HIRAGANA is a phonetic alphabet that is taught to Japanese students in Kindergarten. The name of each letter is the same as the pronunciation of that letter, unlike English, where the names of letters sometimes sound different from their pronunciation.

KATAKANA is also a phonetic alphabet that is used for foreign words. For example, words like *McDonald's, elevator*, and *Christmas* would be written in Katakana. The Japanese have a separate alphabet for foreign words so that they can pronounce them with greater ease.

KANJI are Chinese characters. They do not represent sounds, but pictures. For example, 木 stands for tree.

If one learns to write Kanji, he or she will be able to communicate with Chinese individuals in writing.

ROMAJI is Japanese words written with the English alphabet. This is rarely found in literature or newspapers, and is mostly used by English speaking people.

•Hiragana, Katakana, and Kanji are often used together in one sentence:

I ate ice cream.	私は	アイス クリームを	食べました。
Hiragana -	は	を	べました。
Katakana -		アイス クリーム	
Kanji -	私		食

HIRAGANA

Once this phonetic alphabet is mastered, one can speak any word in Japanese with native-like pronunciation. Unlike English letters, Japanese characters represent one sound only (with the exception of *n*). Further, every sound used in Hiragana, and therefore every sound in the Japanese language, is one familiar to English speaking individuals. This makes pronunciation quite easy!

Each character receives an equal beat in each word.

あ **A**　　　pronounced like the **a** in *water*

い **I**　　　sounds like the **e** in *feet*

う **U**　　　like the **u** in *flute*, with the lips spread instead of rounded

え **E**　　　is like the **e** sound in *egg*

お **O**　　　pronounced like the **o** in *ghost*

•**I** and **U** are often voiceless when preceded by **k**, **t**, **p**, **s**, **shi**, **h**, or **f**.

A, **I**, **U**, **E**, and **O** keep the same sound when paired with a consonant.

か **KA**　　き **KI**　　く **KU**　　け **KE**　　こ **KO**
The **k** sound in Japanese is the same as English.

が **GA**　　ぎ **GI**　　ぐ **GU**　　げ **GE**　　ご **GO**
G also is no different from the English **g** as used in the word *get*.

さ **SA**　　し **SHI**　　す **SU**　　せ **SE**　　そ **SO**
Shi is pronounced the same as the English word **she**. The remaining consonants are like the English sounding **s**.

さ **ZA** 　　じ **JI** 　　ず **ZU** 　　ぜ **ZE** 　　ぞ **ZO**

The **z** consonant in Japanese is like the **z** in *zoo*. The consonant in **ji** is pronounced like the **j** in joke.

た **TA** 　　ち **CHI** 　　つ **TSU** 　　て **TE** 　　と **TO**

The **t** in Japanese is similar to the **t** in English. **Chi** is pronounced like **chee** in *cheese,* but without extending the vowel sound. **Tsu** is a familiar sound to English speaking people. It is used in the word *Mitsubishi*.

だ **DA** 　　で **DE** 　　ど **DO**

The **d** sound is the same as in English. **Di** and **du** do not exist in Japanese.

な **NA** 　　に **NI** 　　ぬ **NU** 　　ね **NE** 　　の **NO**

The initial sounds in these syllables are the same **n** sound as English.

は **HA** 　　ひ **HI** 　　ふ **FU** 　　へ **HE** 　　ほ **HO**

The **h** sound is not as forced in Japanese as English, but otherwise sounds the same. The pronunciation of **f** sounds like a combination of the English **h** and **f**. The lips do not touch the teeth. The sound is similar to that of one blowing out a candle, though not as strong. The lips are slightly parted without being rounded.

ば **BA** 　　び **BI** 　　ぶ **BU** 　　べ **BE** 　　ぼ **BO**

The **b** sound is the same as the English **b**.

ぱ **PA** 　　ぴ **PI** 　　ぷ **PU** 　　ぺ **PE** 　　ぽ **PO**

P is pronounced like the English **p**, using a little less force.

ま **MA**   み **MI**   む **MU**   め **ME**   も **MO**

The initial sounds in these syllables are the same as the English **m.**

や **YA**   ゆ **YU**   よ **YO**

The same as the English **y.**

ら **RA**   り **RI**   る **RU**   れ **RE**   ろ **RO**

The **r** sound in Japanese is between an English **l** and **r.** The tongue quickly touches the top of the mouth just behind the teeth.

わ **WA**

The **w** sound is similar to the English **w,** but more relaxed.

ん **N**

This sound varies, depending on where it is located within a word.

- Preceding *b, p,* or *m,* it is pronounced **m** like in *may.*

- Preceding *z, t, d,* or *n,* it is pronounced **n** like in *new.*

- Preceding *k, g,* or *n*(ん), it is pronounced **ng** like in *sing,* without hearing the final **g** sound.

•**YA, YU, AND YO** can replace *i* after all consonants that are paired with an *i.*

きゃ **KYA**   きゅ **KYU**   きょ **KYO**

ぎゃ **GYA**   ぎゅ **GYU**   ぎょ **GYO**

しゃ **SHA**   しゅ **SHU**   しょ **SHO**

じゃ **JA**　　じゅ **JU**　　じょ **JO**

ちゃ **CHA**　　ちゅ **CHU**　　ちょ **CHO**

にゃ **NYA**　　にゅ **NYU**　　にょ **NYO**

ひゃ **HYA**　　ひゅ **HYU**　　ひょ **HYO**

びゃ **BYA**　　びゅ **BYU**　　びょ **BYO**

ぴゃ **PYA**　　ぴゅ **PYU**　　ぴょ **PYO**

みゃ **MYA**　　みゅ **MYU**　　みょ **MYO**

りゃ **RYA**　　りゅ **RYU**　　りょ **RYO**

DOUBLE VOWELS

Vowel sounds are never blended. If two of the same vowels occur successively, simply extend the vowel an additional beat.

おばさん　obasan (aunt)

おばあさん obaasan (grandmother)

DOUBLE CONSONANTS

When a small っ appears in a word, the consonant directly after it receives an extra beat. Do not repeat the consonant twice; pause briefly before saying the consonant.

いた　　ita (exist)

いった　itta (went)

PARTICLES

は **WA**　　denotes subject

を **O**　　follows objects

へ **E**　　indicates direction

STUDY HINTS

• Try to study a little every day. You will learn much more this way than if you studied for long periods of time inconsistently.

• Try to meet with a Japanese person or fluent Japanese speaker at least once a week.

• Do not move on to the next lesson until you have mastered the current one.

• Remember the correct pronounciation; do not deviate from it.

• Try to incorporate Japanese words into your daily life. Speak and think in Japanese as much as possible.

Ganbatte Kudasai!

Good Luck!

HIRAGANA

あ	**A**	い	**I**	う	**U**	え	**E**	お	**O**
か	**KA**	き	**KI**	く	**KU**	け	**KE**	こ	**KO**
さ	**SA**	し	**SHI**	す	**SU**	せ	**SE**	そ	**SO**
た	**TA**	ち	**CHI**	つ	**TSU**	て	**TE**	と	**TO**
な	**NA**	に	**NI**	ぬ	**NU**	ね	**NE**	の	**NO**
は	**HA**	ひ	**HI**	ふ	**FU**	へ	**HE**	ほ	**HO**
ま	**MA**	み	**MI**	む	**MU**	め	**ME**	も	**MO**
や	**YA**			ゆ	**YU**			よ	**YO**
ら	**RA**	り	**RI**	る	**RU**	れ	**RE**	ろ	**RO**
わ	**WA**							を	**O**
が	**GA**	ぎ	**GI**	ぐ	**GU**	げ	**GE**	ご	**GO**
ざ	**ZA**	じ	**JI**	ず	**ZU**	ぜ	**ZE**	ぞ	**ZO**
だ	**DA**	ぢ	**JI**	づ	**ZU**	で	**DE**	ど	**DO**
ば	**BA**	び	**BI**	ぶ	**BU**	べ	**BE**	ぼ	**BO**
ぱ	**PA**	ぴ	**PI**	ぷ	**PU**	ぺ	**PE**	ぽ	**PO**

きゃ	**KYA**	きゅ	**KYU**	きょ	**KYO**
しゃ	**SHA**	しゅ	**SHU**	しょ	**SHO**
ちゃ	**CHA**	ちゅ	**CHU**	ちょ	**CHO**
にゃ	**NYA**	にゅ	**NYU**	にょ	**NYO**
ひゃ	**HYA**	ひゅ	**HYU**	ひょ	**HYO**
みゃ	**MYA**	みゅ	**MYU**	みょ	**MYO**
りゃ	**RYA**	りゅ	**RYU**	りょ	**RYO**
ぎゃ	**GYA**	ぎゅ	**GYU**	ぎょ	**GYO**
じゃ	**JA**	じゅ	**JU**	じょ	**JO**
びゃ	**BYA**	びゅ	**BYU**	びょ	**BYO**
ぴゃ	**PYA**	ぴゅ	**PYU**	ぴょ	**PYO**
ん	**N**				

KATAKANA

ア A	イ I	ウ U	エ E	オ O
カ KA	キ KI	ク KU	ケ KE	コ KO
サ SA	シ SHI	ス SU	セ SE	ソ SO
タ TA	チ CHI	ツ TSU	テ TE	ト TO
ナ NA	ニ NI	ヌ NU	ネ NE	ノ NO
ハ HA	ヒ HI	フ FU	ヘ HE	ホ HO
マ MA	ミ MI	ム MU	メ ME	モ MO
ヤ YA		ユ YU		ヨ YO
ラ RA	リ RI	ル RU	レ RE	ロ RO
ワ WA				ヲ O
ガ GA	ギ GI	グ GU	ゲ GE	ゴ GO
ザ ZA	ジ JI	ズ ZU	ゼ ZE	ソ ZO
ダ DA	ジ JI	ツ ZU	デ DE	ド DO
バ BA	ビ BI	ブ BU	ベ BE	ボ BO
バ PA	ピ PI	プ PU	ペ PE	ポ PO
キャ KYA		キュ KYU		キョ KYO
シャ SHA		シュ SHU		ショ SHO
チャ CHA		チュ CHU		チョ CHO
ニャ NYA		ニュ NYU		ニョ NYO
ヒャ HYA		ヒュ HYU		ヒョ HYO
ミャ MYA		ミュ MYU		ミョ MYO
リャ RYA		リュ RYU		リョ RYO
ギャ GYA		ギュ GYU		ギョ GYO
ジャ JA		ジュ JU		ジョ JO
ビャ BYA		ビュ BYU		ビョ BYO
ピャ PYA		ピュ PYU		ピョ PYO
ン N				

LESSON ONE
IMA NANJI DESU-KA

In this lesson you will learn:

- Basic sentence formation
- How to tell time
- Numbers one through one hundred

DIALOGUE

A: すみません。　とけいを　もって　いますか.
B: はい.
A: いま　なんじ　ですか.
B: はちじ　はん　です.
A: ありがとう　ございます.
B: どう　いたしまして.

たなか:　　　ジョンソンさん　あなたの　でんわ　ばんごうを
　　　　　おしえて　ください.
ジョンソン:　はい。　わたしの　でんわ　ばんごうは　ろく
　　　　　に　いちの　きゅう　なな　ご　さん　です.
たなか:　　　ありがとう　ございます.

A: *Sumimasen, tokei-o motte imasu-ka.*

A: Excuse me, do you have a watch?

B: *Hai.*

B: Yes.

A: *Ima nanji desu-ka.*

A: What time is it?

B: *Hachiji-han desu.*

B: It is eight thirty.

A: *Arigatoo gozaimasu.*

A: Thank you very much.

B: *Doo itashimashite.*

B: You are welcome.

II

Tanaka: *Jonson-san, anata-no denwa bangoo-o oshiete kudasai.*

Tanaka: Mr. Johnson, please tell me your telephone number.

Jonson: *Hai. Watashi-no denwa bangoo-wa roku ni ichi no kyuu nana go san desu.*

Johnson: Sure. My telephone number is 621-9753.

T: *Arigatoo gozaimasu.*

T: Thank you very much.

GRAMMAR EXPLANATION

1. Wa

Wa is always added to the subject of every sentence. However, in the Hiragana alphabet, one does not use the symbol わ , instead は is used.

> ex. *Tookyoo-**wa** ima roku-ji desu.*
> In Tokyo, it is 6:00.

The basic sentence structure in Japanese is:

> Subject-***wa*** object verb.

2. Ka

Ka changes a sentence from a statement to a question. It is used at the end of a sentence.

> ex. *Yoji desu.*　　　It is 4:00.
> *Yoji desu-**ka**.*　　Is it 4:00?

3. Nani

Nani means "what." *Nani* can be combined with the word following it by dropping the final *i*. For example, "What is it?" in Japanese is said ***nan**desu-ka*, or "what time?" becomes ***nan**ji*.

4. Ban

To state "number one, number two," etc., combine the number with *ban*.

> ex. *ichi**ban***　　　number one
> *ni**ban***　　　　number two

3

anata
you

arigatoo
thank you

asa
morning

ban
number

denwa
telephone

**denwa
bangoo**
telephone
number

desu
is

**doo
itashimashite**
you are
welcome

**doomo
arigatoo**
thank you
very much

gogo
p.m.

gozen
a.m.

hai
yes

han
half

iie
no

ima
now

EXERCISES

1. Memorize numbers 1 - 12:

1	-	*ichi*	7	-	*shichi, nana*
2	-	*ni*	8	-	*hachi*
3	-	*san*	9	-	*kyuu, ku*
4	-	*shi, yon*	10	-	*juu*
5	-	*go*	11	-	*juuichi*
6	-	*roku*	12	-	*juuni*

2. Add *ji* to each number to express the time:

ex. 1:00 - *ichiji*; 2:00 - *niji*; etc.

1:00 -	7:00 -
2:00 -	8:00 -
3:00 -	9:00 -
4:00 -	10:00 -
5:00 -	11:00 -
6:00 -	12:00 -

3. Add *ji* and *han* to each number to express half-past:

ex. 1:30 - *ichiji-han*; 2:30 - *niji-han*

1:30 -	7:30 -
2:30 -	8:30 -
3:30 -	9:30 -

4

4:30 -	10:30 -
5:30 -	11:30 -
6:30 -	12:30 -

Yo, Ku
When telling
time, use *yo* for
4 and *ku* for 9.

4. Use each number in a sentence to state what time it is:

ex. 1:00, 1:30
➡*Ima ichiji desu.*
➡*Ima ichiji-han desu.*

1:00 -	7:00 -
2:30 -	8:30 -
3:00 -	9:00 -
4:30 -	10:30 -
5:00 -	11:00 -
6:30 -	12:30 -

Ji
In English,
"o'clock" is only
said when
referring to a
time directly on
the hour.
However, in
Japanese, *ji* is
always used
whenever telling
time after the
hour is stated,
then *han* or the
minutes are
said

5. Practice saying "The party's from _____ until _____," by substituting the times found below into the underlined sections:

ex. 4:00, 6:00

➡ *Paatii-wa* **4:00** *kara* **6:00** *made desu.*

2:00, 5:00	1:00, 10:00	7:00, 8:00
11:00, 3:00	12:00, 2:00	9:00, 11:00
3:00, 6:00	4:00, 7:00	5:00, 10:00

ji
time

-ka
added to the
end of
sentences to
form a
question

kara
from

kudasai
please

made
until

motte imasu
have, carry

nani
what

-no
shows
possession

-o
denotes
sentence
object

**oshiete
kudasai**
please tell
me, please
teach me

paatii
party

soo desu
that's right

sumimasen
excuse me

6. Memorize numbers 13 - 20:

13-*juusan*	16-*juuroku*	19-*juuku*
14-*juushi*	17-*juushichi*	20-*nijuu*
15-*juugo*	18-*juuhachi*	

7. Learn the multiples of 10:

10-*juu*	40-*yonjuu*	70-*shichijuu, nanajuu*
20-*nijuu*	50-*gojuu*	80-*hachijuu*
30-*sanjuu*	60-*rokujuu*	90-*kyuujuu*
		100-*hyaku*

8. Numbers 21 through 99:

21-*nijuuichi*	30-*sanjuu*
22-*nijuuni*	31-*sanjuuichi*. . .
23-*nijuusan*	41-*yonjuuichi*. . .
24-*nijuushi*	51-*gojuuichi*. . .
25-*nijuugo*	61-*rokujuuichi*. . .
26-*nijuuroku*	71-*shichijuuichi*. . .
27-*nijuushichi*	81-*hachijuuichi*. . .
28-*nijuuhachi*	91-*kyuujuuichi*. . .
29-*nujuuku*	99-*kyuujuuku*

SHORT DIALOGUES

Practice these dialogues changing the underlined words:

1. On the street

No
When saying a telephone number, use *no* when stating where the dash belongs.

ex. sanji-han

    Excuse me now what time is?

    Sumisu: Sumimasen, ima nanji desu-ka.
    Tanaka: Ima **sanji-han** desu. *It is 3:30*
    Sumisu: **Sanji-han** desu-ka. *3:30?*
    Tanaka: Soo desu. *that's right*
    Sumisu: Arigatoo gozaimasu. *thank you*
    Tanaka: Doo itashimashite. *you're welcome.*

    1. rokuji   4. ichiji-han
    2. juuichiji-han   5. goji-han
    3. hachiji

2. At a meeting in New York

ex. rokuji-han, gogo, yoru

    what time is it in Tokyo?

    Sumisu: Tookyoo-wa ima nanji desu-ka.
    Tanaka: **Rokuji-han** desu. *6:30 now*
    Sumisu: **Gogo rokuji han** desu-ka. *p: 6:30 p.m?*
    Tanaka: Hai, soo desu. Tookyoo-wa ima **yoru** desu. *Yes that's right. It is night now.*

    1. goji, gozen, asa   *a.m morning*
    2. hachiji-han, gogo, yoru   *night*
    3. kuji, gogo, yoru
    4. shichiji-han, gozen, asa
    5. juuji, gogo, yoru

tokei
watch, clock

Tookyoo
Tokyo

-wa
denotes
subject

watashi
I, me

yoru
night

SELF-TEST

Translate the following sentences into Japanese:

1. Excuse me, what time is it?

2. The party is from 6:00 until 11:00.

3. Thank you very much.

4. My phone number is 251-9643.

5. Now it is 12:30 a.m.

6. What time is it in Tokyo?

7. It is morning in Tokyo.

8. It is evening in Tokyo.

9. Is it 3:00 p.m.?

10. That's right.

1. Sumimasen, ima nanji-desu ka.
2. Paatii-wa rokuji kara juuichiji made desu.
3. ~~Doomo~~ arigatoo gozaimasu.
watashi-no 4. Denwa bangoo ~~wa~~ ni go ichi ~~kyuu~~ roku no
shi yon san. desu.

5. Ima gozen juniji-han ~~desu~~ desu.

LESSON TWO
IKURA DESU-KA

In this lesson you will learn:

- How to ask for an object
- The days of the week
- The months of the year
- The multiples of one thousand

DIALOGUE

スミス： すみません． あの セーターは いくら
です か．

てんいん： どちらの セーター ですか．

スミス： あれ です．

てんいん： ああ． あの セーターは きゅうせん えん
です．

スミス： そう ですか． この セーターも きゅうせん
えん ですか．

てんいん： いいえ． その セータは はっせん えん
です．

スミス： これを ください．

てんいん： はい． ありがとう ございます．

Sumisu: *Sumimasen. Ano seetaa-wa ikura desu-ka.*

Smith: Excuse me. How much is that sweater?

Ten'in: *Dochira-no seetaa desu-ka.*

Clerk: Which sweater is it?

S: *Are desu.*

S: That one.

T: *Aa. Ano seetaa-wa kyuusen en desu.*

C: Oh. That sweater is 9,000 yen.

S: *Soo desu-ka. Kono seetaa-mo kyuusen en desu-ka.*

S: Really. Is this sweater also 9,000 yen?

T: *Iie. Sono seetaa-wa hassen en desu.*

C: No. That sweater is 8,000 yen.

S: *Kore-o kudasai.*

S: I'd like this please.

T: *Hai. Arigatoo gozaimasu.*

C: Thank you very much.

GRAMMAR EXPLANATION
1. Kore, kono

Kore refers to an object that is close to the speaker. It is usually followed by *wa*, *mo*, or *o* because it is always the subject or object of the sentence.

> *ex.* **Kore-wa** *pen desu.*
> This is a pen.
>
> **Kore-o** *kudasai.*
> I'll take this, please.

Kono has the same meaning as *kore*, but is always paired with a noun.

> *ex.* **Kono pen**-*wa yasui desu.*
> This pen is cheap.

2. Sore, sono

Sore and *sono* refer to objects that are close to the listener. They have the same grammar structure as *kore* and *kono*; *sore* is followed by *wa*, *mo*, or *o*, and *sono* is always paired with a noun.

> *ex.* **Sore-wa** *tokei desu.*
> It is a watch.
>
> **Sono tokei**-*wa ookii desu.*
> That watch is big.

Prices
To state the price of an item, simply state the cost + *en. ex. juu* **en** (10 yen)

Yo
Yo is added at the end of a sentence when the speaker is telling the learner something that the learner probably did not know. *ex. Kore-wa nandesu-ka. Sore-wa tokei desu yo.* What is this? It's a clock (I'm informing you).

11

ano
that (with noun)

are
that

ashita
tomorrow

chigaimasu
is different, wrong

chiisai(i)
small

dochira
which one; choice of two

dono
which one(s), choice of three or more (with noun)

dore
which one(s), choice of three or more

en
yen

-ga
indicates subject or object

ikura
how much

kinoo
yesterday

kono
this (with noun)

3. Are, ano

Are and *ano* are objects that are far from both the speaker and listener. They are used in the same grammatical patterns as *kore* and *kono*.

> ex. **Are-o** *kudasai.*
> I'll take that please.

> **Ano zubon**-*wa ikura desu-ka.*
> How much are those pants?

4. Dore, dono

Dore and *dono* mean "which one(s)" when there are three or more items to choose from. *Dore* is used as the subject or object of the sentence, and *dono* is always paired with a noun.

> ex. **Dore-ga** *anata-no desu-ka.*
> Which one is yours?

> **Dono wanpiisu**-*ga anata-no desu-ka.*
> Which dress is yours?

EXERCISES
1. Days of the week:

Sunday	*nichi yoobi*
Monday	*getsu yoobi*
Tuesday	*ka yoobi*
Wednesday	*sui yoobi*

Thursday	*moku yoobi*
Friday	*kin yoobi*
Saturday	*do yoobi*

The past form of
desu is **deshita**.

2. Months in a year

The months are quite easy to learn. Simply state the number of each month (January = 1) and add *gatsu*:

Dore and
dono+noun are
usually followed
by **ga** instead of
wa.

January	*ichigatsu*
February	*nigatsu*
March	*sangatsu*
April	*shigatsu*
May	*gogatsu*
June	*rokugatsu*
July	*shichigatsu*
August	*hachigatsu*
September	*kugatsu*
October	*juugatsu*
November	*juuichigatsu*
December	*juunigatsu*

-O kudasai
-O kudasai is the
phrase for
letting someone
know that you
want to buy a
certain object.*ex.*
Kono seetaa-o
kudasai. I
would like this
sweater.

3. Multiples of one thousand:

1,000 - *sen*	6,000 - *rokusen*
2,000 - *nisen*	7,000 - *nanasen*
3,000 - *sanzen*	8,000 - *hassen*
4,000 - *yonsen*	9,000 - *kyuusen*
5,000 - *gosen*	

13

kore
this

kyoo
today

-mo
also, too,
either

-o kudasai
I'll take ___
please

ookii(i)
big

pen
pen

sono
it (with noun)

soo desu-ka
Really? Is
that so?

sore
it

takai(i)
high;
expensive

ten'in
sales clerk

yasui(i)
low; cheap

4. Look at the pictures below and ask for each item by saying "_____-o kudasai:"

SHORT DIALOGUES

1. Shopping

   ex. zubon, hassen

   Hayashi: Sono **zubon**-wa ikura desu-ka.
   Ten'in: Kono **zubon**-wa **hassen** en desu.
   Hayashi: Sore-o kudasai.
   Ten'in: Hai, arigatoo gozaimasu.

   1. kutsushita, sen
   2. shatsu, gosen
   3. booshi, nisen
   4. wanpiisu, kyuusen
   5. sukaato, rokusen

2. Two friends shopping together

ex. kooto, kyuusen

> *Michiko: Kono* **kooto**-*wa* **kyuusen** *en desu.*
> *Sumisu: Takai desu, ne.*
> *Michiko: Iie, yasui desu, yo.*
> *Sumisu: Soo desu-ka.*
> *Michiko(to clerk): Kono* **kooto**-*o kudasai.*

1. kutsushita, sen
2. shatsu, gosen
3. booshi, nisen
4. wanpiisu, kyuusen
5. sukaato, rokusen

3. *ex.* kinyoobi

> *A: Kyoo-wa nanyoobi desu-ka.*
> *B: Kyoo-wa* **kinyoobi** *desu.*

1. nichiyoobi
2. doyoobi
3. suiyoobi
4. getsuyoobi
5. mokuyoobi

Mo
Mo can replace
o, ga, or *wa* in a
sentence.

Ne
Ne is often
added to the
end of sentenc-
es or phrases.
It is similar in
meaning to the
Canadian *eh.*

CLOTHES

booshi
hat

kooto
coat

kutsu
shoes

kutsushita
socks

nekutai
tie

seetaa
sweater

shatsu
shirt

sukaato
skirt

wanpiisu
dress

zubon
pants

SELF-TEST

Translate the following sentences into Japanese:

1. Yesterday was Monday.

2. How much is that? (far from speaker and listener)

3. How much is that (far from speaker and listener) shirt?

4. This (close to speaker) dress is expensive.

5. Now, it is March.

Unscramble these sentences:

6. o kooto kudasai kono.

7. are desu wa ka ikura.

8. yasui desu ne sono wa nekutai.

9. ka nanyoobi wa kyoo desu.

10. kudasai o booshi sono.

LESSON THREE
DOKO-NI ARIMASU-KA

In this lesson you will learn:

- How to ask where an object is
- How to state prepositions
- Multiples of one hundred

DIALOGUE

I
たなか：　スミスさん　こんにちは.
スミス：　ああ.　たなかさん　こんにちは.
たなか：　あの　くるまは　スミスさんの　ですか.
スミス：　どの　くるま　ですか.
たなか：　あの　たてものの　まえの　くるま　です.
スミス：　いいえ.　わたしの　くるまは　あの　たてものの
　　　　　　よこに　あります.
たなか：　そう　ですか.　あの　くるまは　いい　くるま
　　　　　　ですね.
II
みちこ：　くみこさん　わたしの　かばんは　どこに
　　　　　　ありますか.
くみこ：　テーブルの　うえに　ありませんか.
みちこ：　はい　ありません.　ああ　つくえの　なかに
　　　　　　ありますよ.

I

Tanaka: *Sumisu-san, konnichi-wa.*

Sumisu: *Aa. Tanaka-san, konnichi-wa.*

T: *Ano kuruma-wa Sumisu-san-no desu-ka.*

S: *Dono kuruma desu-ka.*

T: *Ano tatemono-no mae-*

I

Tanaka: Mr. Smith, good afternoon.

Smith: Oh, Mr. Tanaka, good afternoon.

T: Is that your car, Mr. Smith?

S: Which car?

T: The car in front of

no kuruma desu.

S: *Iie. Watashi-no kuruma-wa ano tatemono-no yoko-ni arimasu.*

T: *Soo desu-ka. Ano kuruma-wa ii kuruma desu, ne.*

II

Michiko: *Kumiko-san, watashi-no kaban-wa doko-ni arimasu-ka.*

Kumiko: *Teeburu-no ue-ni arimasen-ka.*

M: *Hai, arimasen. Aa, tsukue-no naka-ni arimasu yo.*

that building.

S: No. My car is beside that building.

T: Really. That car is very nice.

II

Michiko: Kumiko, where is my hand-bag?

Kumiko: Isn't it on the table?

M: Yes, it's not. Oh, it's in the desk.

Arimasu is used only when talking about non-living objects, and *imasu* is used for living things.

In Japanese, if a question is asked with a negative word, the answer is different than English. For example, "It isn't on the table?" in English is answered, "No, it's not." But in Japanese, they say, *Hai, arimasen.* "Yes (that's right), it's not."

GRAMMAR EXPLANATION

1. **The sentence structure for prepositions:**

Subject-*wa* place-*no* preposition-*ni arimasu* / *imasu.*

ex. *Pen-wa teeburu-no shita-ni arimasu.*
The pen is under the *table.*

Hon-wa tsukue-no naka-ni arimasu.
The book is in the desk.

aa
oh

arimasen
does not
exist

arimasu
exist, have

doa
door

doko
where

enpitsu
pencil

hon
book

ii(i)
good

imasu
exist, have

isu
chair

kaban
purse

kami
paper

kuruma
car

kyoodai
siblings

mado
window

mise
store, shop

ni
at, to

To state someone or something is in a general location, like a country, city, or building, use:

> Subject-*wa* place-*ni arimasu* / *imasu*.

*ex. Tanaka-san-wa Tookyoo-**ni imasu**.*
Mrs. Tanaka is in Tokyo.

*Nooto-wa ie-**ni arimasu**.*
The notebook is in the house.

2. No

When *no* is added to the end of a noun, it shows possession. It is like the English 's.

*ex. Kore-wa Michiko-san-**no** pen desu.*
This is Michiko's pen.

When describing where an object is, *no* is always added to the noun that shows where the object is.

*ex. Nooto-wa teeburu-**no** ue-ni arimasu.*
The notebook is on the table.

3. Arimasu, imasu

Arimasu and *imasu* can be used to show that something exists, or that one has something.

*ex.Kono resutoran-ni-wa sushi-ga **arimasu**-ka?*
Does this restaurant have sushi?

20

*Anata-wa kyoodai-ga **imasu**-ka.*
Do you have any brothers or sisters?

If the subject in
the sentence is
understood, it
can be omitted.

EXERCISES

1. **Looking at the pictures below, identify each item with a Japanese sentence:**

    ex.

    ➡ *Kore-wa **enpitsu** desu.*

2. **Answer the following questions:**

    *ex. **Enpitsu**-wa doko-ni arimasu-ka.*
    ➡ ***Enpitsu**-wa **tsukue**-no ue-ni arimasu.*

    ***Isu**-wa doko-ni arimasu-ka.*
    ***Tsukue**-wa doko-ni arimasu-ka.*
    ***Nooto**-wa doko-ni arimasu-ka.*

Doko desu-ka
Doko desu-ka
means "where
is" something.
However, *doko-
ni arimasu-ka*
means "*exactly*
where is
(something)," or
"where is
(something) *at*."

nooto
notebook

resutoran
restaurant

tatemono
building

teeburu
table

tsukue
desk

uchi
home

yoi
good

PREPOSI-TIONS

aida
during, while, between

mae
before, in front of, ago

naka
in, inside

shita
down, under

soto
out, outside

ue
up, above

ushiro
behind, back

yoko
by, beside

3. Multiples of 100:

100 - *hyaku*	600 - *roppyaku*
200 - *nihyaku*	700 - *nanahyaku*
300 - *sanbyaku*	800 - *happyaku*
400 - *yonhyaku*	900 - *kyuuhyaku*
500 - *gohyaku*	

SHORT DIALOGUES

1. *ex.* enpitsu, tsukue, naka

> Emiko: Michiko-san, **enpitsu**-*wa doko-ni arimasu-ka.*
>
> Michiko: **Enpitsu**-*wa* **tsukue**-*no* **naka**-*ni arimasu.*

1. pen, teeburu, ue
2. kami, teeburu, shita
3. kuruma, uchi, soto
4. nooto, isu, ue
5. anata-no zubon, teeburu, yoko
6. shatsu, doa, mae

2. *ex.* Naomi, uchi, naka

> A: ***Naomi***-*san-wa doko-ni imasu-ka.*
> B: ***Naomi***-*san-wa **uchi**-no **naka**-ni imasu.*

> 1. Kaoru, doa, ushiro
> 2. Jonson, uchi, soto
> 3. Sumisu, kuruma, yoko
> 4. Nobutaka, doa, mae
> 5. Tokuichiro, kuruma, naka

Ii
Both *yoi* and *ii* mean good; however, *ii* is generally used in conversation, while *yoi* is used primarily in writing.

3. *ex.* enpitsu, 50

> A: *Ano mise-ni-wa **enpitsu**-ga arimasu-ka.*
> B: *Hai, arimasu.*
> A: *Ikura desu-ka.*
> B: ***Gojuu** en desu.*

> 1. nooto, 100
> 2. kami, 200
> 3. pen, 150

SELF-TEST

Fill in the missing particles with *wa, no, ni, san,*
and *ka*:

1. Enpitsu ___ kaban ___ naka ___ arimasu.

2. Anata ___ hon ___ teeburu ___ ue ___
   arimasu___.

3. Michiko ___ ___ kuruma ___ mae ___ imasu.

4. Emiko ___ ___ doko desu ___.

5. Isu ___ teeburu ___ ushiro ___ arimasu.

Unscramble the sentences:

6. naka no Jonson san arimasu wa nooto no ni
   tsukue.

7. arimasu doko watashi pen no wa ni ka.

8. wa kami tsukue shita no ni arimasu.

9. kutsu doko arimasu ni no ka Hara san wa.

10. Jonson san ni imasu resutoran wa.

LESSON FOUR
NANI-O SHIMASHITA-KA

In this lesson you will learn:

- Common verbs
- The past tense of verbs
- How to link two sentences

DIALOGUE

はら：　　おはよう　ございます．
スミス：　おはよう　ございます．
はら：　　きのう　スミスさんは　なにを　しましたか．
スミス：　きのう　にほんごを　べんきょう　しました．
はら：　　そう　ですか．　テレビも　みましたか．
スミス：　はい．　テレビも　みました．　はらさんは　なにを
　　　　　しましたか．
はら：　　てがみを　かきました．　それ　から　ほんを
　　　　　よみました．　ところで　きょうは　どこに
　　　　　いきますか．
スミス：　おおさかに　いきます．　そうして　みちこさんに
　　　　　あいます．　あなたは　どこに　いきますか．
はら：　　とうきょうに　いきます　そうして　とけいを
　　　　　かいます．
スミス：　それ　では　さようなら．
はら：　　さようなら．

Hara: *Ohayoo gozaimasu.*　　Hara: Good morning.

Sumisu: *Ohayoo gozaimasu.*　　Smith: Good morning.

H: *Kinoo, Sumisu-san-wa nani-o shimashita-ka.*　　H: Mr. Smith, what did you do yesterday?

S: *Kinoo nihongo-o benkyoo shimashita.*　　S: Yesterday I studied Japanese.

H: *Soo desu-ka. Terebi-mo mimashita-ka.*　　H: Really. Did you also watch television?

S: *Hai. Terebi-mo mimashita. Hara-san-wa nani-o shimashita-ka.*

S: Yes, I also watched television. What did you do Mr. Hara?

H: *Tegami-o kakimashita, sore kara hon-o yomimashita. Tokorode, kyoo-wa doko-ni ikimasu-ka.*

H: I wrote a letter and then I read a book. By the way, where will you go today?

S: *Oosaka-ni ikimasu, soshite Michiko-san-ni aimasu. Anata-wa doko-ni ikimasu-ka.*

S: I will go to Osaka and I will meet Michiko. Where will you go today?

H: *Tookyoo-ni ikimasu, soshite tokei-o kaimasu.*

H: I will go to Tokyo and buy a watch.

S: *Sore dewa, sayoonara.*

S: Well, goodbye.

H: *Sayoonara.*

H: Goodbye.

O
Objects of sentences are always followed by *o. ex. Watashi-wa miruku-o nomimasu.* I drink milk. *Watashi-wa sushi-o tabemasu.* I eat sushi.

O-
O can be used as a prefix to many nouns to add honor or respect. *ex. sake, o-sake.*

GRAMMAR EXPLANATION
1. -Mashita

To change verbs to the past tense, simply change *masu* to *mashita.*

    *ex. iki**masu***   go

         *iki**mashita***   went

         *hanashi**masu***   speak

         *hanashi**mashita***   spoke

Amerika
America

bideo
video

ee
yes (less
formal than
hai)

eigo
English

ie
house

miruku
milk

mizu
water

Nihon
Japan

nihongo
Japanese
language

rajio
radio

sake
rice wine;
alcohol

sore dewa
in that case

sore kara
then, after
that

soshite
and

tegami
letter

2. Ni

Ni always precedes *ikimasu, kaerimasu*, and *kimasu* after a place is stated. In these instances, *ni* is used like the English "to." The grammar pattern is as follows:

> Subject-*wa* place-***ni*** *ikimasu (kimasu*, or *kaerimasu)*

> *ex. Watashi-wa Hara-san-no ie-**ni** ikimasu.*
> I go to Hara's house.

> *Harada-san-wa Amerika-**ni** kimashita.*
> Mr. Harada came to America.

> *Mori-san-wa uchi-**ni** kaerimashita.*
> Mrs. Mori returned home.

Additionally, *ni* always precedes *aimasu*.

> *ex. Sumisu-san-**ni** aimashita.*
> I met Mr. Smith.

> *Tanaka-san-wa Sumisu-san-**ni** aimashita-ka.*
> Did Mr. Tanaka meet Mr. Smith?

3. Soshite

Soshite is a word that means "and;" it is always used to link two sentences together.

> *ex. Watashi-wa Tookyoo-ni ikimasu.*
> I go to Tokyo.

Watashi-wa nihongo-o benkyoo shimasu.
I study Japanese.

Watashi-wa Tookyoo-ni ikimasu, **soshite**
nihongo-o benkyoo shimasu.
I go to Tokyo **and** study Japanese.

There is no
difference
between present
tense verbs and
future tense in
Japanese.
Whether or not
the action takes
place currently
or in the future
depends on the
context of the
sentence.

EXERCISES
1. Verbs

Identify each verb in the pictures below:

terebi
television

tokorode
by the way

VERBS
aimasu
meet

arukimasu
walk

benkyoo
shimasu
study

hanashimasu
speak

hashirimasu
run

ikimasu
go

kaerimasu
return (go
back)

kaimasu
buy

kakimasu
write

kikimasu
listen

kimasu
come

mimasu
see

nemasu
sleep

nomimasu
drink

2. Past tense

Change the following verbs into past tense by placing them into the following sentence:

ex. imasu
➡*Hara-san-wa **imashita**.*

arukimasu   hashirimasu
wakarimasu   nemasu

ex. nihongo, benkyoo shimasu
➡*Watashi-wa **nihongo**-o **benkyoo shimashita**.*

mizu, nomimasu
rajio, kikimasu
terebi, mimasu
kuruma, unten shimasu
kutsushita, kaimasu
eigo, oshiemasu
sushi, tabemasu
bideo, mimasu

ex. Kyooto, ikimasu
➡*Anata-wa **Kyooto**-ni **ikimashita**-ka.*
*Ee, **Kyooto**-ni **ikimashita**.*

Nihon, kimasu
ie, kaerimasu
Yamada-san, aimasu
Amerika, ikimasu

30

SHORT DIALOGUES

1. Two friends talking

ex. nichiyoobi, benkyoo shimashita

> Tanaka: *Jonson-san-wa **nichiyoobi** nani-o*
> *shimashita-ka.*
> Jonson: ***Nichiyoobi** watashi-wa **benkyoo***
> ***shimashita.***

    1. mokuyoobi, Michiko-san-ni aimashita
    2. getsuyoobi, Tookyoo-ni ikimashita
    3. suiyoobi, Nihon-ni kimashita
    4. kinoo, hon-o yomimashita

2. Two friends talking

ex. hon-o yomimashita

> Tanaka: *Sumisu-san, kinoo-wa **hon-o***
> ***yomimashita**-ka.*
> Sumisu: *Hai, **hon-o yomimashita.***
> Tanaka: *Nihongo-mo benkyoo*
> *shimashita-ka.*
> Sumisu: *Hai, Nihongo-mo benkyoo*
> *shimashita.*

    1. o-sake-o nomimashita
    2. terebi-o mimashita
    3. rajio-o kikimashita
    4. eigo-o oshiemashita

Oshiemasu
Oshiemasu means "teach," but it also means "tell." If you want a person to tell you information about something, use *oshiemasu*.

Aimasu
Aimasu is used not only when you meet someone for the first time, but also whenever you see someone. For example, one would say "I saw Kate at the mall," in English, but in Japanese, one would use *aimasu* (meet) instead of *mimasu* (see).

31

VERBS
(cont.)

oshiemasu
teach

shimasu
do

tabemasu
eat

unten
shimasu
drive

wakarimasu
understand

yomimasu
read

3. *ex.* Tookyoo, juuichiji

> *Yuki:*   *Doko-ni ikimashita-ka.*
> *Hiroko:*   ***Tookyoo**-ni ikimashita.*
> *Yuki:*   *Nanji-ni kaerimashita-ka.*
> *Hiroko:*   ***Juuichiji**-ni kaerimashita.*

1. Oosaka, juuniji
2. Yokohama, juuichiji
3. Kyooto, niji

SELF-TEST

Fill in the missing particles with *wa, no, ni, san, o,* and *ka*:

1. Jonson ___ ___ sushi ___ tabemashita.

2. Watashi ___ mizu ___ nomimashita.

3. Michiko ___ ___ Tookyoo ___ kimashita.

4. Watashi ___ nihongo ___ benkyoo shimasu.

5. Kinoo, Jonson ___ ___ terebi ___ mimashita ___.

Translate the following sentences into Japanese:

6. Today, I teach English.

7. Yesterday, Michiko came to America.

8. Does Mrs. Smith run?

9. I read (past) a book.

10. I speak Japanese.

LESSON FIVE
NIHONGO-O HANASHIMASEN

In this lesson you will learn:

- Family terms
- The negative form of verbs
- The plain form of verbs

DIALOGUE

I

A: スミスさん こちらは たなかさん です.

たなか: はじめまして たなか です.

スミス: はじめまして スミス です. どうぞ よろしく.

たなか: にほんに どの くらい いますか.

スミス: ごかげつ です. その あいだに えいごを
おしえて いました.

たなか: かぞくも きましたか.

スミス: おとうとは きました.

たなか: おとうとさんは にほんごを はなしますか.

スミス: いいえ. おとうとは にほんごを はなしません.

II

A: あの おんなのひとは だれ ですか.

B: その おんなのひとは どこに いますか.

A: くるまの そとに います.

B: ああ. かのじょは やましたさんの おくさん です.

I

A: *Sumisu-san, kochira-
wa Tanaka-san desu.*

T: *Hajimemashite,
Tanaka desu.*

I

A: Mr. Smith, this is
Mr. Tanaka.

T: How do you do, I'm
Mr. Tanaka.

S: *Hajimemashite, Sumisu desu. Doozo, yoroshiku.*

S: How do you do, I'm Mr. Smith. Pleased to meet you.

T: *Nihon-ni dono kurai imasu-ka.*

T: How long have you been in Japan?

S: *Gokagetsu desu. Sono aida-ni, eigo-o oshiete imashita.*

S: Five months. During that time, I have been teaching English.

T: *Kazoku-mo kimashita-ka.*

T: Did your family also come?

S: *Otooto-wa kimashita.*

S: My younger brother came.

T: *Otooto-san-wa nihongo-o hanashimasu-ka.*

T: Does your brother speak Japanese?

S: *Iie. Otooto-wa nihongo-o hanashimasen.*

S: No, he does not speak Japanese.

II

II

A: *Ano onnanohito-wa dare desu-ka.*

A: Who is that woman over there?

B: *Sono onnanohito-wa doko-ni imasu-ka.*

B: Where is the woman?

A: *Kuruma-no soto-ni imasu.*

A: Outside of the car.

B: *Aa. Kanojo-wa Yamashita-san-no oku-san desu.*

B: Oh. She is Mr. Yamashita's wife.

Sensei
Sensei is a term that means "teacher," but is not solely used when referring to a teacher; any person who is in a position of high authority or respect can be addressed as *sensei*.

Mada
When *mada* is used to mean "yet," it is always paired with a negative verb. *Sumisu-san-wa* **mada** *kimasen.* Mr. Smith did not come yet.

dare
who

*dono
(g)kurai*
how long

*doozo
yoroshiku*
I'm pleased to
meet you (lit. -
please be good
to me)

gakusei
student

gokagetsu
five months

*hajime-
mashite*
how do you do
(lit. - for the
first time)

hito
person

kanojo
she

kare
he

kata
person
(polite)

kochira
this way,
polite for *kore*

kodomo
child

kodomotachi
children

GRAMMAR EXPLANATION
1. Negative verbs

To change verbs to a negative, change the *su* at the end of the verb to *sen*.

*ex. ikima**su***	go
*ikima**sen***	don't go
*unten shima**su***	drive
*unten shima**sen***	don't drive

The negative form of *desu* is *dewa arimasen*.

*Sensei **dewa arimasen**.*
Is not a teacher.

*Gakusei **dewa arimasen**.*
Is not a student.

2. Asking Names

To ask someone their name, say:
Anata-no namae-wa nandesu-ka.
To answer:
Watashi-no namae-wa _____ desu.

> *ex. Anata-no namae-wa nandesu-ka.*
> *Watashi-no namae-wa **Hiroko** desu.*

This question is usually asked by a person of higher position to their subordinate, like a teacher asking a student.

EXERCISES

1. **Look at the picture below, and state each person's family name:**

2. **Look at the pictures below, and identify man, woman, girl, boy, and baby:**

3. **Change the following verbs to negatives:**

ex. arukimasu
➡ *arukimasen*

aimasu	*unten shimasu*
imasu	*yomimasu*
hanashimasu	*tabemasu*
ikimasu	*wakarimasu*
kaerimasu	*shimasu*
kakimasu	*oshiemasu*
kikimasu	*hashirimasu*
nemasu	*nomimasu*
benkyoo shimasu	

Onnano
Onnano means "female;" *hito* means "person;" *ko* is "child." Therefore, *onnano+hito* means "woman," and *onnano+ko* means "girl."

Otokono
Otokono means "male;" therefore, *otokono+hito* means "man," and *otokono+ko* means "boy."

37

mada
(not) yet; still

namae
name

onnanohito
woman

onnanoko
girl

*oshiete
imashita*
have been
teaching

otokonohito
man

otokonoko
boy

Oosutoraria
Australia

sensei
teacher

tomodachi
friend

4. The plain form of the verbs is as follows:

aimasu	*au(-u)*
arimasu	*aru(-u)*
arukimasu	*aruku(-u)*
benkyoo shimasu	*benkyoo suru*
chigaimasu	*chigau(-u)*
desu	*da*
hanashimasu	*hanasu(-u)*
hashirimasu	*hashiru(-ru)*
ikimasu	*iku(-u)*
imasu	*iru(-ru)*
kaerimasu	*kaeru(-u)*
kaimasu	*kau(-u)*
kakimasu	*kaku(-u)*
kikimasu	*kiku(-u)*
kimasu	*kuru(irregular)*
mimasu	*miru(-ru)*
nemasu	*neru(-u)*
nomimasu	*nomu(-u)*
oshiemasu	*oshieru(-ru)*
shimasu	*suru(irregular)*
tabemasu	*taberu(-ru)*
unten shimasu	*unten suru*
wakarimasu	*wakaru(-u)*
yomimasu	*yomu(-u)*

From this point forward, verbs will be introduced in their plain form.

To conjugate the plain form into the *-masu* form:

• For *-u* verbs, drop the final *u* and add *imasu*

*ex. a***u**	*a***imasu**
nom***u***	nom***imasu***

• The *si* sound does not exist in Japanese; one can only say *shi*. Therefore, when *-u* verbs end in *su*, *shimasu* must be addded.

*ex. hana***su**	*hana***shimasu**

• For *-ru* verbs, if the letter preceding the final *ru* is an *i* or *e*, drop *ru* and add *masu*

*ex. mi***ru**	*mi***masu**
oshie***ru***	oshie***masu***

• If the letter preceding the final *ru* is an *a* or *o*, drop *ru* and add *rimasu*

*ex. a***ru**	*a***rimasu**

SHORT DIALOGUES
1. At school

ex. Megumi

> Sensei: *Anata-no namae-wa nandesu-ka.*
> Gakusei: *Watashi-no namae-wa **Megumi** desu.*

1.	Takeshi	2.	Keigo
3.	Masaaki	4.	Nobutaka
5.	Tokuichiro		

Dare
If *dare* is the subject and the person is unknown, use *ga* after *dare*; if the person is known, use *wa*.

Pronouns
The personal pronouns *kanojo* and *kare* are not used in Japanese as frequently as the English "she" and "he," as they are considered informal words. First or last names + *san* are used more often.

39

FAMILY TERMS

okaa-san
mother

otoo-san
father

oku-san
wife

go-shujin
husband

onee-san
older sister

imooto-san
younger sister

onii-san
older brother

otooto-san
younger brother

obaa-san
grandmother
(old woman)

oba-san
aunt

ojii-san
grandfather
(old man)

oji-san
uncle

kazoku
family

akachan
baby

2. At a party

ex. Jonson, Tanaka, Amerika

Intro: __Jonson__-san, kochira-wa __Tanaka__-san desu.

A: Hajimemashite, __Tanaka__ desu.

B: Hajimemashite, __Jonson__ desu. Doozo yoroshiku.

A: __Jonson__-san-wa __Amerika__-no kata desu-ka.

A: Hai, __Amerika__ kara kimashita.

1. Jonson, Hirakawa, Amerika
2. Sumisu, Nishiyama, Oosutoraria
3. Aoki, Tanaka, Tookyoo
4. Hanabusa, Tanaka, Tookyoo
5. Tanaka, Mouri, Kyooto

3. At school

ex. eigo-o, benkyoo suru

A: Kyoo, anata-wa __eigo-o benkyoo shimasu__-ka.

B: Iie, __benkyoo shimasen__.

A: Nani-o shimasu-ka.

B: Mada wakarimasen.

1. Kyooto-ni, iku
2. bideo-o, miru
3. o-sake-o, nomu
4. hon-o, yomu

SELF TEST

Translate the following into Japanese:

1. This is Michiko's grandmother.

2. How do you do?

3. Nice to meet you.

4. What is your name?

5. Today, his father does not study English.

Unscramble the following sentences:

6. wa o no imooto san Mitsumura san tabemasen sushi.

7. yomimashita onii san Tanaka san hon no kinoo o wa.

8. no namae Jonson desu watashi wa.

9. no no no ni wa oba san naka arimasen anata hon tsukue.

10. watashi wa ni aimashita tomodachi kinoo.

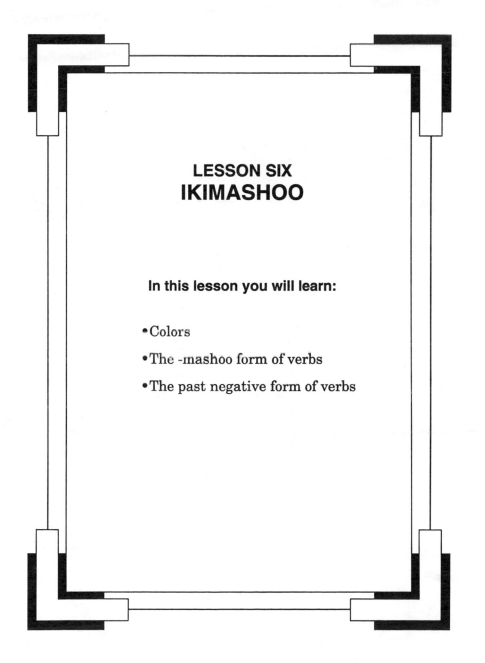

LESSON SIX
IKIMASHOO

In this lesson you will learn:

• Colors

• The -mashoo form of verbs

• The past negative form of verbs

DIALOGUE

I

A: きのう　おともだちに　あいましたか．

B: いいえ　あいません　でした．

A: なにを　しましたか．

B: えいがかんに　いきました．　ターミネータ　ツを
みました．えいごは　よく　わかりませんでした．　でも
とても　いい　えいが　でした．　あなたは　なにを
しましたか．

A: わたしは　マクドナルドに　いきました．　それ　から
デパートに　いきました．

B: そうですか．　なにを　かいましたか．

A: きいろい　セーターを　かいました．

B: ずぼんも　かいましたか．

A: いいえ．　かいません　でした．

II

A: これ　から　どこに　いきましょうか．

B: そう　ですね．　いせたん　デパートに　いきましょうか．
バーゲンが　あります．

A: それは　いい　ですね．　そこに　いきましょう．

I	I
A: *Kinoo o-tomodachi-ni aimashita-ka.*	A: Yesterday, did your meet your friend?
B: *Iie, aimasen deshita.*	B: No, I didn't.
A: *Nani-o shimashita-ka.*	A: What did you do?

B: *Eigakan-ni ikimashita. Taamineeta-tsu-o mimashita. Eigo-wa yoku wakarimasen deshita, demo totemo ii eiga deshita. Anata-wa nani-o shimashita-ka.*

B: I went to the movie theater. I saw Terminator 2. I didn't understand the English very well, but it was a very good movie. What did you do?

A: *Watashi-wa Makudonarudo-ni ikimashita. Sore kara, depaato-ni ikimashita.*

A: I went to McDonald's. Then, I went to a department store.

B: *Soo desu-ka. Nani-o kaimashita-ka.*

B: Really. What did you buy?

A: *Kiiroi seetaa-o kaimashita.*

A: I bought a yellow sweater.

B: *Zubon-mo kaimashita-ka.*

B: Did you buy pants too?

A: *Iie. Kaimasen deshita.*

A: No, I didn't

II

II

A: *Kore-kara doko-ni ikimashoo-ka.*

A: Where shall we go from here?

B: *Soo desu-ne. Isetan depaato-ni ikimashoo-ka. Baagen-ga arimasu.*

B: Well, should we go to Isetan? They are having a sale.

A: *Sore-wa ii desu, ne. Soku-ni ikimashoo.*

A: That's great. Let's go there.

As you will note by reading the dialogue, many of the places listed are foreign words changed to fit into the Japanese phonetic system. For instance, "McDonald's" becomes *Makudonarudo.* "Seven-Eleven" becomes *Sebun Irebun.*

-Jin
To say that someone is Japanese, Australian, etc., add *-jin* to the country's name. ex. *nihonjin,* Japanese person; *oosutorariajin,* Australian.

asoko
over there

baagen
bargain
(sale)

biiru
beer

demo
but

eiga
movie

gohan
rice; meal

Isetan
a depart-
ment store
in Japan

koko
here

koohii
coffee

ocha
tea

shinbun
newspaper

soko
there

totemo
very

yoku
well

GRAMMAR EXPLANATION

1. Colors

Only six colors can stand alone as adjectives: *akai, aoi, chairoi, kiiroi, kuroi,* and *shiroi.*

> *ex. Kuruma-wa **akai** desu.*   ***akai** kuruma*
> The car is red.   red car
>
> *Hon-wa **kuroi** desu.*   ***kuroi** hon*
> The book is black.   black book

To use these color words as nouns, drop the final *i:*

> *ex. **Aka**-wa ii iro desu.*
> Red is a nice color.

Other color adjectives cannot stand alone. When these colors are used as predicate adjectives, state the color + *iro.*

> *ex. Kuruma-wa **orenji iro** desu.*
> The car is orange.
>
> *Hon-wa **midori iro** desu.*
> The book is green.

When these colors directly modify nouns, state the color + *iro-no.*

> *ex. **orenji iro-no** kuruma*
> orange car
>
> ***midori iro-no** hon*
> green book

To use these colors as nouns, use the color + *iro*:

> ex. **Murasaki iro**-*wa ii iro desu.*
> Purple is a nice color.

2. -Mashoo

To change a verb to mean let's+verb, change the *masu* to *mashoo*.

> ex. *iki***masu**
> *iki***mashoo**   Let's go.
>
> *nomi***masu**
> *nomi***mashoo**   Let's drink.

3. Verbs, Past Negative Tense

To change a verb to past negative tense (did not + verb), change the *masu* to *masen* and add *deshita*.

> ex. *Watashi-wa yakkyoku-ni iki***masu**.
> I go to the pharmacy.
>
> *Watashi-wa yakkyoku-ni iki***masen deshita**.
> I didn't go to the pharmacy.
>
> *Kare-wa koohii-o nomi***masen**.
> He doesn't drink coffee.
>
> *Kare-wa koohii-o nomi***masen deshita**.
> He didn't drink coffee.
>
> *biyooin dewa ari***masen deshita**
> was not a beauty shop

Baagen
The word *baagen* is borrowed from the English word "bargain." In Japan, when a store is having a sale, they refer to it as a bargain instead of a sale.

Mashoo
When *mashoo* is added to a verb, the meaning becomes "let's + verb." However, when one uses this verb form and adds *ka*, the nuance changes to "shall we ____?"

When Japanese people state their names, they say their last name first, then their first name. Additionally, unless you are very familiar with a Japanese individual, always use their last name only.

PLACES

apaato
apartment

biyooin
beauty shop

byooin
hospital

depaato
department
store

eigakan
movie
theater

eki
station

gakkoo
school

ginkoo
bank

hoteru
hotel

*suupaa-
maaketto*
supermarket

*yakkyoku,
kusuriya*
pharmacy

*yuubin-
kyoku*
post office

EXERCISES

1. -Mashoo

Change the following verbs into the *mashoo* form:

> *ex. arukimasu*
> ➡ *arukimashoo*

aimasu	*nemasu*
tabemasu	*shimasu*
hanashimasu	*ikimasu*
benkyoo shimasu	

2. Past negative

Substitute the given words into the following sentences:

> *ex. arukimasu*
> ➡ *Hanabusa-san-wa* **arukimashita**-*ka.*
> *Iie, Hanabusa-san-wa* **arukimasen deshita.**

kaerimasu	*unten shimasu*
kakimasu	*wakarimasu*
kikimasu	*yomimasu*
mimasu	*nomimasu*

SHORT DIALOGUES

1. *ex.* hon, yomu

> Masaaki: *Keigo-san, nani-o shimashoo-ka.*
> Keigo: **Hon**-o **yomimashoo**.

1. gohan, taberu
2. terebi, miru
3. nihongo, benkyoo suru
4. o-sake, nomu

2. *ex.* eigakan

> Megumi: *Takeshi-san, doko-ni ikimashoo-ka.*
> Takeshi: **Eigakan**-ni ikimashoo.

1. yuubinkyoku
2. ginkoo
3. depaato
4. suupaamaaketto
5. Tookyoo

3. *ex.* terebi, miru, bideo

> A: *Kinoo, nani-o shimashita-ka.*
> B: **Terebi**-o **mimashita**.
> A: **Bideo**-mo **mimashita**-ka.
> B: *Iie,* **mimasen** deshita.

1. hon, yomu, shinbun
2. biiru, nomu, o-sake
3. eiga, miru, terebi
4. shatsu, kau, kutsu

Soo Desu Ne
This expression can also mean "let me see. . ." Additionally, it is sometimes used as an indirect refusal; often times Japanese people consider it impolite to say "no" in a straight-forward manner. Be very sensitive when speaking to a Japanese person who uses this phrase. He or she may need time to think over what has been said, or may be politely trying to tell you "no."

COLORS
akai(i)
red

aoi(i)
blue

chairoi(i)
brown

iro
color

kiiroi(i)
yellow

kuroi(i)
black

midori iro
green

murasaki iro
purple

orenji iro
orange

shiroi(i)
white

4. *ex.* midori

A: *Jonson-san-no kuruma-wa nani iro desu-ka.*
B: *Jonson-san-no kuruma-wa __midori iro__ desu.*
A: *Anata-no ie-ni-mo __midori iro-no__ kuruma-ga arimasu-ka.*
B: *Hai, arimasu.*

1. akai   4. ao
2. chairo   5. kuroi
3. kiiro   6. orenji

_____

SELF-TEST
Translate the following sentences into Japanese:

1. Let's sleep.

2. Let's go to the movie theater.

3. I didn't go to the hospital.

4. Didn't you drink tea?

5. I didn't drive a blue car.

6. I see a purple desk.

7. Did you go to the beauty salon?

8. That woman reads a red book.

9. That (far from speaker and listener) white building is a bank.

10. He is in the restaurant.

LESSON SEVEN
KANTAN DESU

In this lesson you will learn:

- Common adjectives
- How to state successive adjectives
- How to express likes and dislikes

DIALOGUE

I

A: きょうは　レストランに　いきましょうか.

B: どこの　レストランに　いきましょうか.

A: レッド　ロブスターは　どう　ですか.

B: そう　ですね.　ほかの　レストランは　どう　ですか.

A: それ　では　にほん　しょくの　レストランに
　　いきましょう.

B: はい.

A: この　レストランの　しょくじは　おいしい　ですか.

B: はい.　ここは　おいしくて　やすい　です.

A: ここには　おはしが　ありますか.

B: はい　あります.

A: むずかしい　ですか.

B: いいえ.　かんたん　です.

II

A: きれいな　セーター　ですね.　あたらしいの　ですか.

B: はい.　きのう　かいました.

A: どこで　かいましたか.

B: いせたんで　かいました.

I

A: *Kyoo-wa resutoran-ni ikimashoo-ka.*

B: *Doko-no resutoran-ni ikimashoo-ka.*

A: *Reddo Robusutaa-wa doo desu-ka.*

I

A: Shall we go to a restaurant today?

B: Where (restaurant) shall we go?

A: How about Red Lobster?

B: *Soo desu ne. Hoka-no resutoran-wa doo desu-ka.*

B: Well . . . what about another restaurant?

A: *Sore dewa Nihon shoku-no resutoran-ni ikimashoo.*

A: In that case, let's go to a Japanese restaurant.

B: *Hai.*

B: O.K.

A: *Kono resutoran-no shokuji-wa oishii desu-ka.*

A: Is the food in this restaurant good?

B: *Hai. Koko-wa oishikute yasui desu.*

B: Yes. It's delicious and reasonably priced.

A: *Koko-ni-wa o-hashi-ga arimasu-ka.*

A: Do they use chopsticks here?

B: *Hai, arimasu.*

B: Yes, they do.

A: *Muzukashii desu-ka.*

A: Are they difficult?

B: *Iie. Kantan desu.*

B: No. They are simple.

II

II

A: *Kireina seetaa desu, ne. Atarashii-no desu-ka.*

A: That is a pretty sweater. Is it a new one?

B: *Hai. Kinoo kaimashita.*

B: Yes. I bought it yesterday.

A: *Doko-de kaimashita-ka.*

A: Where did you buy it?

B: *Isetan-de kaimashita.*

B: I bought it at Isetan.

Fast Food
Many American fast food chains exist in Japan, like McDonald's, Kentucky Fried Chicken, Taco Bell, and Pizza Hut. Usually the names of the food items are the same as they are in America, but they are written in *Katakana* and pronounced within the Japanese phonetic system. Some examples are: *hanbaagaa* (hamburger), *pepushi* (pepsi), *koka koora* (coke), *furaido poteto* (french fries)

akarui(i)
bright

amari
(not) much

atarashii(i)
new

atsui(i)
hot

daisuki(na)
like very
much

-de
indicates an
action's
location

doo
what way;
how about

(o)hashi
chopsticks

hayai(i)
fast; early

hiroi(i)
spacious

hoka-no
other

kantan(na)
simple

karai(i)
spicy hot

kirei(na)
beautiful

kirai(na)
dislike; hate

GRAMMAR EXPLANATION
1. I and Na Adjectives

•*i* adjectives: The final *i* is used when stating an adjective in the present tense, regardless of its position in the sentence.

> *ex. oishii*
> *oishii tenpura*
> *Tenpura-wa oishii desu.*

•*na* adjectives: When a *na* adjective is used directly before a noun, use *na*. However, when it stands alone, do not say *na*.

> *ex. kirei*
> *kireina seetaa*
> *Seetaa-wa kirei desu.*

2. Two Successive Adjectives

In English, when using two adjectives, the word "and" usually connects them. However, in Japanese, the word *to* is not used. The word *to* usually connects nouns only.

When stating successive adjectives, if the first adjective is an *i* adjective, drop the final *i* and add *kute*.

> *ex. Kuruma-wa **akakute ookii** desu.*
> The car is red and big.

> *Nihon-no ie-wa **chiisakute takai** desu.*
> Japanese houses are small and expensive.

If the first adjective is a *na* adjective, simply add *de* to the end of it.

> *ex. Amerika-wa **kirei-de hiroi** desu.*
> America is beautiful and spacious.

3. Suki desu, Kirai desu

When stating that you like or dislike something, the following sentence pattern is always used:

_____-ga *suki desu.* _____-ga *kirai desu.*

> *ex. Pan-**ga suki desu**.*
> I like bread
>
> *Biiru-**ga kirai desu**.*
> I strongly dislike beer.

4. -De

When stating a location where an action was performed, the article *de* always follows the place's name. It is similar to the English "at."

> *ex. Gakkoo-**de** nihongo-o benkyoo shimashita.*
> At school, I studied Japanese.
>
> *Eigakan-**de**, Michiko-san-ni aimasen deshita.*
> At the theater, I did not meet (see) Michiko.

Amari
Amari is always paired with a negative verb and usually comes directly before the verb. *ex. Watashi-wa nihongo-o **amari** benkyoo shimasen deshita.* I did not study Japanese very much.

Doo
Doo is in another set of *kosoado* words. *Koo* (this way), *soo* (that way), and *aa* (that way), are the others.

55

kurai(i)
dark

muzukashii(i)
difficult

oishii(i)
delicious

omoshiroi(i)
interesting;
fun

osoi(i)
slow; late

samui(i)
cold

shokuji
a meal;
dinner

suki(na)
likeable

to
and, with

tokoro
place

yasashii(i)
easy

EXERCISES

1. Adjectives

Combine the following adjectives:

> *ex. ookii, takai desu*
> ➤*ookikute takai desu*

> *chiisai, yasui desu*
> *kireina, omoshiroi desu*
> *hayai, chiisai desu*
> *osoi, shiroi desu*
> *akai, atsui desu*
> *akarui, ookii desu*

2. Suki desu, kirai desu

Use the following words in either of these sentences:

_____-ga suki desu.	_____-ga kirai desu.
sushi	akai kuruma
byooin	oishii tabemono
miruku	nihongo
pan	kono hon
ringo	murasaki iro-no zubon

3. -De

Match the following phrases:

1. *gakkoo-de*	a. *terebi-o mimashita*
2. *eigakan-de*	b. *benkyoo shimashita*
3. *resutoran-de*	c. *nemashita*
4. *uchi-de*	d. *eiga-o mimashita*
5. *hoteru-de*	e. *gohan-o tabemashita*

SHORT DIALOGUES

1. *ex.* sushi, oishii

> A: *Kono resutoran-ni-wa* **sushi***-ga arimasu-ka.*
> B: *Hai,* **sushi***-ga arimasu.*
> A: **Oishii** *desu-ka.*
> B: *Hai, totemo* **oishii** *desu.*
>
> 1. akai budooshu, takai
> 2. karei, karai
> 3. o-sashimi, oishii

2. *ex.* Toyota-no kuruma, Yugo-no kuruma

> A: *Sumisu-san-wa* **Toyota-no kuruma***-ga*
> *suki desu-ka.*
> B: *Hai, daisuki desu.*
> A: **Yugo-no kuruma***-mo suki desu-ka.*
> B: *Iie, amari suki dewa arimasen.*
>
> 1. atsui sake, biiru
> 2. hayai kuruma, ookii kuruma
> 3. Nihon, Nihon-no shokuji
> 4. nihongo, kanji
> 5. o-sakana, o-sashimi

If you do not like a particular food, and do not wish to offend the person you are speaking to, do not use the word *kirai* because it is too strong. Instead, you should say *amari suki dewa arimasen.* This means "I do not really care for it," or "I don't like it very much."

Ya
Ya is often added to the end of a word to change that word into a store name. *ex. kusuri,* medicine, *kusuriya,* pharmacy; *sakana,* fish, *sakanaya,* fish store; *niku,* meat, *nikuya,* meat store; *hon,* book, *honya,* book store.

FOOD

budooshu
wine

juusu
juice

karei
curry

niku
meat

(o)kashi
snack

pan
bread

ringo
apple

(o)sakana
fish

(o)sashimi
raw fish dish

sukiyaki
meat dish

tabemono
food

tenpura
fried shrimp
and vegeta-
bles

wasabi
very hot
mustard

3. *ex.* ookii, kirei, o-sake-o nomu

A: *Tanaka-san-no ie-wa **ookikute kirei**
desu, ne.*
B: *Iie, uchi-wa chiisai desu.*
A: *Koko-de **o-sake-o nomimashoo**-ka.*
B: *Hai soo shimashoo.*

1. kirei, hiroi, gohan-o taberu
2. hiroi, kirei, ocha-o nomu
3. kirei, ookii, bideo-o miru

SELF-TEST

Fill in the missing blanks with *san, wa, ga, de, o,
kute, no, ni,* or *ka*:

1. Kuruma ___ kiiro ___ chiisai desu.

2. Akai budooshu ___ arimasu ___.

3. Asoko ___ gohan ___ tabemashita.

4. Tanaka ___ ___ ie ___ yasashii hon ___
yomimashita.

5. Sumisu ___ ___ ___-sashimi ___ suki desu ___.

Translate the following sentences into Japanese:

6. It is beautiful and expensive.

7. Is karashi delicious?

8. I don't really care for red wine.

9. At school, I didn't study Japanese.

10. I like Tokyo very much.

58

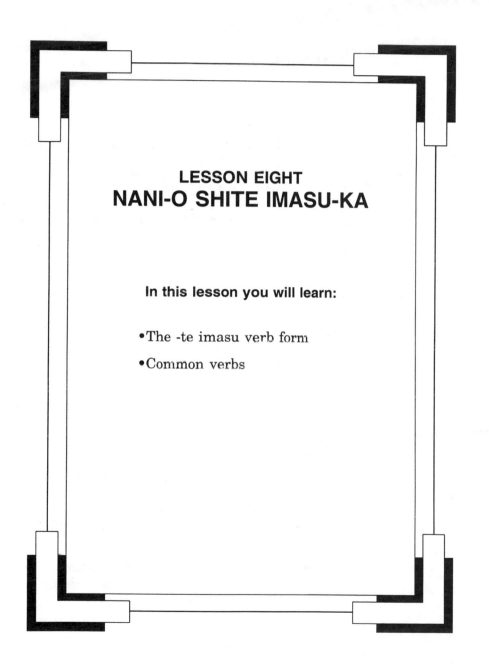

LESSON EIGHT
NANI-O SHITE IMASU-KA

In this lesson you will learn:

- The -te imasu verb form
- Common verbs

DIALOGUE

I
A: いま ひらかわさんと でんわで はなしました.
B: そう ですか. それで ひらかわさんは なにを して
いますか.
A: ひらかわさんは いま ごはんを つくって います.
B: ひらかわさん おげんき ですか.
A: はい げんき です.
B: ちょっと まって ください. いま おちゃを いれて
います から.
A: どうぞ おかまいなく.
II
はら: もりたさん こんにちは.
もりた: こんにちは. あなたの ごかぞくは いかが
ですか. いそがしい ですか.
はら: とても いそがしい です. しゅじんは ふじ
ぎんこうに つとめて います. むすめは
じゅくで べんきょう して います. むすこは
サッカーを して います. そして わたしは
いろいろな ことを して います.
もりた: そう ですか. それは たいへん ですね.

I

A: *Ima Hirakawa-san-to denwa-de hanashimashita.*

B: *Soo desu-ka. Sorede Hirakawa-san-wa nani-o shite imasu-ka.*

I

A: I just talked with Mrs. Hirakawa on the phone.

B: Really. What is Mrs. Hirakawa doing?

A: *Hirakawa-san-wa ima gohan-o tsukutte imasu.*

A: Now Mrs. Hirakawa is making a meal.

B: *Hirakawa-san-wa o-genki desu-ka.*

B: Is Mrs. Hirakawa healthy?

A: *Hai, genki desu.*

A: Yes, she's healthy.

B: *Chotto matte kudasai. Ima ocha-o irete imasu kara.*

B: Just a moment please. (Because) I'm pouring some tea.

A: *Doozo okamainaku.*

A: Please don't trouble yourself.

II

Hara: *Morita-san, konnichi-wa.*

Hara: Mrs. Morita, good afternoon.

Morita: *Konnichi-wa. Anata-no go-kazoku-wa ikaga desu-ka. Isogashii desu-ka.*

Morita: Good afternoon. How is your family? Are they busy?

H: *Totemo isogashii desu. Shujin-wa Fuji ginkoo-ni tsutomete imasu. Musume-wa juku-de benkyoo shite imasu. Musuko-wa sakkaa-o shite imasu. Soshite watashi-wa iroirona koto-o shite imasu.*

H: Very busy. My husband is working at Fuji Bank. My daughter is studying at juku. My son is playing soccer, and I'm doing a variety of things.

M: *Soo desu-ka. Sore-wa taihen desu ne.*

M: Really. That's tough, isn't it.

Chotto matte kudasai
This phrase means "please wait a moment."

Doozo
Doozo can take on a wide variety of meanings, depending on how it is used. Generally speaking, it means "please accept this," or "please go ahead." Japanese people frequently say *doozo* when presenting one with a gift, telling someone to go ahead and eat or drink, or when inviting someone into their home.

61

VERBS

ageru(-ru)
to give

asobu(-u)
to play

dekakeru(-ru)
to leave; go
out

dekiru(-ru)
can do; is
possible to
do

*denwa-o
kakeru*
to talk on
the phone

furu(-u)
to fall (rain
or snow)

hairu(-u)
to enter

ireru(-u)
to put in; to
pour

iu(-u)
to say

matsu(-u)
to wait

narau(-u)
to learn

naru(-u)
to become

noru(-u)
to ride

okiru(-ru)
to awake;
wake up

GRAMMAR EXPLANATION

1. -Te imasu

This verb tense is the same as the English verb+ing.

> ex. *Watashi-wa **matte imasu**.*
> I am waiting.

> *Ame-ga **futte imasu**.*
> It is raining.

> *Tanaka-san-wa benkyoo **shite imasu**.*
> Mr. Tanaka is studying.

Shite imasu also describes something that one has been doing in the past, and continues to do now, like the English "I have been _____ing."

> ex. *Hirakawa-san-wa Amerika-ni **sunde imasu**.*
> Mr. Hirakawa has been living in America.

> *Ichinenkan nihongo-o **benkyoo shite imasu**.*
> I have been studying Japanese for one year.

2. Conjugating verbs into present continuous

- For *-u* verbs change:

bu to *-nde*	*asobu*	*ason**de***
gu to *-ide*	*isogu*	*iso**ide*** (L. 12)
ku to *-ite*	*kiku*	*ki**ite***
mu, nu to *-nde*	*nomu*	*non**de***
ru to *-tte*	*hashiru*	*hashi**tte***
su to *-shite*	*hanasu*	*hana**shite***

tsu to *-tte*	*matsu*	*ma**tte***	
u to *-tte*	*narau*	*nara**tte***	

- For *-ru* verbs change:

ru to *-te*	*miru*	*mi**te***	
	taberu	*tabe**te***	

- Irregular verbs:

iku	***itte***	*kuru*	***kite***
suru	***shite***		

EXERCISES
1. -Te imasu

Change the following verbs into present continuous tense:

> ex. *iku*
> ➡ *itte imasu*

au	*kiku*
aruku	*kuru*
asobu	*matsu*
benkyoo suru	*narau*
dekakeru	*neru*
furu	*nomu*
hairu	*okiru*
hanasu	*oshieru*
hashiru	*suru*
ireru	*taberu*
kaeru	*tsutomeru*
kau	*unten suru*
kaku	*yomu*

-Ni noru
To state that one rides in a vehicle, use vehicle + *ni noru*. ex. *Kuruma-**ni** norimashita.* Rode in a car.

Juku
Juku is attended by most Japanese students, especially during junior high school and high school. *Juku* generally consists of classes held after school that prepare Japanese students for school entrance examinations. *Juku* is very rigorous, and students perform many memoriza-tion drills. Some students preparing for exams attend *juku* weekdays until ten or eleven o'clock every night.

VERBS
(cont.)
tsukuru(-u)
to make

tsutomeru(-ru)
to work

ADDITIONAL
WORDS
ame
rain

chotto
a little,
moment

doozo
please

furui(i)
old (things,
not people)

genki(na)
healthy

go-
honorific
prefix

ichinen
one year

ichinenkan
for one year

ikaga
how

iroiro(na)
various

isogashii(i)
busy

2. -Te imasu

Substitute the phrases into the conversation:

> *ex. hon-o yomu*
> ➡*Nani-o shite imasu-ka.*
> **Hon-o yonde** *imasu.*

> *nihongo-o benkyoo suru*
> *rajio-o kiku*
> *sake-o nomu*
> *gohan-o taberu*
> *pen-o kau*
> *aruku*
> *ocha-o ireru*

SHORT DIALOGUES

1. *ex.* terebi-o miru

> *Kumiko: Michiko-san ima isogashii desu-ka.*
> *Michiko: Sukoshi isogashii desu.*
> *Kumiko: Nani-o shite imasu-ka.*
> *Michiko:* **Terebi-o mite** *imasu.*

1. gohan-o taberu	6. sukaato-o kau
2. biiru-o nomu	7. toranpu-de asobu
3. shinbun-o yomu	8. bideo-o miru
4. ocha-o ireru	9. murasaki iro-no
5. eigo-o benkyoo suru	kutsushita-o kau

2. *ex.* hon, atarashii, furui

    *A: Anata-no **hon**-wa **atarashii** desu, ne.*
    *B: Iie. Watashi-no **hon**-wa **furui** desu, yo.*

      1. kuruma, hayai, osoi
      2. ie, ookii, chiisai
      3. seetaa, atarashii, furui

3. *ex.* terebi-o miru, eigo-o benkyoo suru

    A: Hiroko-san.
    B: Hai.
    *A: Ima, **terebi-o mite imasu**-ka.*
    *B: Iie, **terebi-o mite imasen. Eigo-o benkyoo shite imasu**.*

      1. Okaa-san-to hanasu, otoo-san-to hanasu
      2. Tookyoo-ni iku, Oosaka-ni iku
      3. Ame-ga furu, yuki-ga furu

Iu
Iu is an irregular verb. It is conjugated to *iimasu*. In Hiragana, it is written as *iu*, but is sometimes pronounced *yuu* in informal situations.

Taihen
Taihen can mean "difficult" or "very," depending on the context. However, do not confuse it with *muzukashii*. *Muzukashii* refers to something being intellectually difficult to grasp or understand; *taihen* refers to a difficult situation.

65

juku
cram school

kara
because,
since

koto
thing

musuko
son

musume
daughter

okamainaku
don't trouble
yourself

sakkaa
soccer

sorede
and

sukoshi
a little

taihen(na)
difficult,
tough, very

toranpu
playing
cards

wakai(i)
young

yuki
snow

SELF-TEST

Fill in the blanks using *san, wa, ga, o, ni, to, ka* or *de*:

1. Oji ___ ___ eigakan ___ eiga ___ mite imasu.

2. Onii ___ ___ ginkoo ___ matte imasu.

3. Keigo ___ ___ Masaaki ___ ___ sakkaa ___ shite imasu.

4. Ame ___ futte imasu.

5. Michiko ___ ___ doko ___ ocha ___ nonde imasu ___.

Unscramble the following sentences:

6. o unten imasu kanojo akakute wa kuruma hayai shite.

7. imasu ringo o tabete oishii kare wa.

8. o wa imasu watashi naratte nihongo.

9. shite Michiko san imasen wa o benkyoo eigo.

10. de ni wa iroirona aimashita hito watashi depaato.

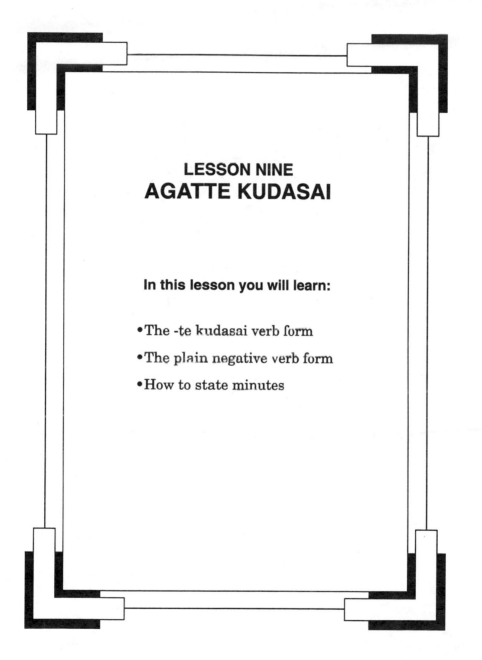

LESSON NINE
AGATTE KUDASAI

In this lesson you will learn:

- The -te kudasai verb form
- The plain negative verb form
- How to state minutes

DIALOGUE

I

ジョンソン： ばいてんは　どちら　ですか。

たなか： あちら　です。　こまかい　おかねを　もって
いますか。

ジョンソン： はい　ひゃく　ご　じゅう　えん　ぐらい
もって　います。　とうきょうに　いきます。
どの　くらい　じかんが　かかりますか。

たなか： にじゅうごふん　ぐらい　かかります。

ジョンソン： あなたは　しごとに　いきますか。

たなか： はい　しごとに　いきます。

ジョンソン： どようびと　にちようびにも　しごとに
いきますか。

たなか： ときどき　どようびに　いきます。
にちようびには　いきません。

II

スミス： ごめん　ください。

いまい： ああ　スミスさん　どうぞ　あがって　ください。

スミス： おじゃま　します。

いまい： どうぞ　すわって　ください。　おちゃを
どうぞ。

スミス： ありがとう　ございます。

I

Jonson: *Baiten-wa dochira desu-ka.*

Tanaka: *Achira desu. Komakai okane-o motte imasu-ka.*

I

Johnson: Which way is the ticket stand?

Tanaka: It is over that way. Do you have small change?

J: *Hai, hyaku go juu en gurai motte imasu. Tookyoo-ni ikimasu. Dono kurai jikan-ga kakarimasu-ka.*

J: Yes, about 150 yen. I am going to Tokyo. About how long will it take?

T: *Nijuugofun gurai kakarimasu.*

T: About 25 minutes.

J: *Anata-wa shigoto-ni ikimasu-ka.*

J: Are you going to work?

T: *Hai, shigoto-ni ikimasu.*

T: Yes.

J: *Doyoobi-to nichiyoobi-ni-mo shigoto-ni ikimasu-ka.*

J: Do you go there also on Saturdays and Sundays?

T: *Tokidoki doyoobi-ni ikimasu. Nichiyoobi-ni-wa ikimasen.*

T: Sometimes I go on Saturday. I don't go on Sundays.

II

Sumisu: *Gomen kudasai.*

Smith: Excuse me.

Imai: *Aa, Sumisu-san, doozo agatte kudasai.*

Imai: Oh, Ms. Smith, please come in.

S: *Ojama shimasu.*

S: I am intruding.

I: *Doozo, suwatte kudasai. Ocha-o doozo.*

I: Please sit down. Please have some tea.

S: *Arigatoo gozaimasu.*

S: Thank you very much.

Motte
Motte means "to hold," or "to have with you." Therefore, *motte itte* literally means "to have with you when you go," or "take." *Motte kite* means "to have with you when you come," or "bring."

Mo
Mo cannot replace *ni, e,* or *de*; it is stated after these particles.
ex. *Doyoobi-ni-mo shigoto-ni ikimasu-ka.*
Do you also go to work on Saturdays?

69

achira
that way

agaru(-u)
to step up,
rise

baiten
ticket/news
stand

dasu(-u)
to take out

dochira
which way

-e
indicates
direction

fun, pun
minutes

geimu
game

**gomen
kudasai**
please
excuse me

**gurai,
kurai**
approxi-
mately,
about

Hiruton
Hilton

jaa
well

jikan
time

kaisha
company

GRAMMAR EXPLANATION

1. -Te Kudasai

The verb form *-te kudasai* is used when requesting someone to please do something.

> *ex. Gohan-o **tabete kudasai.***
> Please eat the food.

> *Kaisha-ni **kite kudasai**.*
> Please come to my company.

Once you know how to conjugate verbs to verb+*imasu*, it is very easy to learn the verb+*kudasai* form. Use the same base verb, drop *imasu*, and add *kudasai*.

ex. mite imasu	is looking
*mite **kudasai***	please look
yonde imasu	is reading
*yonde **kudasai***	please read

2. -Nai

To change the plain form of verbs into negative, the following rules apply:

- *ru* verbs - drop *ru* and add *nai*

taberu	*tabe**nai***
miru	*mi**nai***

- *u* verbs - replace the final *u* with *anai*:

iku	*ik**anai***
yomu	*yom**anai***

hanasu	*hanas**anai***
wakaru	*wakar**anai***

• -*u* verbs with a vowel before *u* - drop *u* and add *wanai*

iu	*iw**anai***

Exceptions:

kuru	*ko**nai***
suru	*shi**nai***
desu	*dewa **nai**, ja **nai*** (informal)

3. Ni

When **specific** time periods, days, dates, months, or years are said to describe when one did or will do something, *ni* always follows.

> *ex. Oku-san-wa nichiyoobi-**ni** Amerika-ni ikimasu.*
> Mr. Oku will go to America on Sunday.

> *Hara-san-wa sanji-**ni** uchi-ni kaerimashita.*
> Mr. Hara returned home at 3:00.

However, when you say **general** times such as yesterday, today, tomorrow, last week, last month, last year, last month, etc., *ni* is not used.

> *ex. Mainichi takusan benkyoo shite imasu.*
> Everyday, I (am) study(ing) a lot.

When you drop the *re* from *kore*, *sore*, *are*, and *dore*, and add *chira*, to form *kochira*, *sochira*, *achira*, and *dochira*, the meanings change to "this way" (close to speaker), "that way" (close to listener), "that way" (far from speaker and listener), and "which way." They also are polite words for *kore*, *sore*, *are*, and *dore*.

E
e can be interchanged with *ni* when indicating direction. *ex. gakko-e ikimasu, doko-e ikimasu-ka.*

71

kaijoo
meeting place

kakaru(-u)
to require, take

kikan
time period

kippu
ticket

komakai
small change

kudamono
fruit

mainichi
every day

motsu(-u)
to hold, have with you

nigiyaka(na)
lively

ojama shimasu
I am in your way

okane
money

onegai shimasu
I plead with you

reizooko
refrigerator

shigoto
work

EXERCISES

1. -Te kudasai

Change the following verbs into the *-te kudasai* form:

ex. machimasu
➥*matte kudasai*

agemasu	*kikimasu*
aimasu	*kakimasu*
arukimasu	*tsutomemasu*
naraimasu	*yomimasu*
nomimasu	*iremasu*
okimasu	*hairimasu*
hanashimasu	*shimasu*
hashirimasu	*tabemasu*
yarimasu	*oshiemasu*

2. Negative plain verbs

Substitute the phrases into the given sentences:

ex. kuruma-o unten suru

➥*Okaa-san: Nobutaka-san-wa* **_kuruma-o unten suru_**-no.
Musoko: Iie, Nobutaka-san-wa **_kuruma-o unten shinai_**.

asobimasu	*enpitsu-o kaimasu*
benkyoo shimasu	*uchi-ni kimasu*
dekakemasu	*bideo-o mimasu*
ikimasu	*eigo-o naraimasu*
nemasu	*kaerimasu*
sakkaa-ga dekimasu	

3. Minutes

The way to express minutes when telling time is as follows:

1 minute - *ippun*	6 minutes - *roppun*
2 minutes - *nifun*	7 minutes - *nanafun*
3 minutes - *sanpun*	8 minutes - *happun*
4 minutes - *yonpun*	9 minutes - *kyuufun*
5 minutes - *gofun*	10 minutes - *jippun*

This pattern continues regularly until 60.

ex. 6:35   *rokuji sanjuugofun*
9:13   *kuji juusanpun*

4. Practice saying the following times:

3:15	6:47	11:06
4:38	1:22	2:59
10:21	12:44	

sochira
that way;
that
direction

suwaru(-u)
to sit

takusan
much

tariru(-ru)
to be enough

tokidoki
sometimes

tsukeru
(-ru)
to turn on

yaru(-u)
to do

yuube
last night

yuugata
evening
(sunset)

SHORT DIALOGUES

1. *ex.* terebi-o miru, terebi-o tsukeru

> Yamada: *Nanika shimashoo-ka.*
> Buraun: *Hai, ii desu yo.*
> Yamada: *Jaa, **terebi-o mimashoo**-ka.*
> Buraun: *Soo desu, ne.*
> (telephone rings)
> Yamada: *Sumimasen. **Terebi-o tsukete** kudasai.*

   1. ocha-o nomu, ocha-o ireru
   2. kudamono-o taberu, reizooko-kara ringo-o dasu
   3. hon-o yomu, hon-o motte kuru
   4. bideo-o miru, bideo-o ireru

2. *ex.* omoshiroi, Kyooto-no resutoran, Yamamoto

> Imai: *Kinyoobi-no paatii-wa doo deshita-ka.*
> Jonson: ***Omoshiroi** paatii deshita. Kaijoo-wa **Kyooto-no resutoran** deshita, yo.*
> Imai: *Soo desu-ka. **Yamamoto**-san-to hanashimashita-ka.*
> Jonson: *Hanashimasen deshita. Jikan-ga arimasen deshita yo.*

   1. nigiyakana, Tookyoo-no hoteru, Kitamura
   2. omoshiroi, Shinjuku-no resutoran, Morita
   3. nigiyakana, Osaka-no hoteru, Ishibashi

3. *ex.* terebi-o miru, 10

> *Okaa-san:*   *Benkyoo shite iru-no.*
> *Musuko:*   *Benkyoo shite inai, yo.* **_Terebi-o_**
>   **_mite iru_**, *no.*
> *Okaa-san:*   *Soo. Ato dono gurai* **_miru_**-*no.*
> *Musuko:*   **_Jippun_** *gurai.*

1. hon-o yomu, 15
2. terebi geimu-o suru, 2
3. gohan-o taberu, 7
4. sakkaa-o suru, 13

SELF-TEST

Translate the following sentences into Japanese:

1. Please eat the tempura.

2. Please come to my house at about 2:15.

3. Which way is the bank?

4. Please buy a ticket.

5. 2,000 yen is not enough.

6. Is your grandmother healthy?

7. Please wait until 5:39.

8. Do you have small change?

9. Do you go to work everyday?

10. Please come this way.

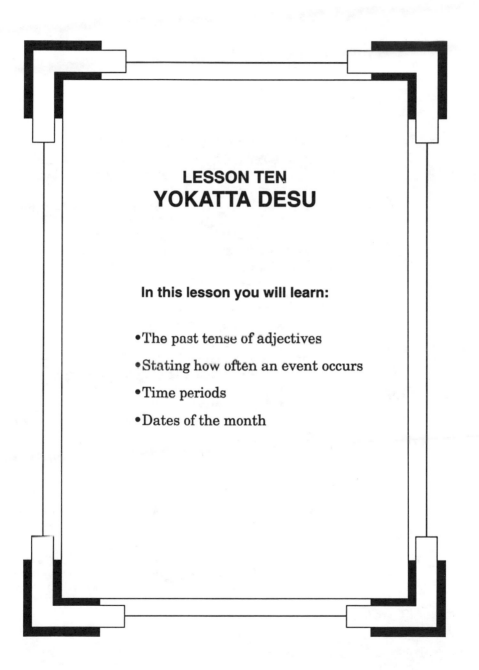

LESSON TEN
YOKATTA DESU

In this lesson you will learn:

- The past tense of adjectives
- Stating how often an event occurs
- Time periods
- Dates of the month

DIALOGUE

I

A: ゆうべは ありがとう ございました.

B: どう いたしまして.

A: こんど わたしの うちに きて ください. いつ おひま ですか.

B: そう ですね. わたしは あたらしい プロジェクトを はじめます ので らいしゅうは いそがしい です.

A: いつ ごろ おわりますか.

B: らいしゅうの きんようびには おわります.

A: あした いっしょに どこかへ いきましょうか.

B: いいえ あしたは いちにち じゅう いそがしい です.

A: ざんねん ですね.

II

A: ゆうべの えいがは どう でしたか.

B: えいがは おもしろくて とても よかった です.

A: つきに どの くらい えいがを みますか.

B: つきに いっかい ぐらいは みます. あなたは どう ですか.

A: にかげつに いっかい ぐらいは みます.

B: いつか いっしょに いきましょうか.

A: それは いい ですね.

I

A: *Yuube-wa arigatoo gozaimashita.*

B: *Doo itashimashite.*

A: *Kondo, watashi-no uchi-ni kite kudasai. Itsu o-hima desu-ka.*

I

A: Thank you very much for (supper) last evening.

B: You're welcome.

A: Next time, please come to my house. When will you be free?

B: *Soo desu ne. Watashi-wa atarashii purojekuto-o hajimemasu node, raishuu-wa isogashii desu.*

B: Well, I will start a new project, so I will be very busy next week.

A: *Itsu goro owarimasu-ka.*

A: When will you finish it?

B: *Raishuu-no kinyoobi-ni-wa owarimasu.*

B: I will finish next Friday.

A: *Ashita issho-ni dokoka-e ikimashoo-ka.*

A: Shall we go somewhere tomorrow?

B: *Iie, ashita-wa ichi nichi juu isogashii desu.*

B: No, tomorrow I'm busy all day long.

A: *Zannen desu, ne.*

A: That's too bad.

II

A: *Yuube-no eiga-wa doo deshita-ka.*

A: How was the movie last night?

B: *Eiga-wa omoshirokute totemo yokatta desu.*

B: It was interesting and very good.

A: *Tsuki-ni dono kurai eiga-o mimasu-ka.*

A: How many times a month do you see a movie?

B: *Tsuki-ni ikkai gurai-wa mimasu. Anata-wa doo desu-ka.*

B: I usually see one about once a month. How about you?

A: *Nikagetsu-ni ikkai gurai-wa mimasu.*

A: I usually see one about once every two months.

B: *Itsuka issho-ni ikimashoo-ka.*

B: Sometime, shall we go together?

A: *Sore-wa ii desu ne.*

A: That would be good.

-Go-ni
When stating a change that will occur **after** a specific time period, add *-go-ni* to the time frame. ex. *Nishuukan-go-ni Amerika-ni kaerimasu.* I will go back to American in two weeks. However, when talking about a general time frame, such as next month, etc., use *kara* (which means "after" in this case). ex. *Raishuu kara, Amerika-ni kaerimasu.* After next week, I will go back to America.

asagohan
breakfast

arigatoo
gozaimashita
thank you
for what you
did

asobi-ni
to see
someone

da
plain form of
desu

dareka
someone

-do
number of
times

dokoka
some place,
somewhere

goro
approxi-
mately,
around

hajimeru(-u)
to begin
(requires
object)

hima
free;
available

hiru
noon

hirugohan
lunch

hontoo
real, true

GRAMMAR EXPLANATION

1. Adjectives to past tense

In Japanese, when sentences in the past tense contain *i* adjectives directly before the verb, the adjectives are changed instead of the verb.

To change an *i* adjective to past tense, drop the final *i* and add *katta*.

> ex. *Koebi-wa oishii desu.*
> The shrimp is delicious.
>
> *Koebi-wa oishikatta desu.*
> The shrimp was delicious.

For *na* adjectives, change *desu* to *deshita*.

> ex. *Sono onnanohito-wa kirei desu.*
> That woman is pretty.
>
> *Sono onnanohito-wa kirei deshita.*
> That woman was pretty.

2. How Often

The grammar structure for stating how often something occurs is as follows:

> (time period) ***kan-ni*** (how often)-***do/kai*** (verb).

> ex. *Isshuukan-ni ni-kai unten shimasu.*
> *Isshuukan-ni ni-do unten shimasu.*
> I drive 2 times a week.

*Nishuu**kan-ni** san-do taitei resutoran-ni ikimasu.*

*Nishuu**kan-ni** san-kai taitei resutoran-ni ikimasu.*

I usually go to a restaurant three times every two weeks.

3. Issho-ni

Use *to* (and) with *issho-ni* when stating you did or will do something together with a person or thing.

> *ex. Sumisu-san-wa Tanaka-san-**to issho-ni** ikimashita.*
>
> Mr. Smith and Mr. Tanaka went together.
>
> *Hara-san-wa watashi-**to issho-ni** sugu benkyoo shimasu.*
>
> Mrs. Hara and I will soon study together.

To ask how many times an event occurs, one can use *nando* or *nankai. ex. Isshuukan-ni **nando** sake-o nomimasu-ka? Isshuukan-ni **nankai** sake-o nomimasu-ka?* How many times in one week do you drink sake?

EXERCISES

1. Adjectives to past tense

Change the following adjectives to past tense:

ex. oishii desu

➡ *oishi**katta** desu*

atsui desu	*omoshiroi desu*
hayai desu	*osoi desu*
hiroi desu	*samui desu*
muzukashii desu	*yasashii desu*

Kan
Kan states the time period; *isshuukan*, for one week; *ichijikan*, for one hour; *nishuukan*, for two weeks; *sanjuppunkan*, for 30 minutes.

**ichi nichi
juu**
all day long

ikkai
once

issho-ni
together

isshuukan
one week

itsu
when

itsuka
some time

-kai
number of
times

koebi
shrimp

kondo
next time

maiasa
every
morning

mata
again

moo
already

-nen
counter for
years

nishuukan
two weeks

node
because, since
(more polite
than *kara*)

2. Time periods:

Days

One day - *ichinichi*	Six days - *muika*
Two days - *futsuka*	Seven days - *nanoka*
Three days -*mikka*	Eight days - *yooka*
Four days - *yokka*	Nine days - *kokonoka*
Five days - *itsuka*	Ten days - *tooka*

•The additional numbers are the same as used in counting,+*nichi*.
    ex. juuichinichi   11 days

Weeks

One week	*isshuu*
Two weeks	*nishuu*
Three weeks	*sanshuu*
Four weeks	*yonshuu*
Five weeks	*goshuu*

•This pattern continues regularly, number +*shuu*.

Months

One month	*ikkagetsu, tsuki, hitotsuki*
Two months	*nikagetsu*
Three months	*sankagetsu*
Four months	*yonkagetsu*
Five months	*gokagetsu*

•The pattern continues, number + *kagetsu*.
    ex. Ten months   *jukkagetsu*
        Eleven months *juuikkagetsu*

Years

    One year - *ichinen*   Four years - *yonen*

    Two years - *ninen*   Five years - *gonen*

    Three years - *sannen*

•This pattern continues regularly, number + *nen*.

3. Dates of the month:

first - *tsuitachi*	sixth - *muika*
second - *futsuka*	seventh - *nanoka*
third - *mikka*	eighth - *yooka*
fourth - *yokka*	ninth - *kokonoka*
fifth - *itsuka*	tenth - *tooka*

•The rest of the numbers are stated the same as when counting, plus *nichi*.
    ex. *juuichinichi*

To say the date, state the year, month, then the day.

    ex. *Sen kyuuhyaku kyuujuuyo nen shigatsu muika*
    1994, April 6

    Sen kyuuhyaku kyuujuuyo nen kugatsu juusannichi
    1994, September 13

    Ichigatsu tsuitachi-wa yasumi desu.
    January 1 is a holiday.

Mai
When *mai* is added to the beginning of a word that indicates a day or time, it becomes every _____. *ex. mainichi,* every day; *maishuu,* every week, *maitsuki,* every month

When an adjective appears *directly* before a noun, do not change the adjective to past tense, only change the verb. *ex. omoshiroi paatii deshita.*

owaru(-u)
to finish (no
object)

purojekuto
project

raishuu
next week

senshuu
last week

sugoi(i)
great

sugu
immediately,
soon

taitei
usually

tesuto
test

tsuki
one month's
time

ukeru(-ru)
to take (a
test)

yasumi
holiday, rest
time, break
time

yuuhan
supper

zannen(na)
too bad

4. Practice

State the following times Mr. Smith eats sushi:

ex. once a week
➡*Sumisu-san-wa **isshuu**kan-ni **ichi**-do
sushi- o tabemasu.*

once a year, month
twice a year, week, month
three times a year, week, month

SHORT DIALOGUES

1. *ex.* eiga-o, miru, omoshiroi

Yuki:	*Sono-**eiga-o** moo **mimashita**-ka.*
Hiroko:	*Hai, senshuu-no kinyoobi-ni **mimashita**.*
Yuki:	*Doo deshita-ka.*
Hiroko:	***Omoshirokatta** desu.*

1. atarashii resutoran-ni, iku, oishii
2. tesuto-o ukeru, muzukashii
3. atarashii depaato-ni, iku, takai
4. rajio-o kiku, sugoi

2. *ex.* ikkagetsu, eiga-o miru, nikai

> *Tanaka:* *Sumisu-san-wa* ***ikkagetsu****-ni dono*
> *gurai* ***eiga-o mimasu****-ka.*
> *Sumisu:* *Soo-desu ne.* ***Ikkagetsu****-ni* ***nikai***
> *gurai* ***eiga-o mimasu****.*
> *Tanaka:* *Hontoo desu-ka. Jaa, kondo issho-ni*
> *ikimashoo.*
> *Sumisu:* *Hai. Soo shimashoo.*

> 1. isshuukan, eiga-o miru, sankai
> 2. ichinen, Kyooto-ni iku, ichido
> 3. isshuukan, resutoran-de taberu, yonkai
> 4. isshuukan, sake-o nomu, nikai

Rai
Rai is a prefix meaning "next," and is combined with words like week, month, and year to form *raishuu* (next week), *raigetsu* (next month), and *rainen* (next year).

3. *ex.* nishuukan-go-ni, tsuitachi, hirugohan

> *Kaori:* *Kondo itsu aimashoo-ka.*
> *Kumiko:* *Soo desu ne.* ***Nishuukan-go-ni***
> *hima desu yo.*
> *Kaori:* *Sore dewa, nigatsu* ***tsuitachi****-ni*
> *aimashoo-ka.*
> *Kumiko:* *Hai. Soo shimashoo.*
> *Kaori:* ***Hirugohan****-o issho-ni tabemashoo-ka.*
> *Kumiko:* *Ii desu yo.*

> 1. nishuukan-go-ni, mikka, asagohan
> 2. raishuu, kokonoka, yuuhan
> 3. raishuu, yooka, hirugohan
> 4. sanshuukan-go-ni, futsuka, yuuhan

Verbs that are paired with *suru* can be used with *suru* or *-o suru.* *ex. unten suru* or *unten-o suru.* Additionally, the first word in the verb pair can stand alone as a noun.

SELF TEST

Use *wa, ga, o, ni, de, do, kai, san, ka,* or X in the
 following blanks:

1. Maiasa ___ nihongo ___ benkyoo shite imasu.

2. Isshuukan ___ san ___ resutoran ___ tabemasu.

3. Watashi ___ nikagetsukan ___ ikkai Kyooto ___
 ikimasu.

4. Senshuu ___ kinyoobi ___ tesuto ___
 muzukashikatta ___ desu.

5. Raishuu ___ mokuyoobi ___ shigoto ___
 hajimemasu.

Translate the following sentences into Japanese:

6. Friday is not a holiday.

7. I go to the department store once a week.

8. Today is December fifth.

9. On Friday, I took a difficult test.

10. Mr. Tanaka and (I) together ate lunch.

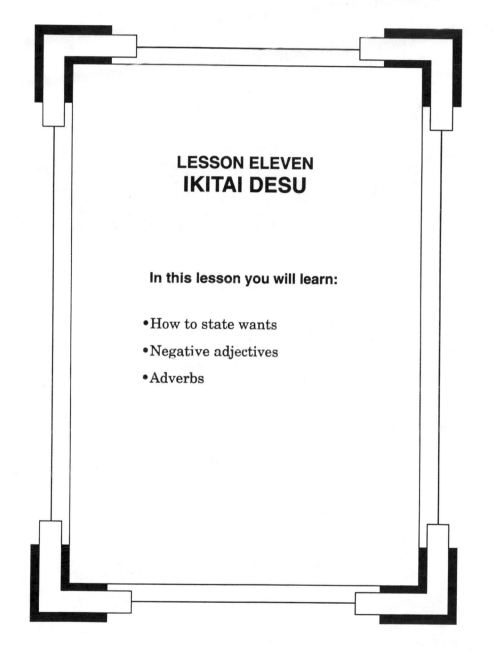

LESSON ELEVEN
IKITAI DESU

In this lesson you will learn:

- How to state wants
- Negative adjectives
- Adverbs

DIALOGUE

I

A: あなたは　こうこうせい　ですか.

B: はい　そう　です.

A: ひらかわ　けいごくんを　しって　いますか.

B: ひらかわ　けいご　くん...

A: かれは　せが　たかい　です.

B: ああ　そうそう.　かれは　わたしの　せんぱい　です.

A: おねえさんは　アメリカで　だいがくに　はいって
いますか.

B: はい　はいって　います.　せんもんは　ビジネス　です.

A: そう　ですか.　おねえさんは　にほんごも　べんきょう
して　いますか.

B: まえに　にほんごを　べんきょう　して　いた　けど　もう
やめました.　でも　かのじょは　にほんに　いきたいと
いって　いました.

A: いつ　ごろ　おねえさんは　だいがくを　そつぎょう
しますか.

B: にねん　ぐらいで　そつぎょう　する　かも　しれません.

II

A: こんばん　げきを　めませんか.

B: ああ　こんばんの　おんがくがいの　きっぷが　あります.
すっかり　わすれて　いました.　いきませんか.

A: いい　ですよ.　なんじに　はじまりますか.

B: しちじに　はじまります.

A: きっぷは　たかい　ですか.

B: いいえ　あまり　たかく　ありません.

I	I
A: *Anata-wa kookoo-sei desu-ka.*	A: Are you a high school student?
B: *Hai, soo desu.*	B: Yes I am.
A: *Hirakawa Keigo-kun-o shitte imasu-ka.*	A: Do you know Keigo Hirakawa?
B: *Hirakawa Keigo-kun . . .*	B: Keigo Hirakawa . . .

A: *Kare-wa se-ga takai desu.*

A: He is tall.

B: *Aa, soo soo. Kare-wa watashi-no senpai desu.*

B: Oh yes, he is ahead of me.

A: *Onee-san-wa Amerika-de daigaku-ni haitte imasu-ka.*

A: Is your older sister in college in America?

B: *Hai, haitte imasu. Senmon-wa bijinesu desu.*

B: Yes. Her major is business.

A: *Soo desu-ka. Onee-san-wa nihongo-mo benkyoo shite imasu-ka.*

A: Really. Is she also studying Japanese?

B: *Mae-ni nihongo-o benkyoo shite ita kedo, moo yamemashita. Demo kanojo-wa Nihon-ni ikitai-to itte imashita.*

B: She was before, but she gave up. However, she said she would like to come to Japan.

A: *Itsu goro onee-san-wa daigaku-o sotsugyoo shimasu-ka.*

A: When will she graduate from college?

B: *Ninen gurai-de sotsugyoo suru kamo shiremasen.*

B: I'm not sure, but maybe in about 2 years.

II

II

A: *Konban geki-o mimasen-ka.*

A: Would you like to see a play tonight?

B: *Aa, konban-no ongakukai-no kippu-ga arimasu. Sukkari wasurete imashita. Ikimasen-ka.*

B: Oh, I have tickets to a concert tonight. I completely forgot about it. Would you like to go?

A: *Ii desu yo. Nanji-ni hajimarimasu-ka.*

A: That's fine. What time does it start?

B: *Shichiji-ni hajimarimasu.*

B: It starts at 7:00.

A: *Kippu-wa takai desu-ka.*

A: Were the tickets expensive?

B: *Iie, amari takaku arimasen.*

B: No, not very expensive.

To state that one is working somewhere, say the name of the company or place, then add *-ni tsutomete imasu. ex. Tanaka-san-wa Mitsubishi-ni tsutomete imasu.* Mr. Tanaka works at Mitsubishi. *Watashi-wa toshokan-ni tsutomete imasu.* I work at a library.

aa, soo soo
Oh, that's
right

bijinesu
business

daigaku
college

daredemo
everyone

dokodemo
everywhere

ga
but

geki
play

gekijoo
theater
where plays
are

hajimaru(-u)
to start (no
object)

ita
imashita
(plain)

itsudemo
any time

**kamo
shirenai**
I'm not sure

kedo
but, though

konban
this evening

kono goro
these days

GRAMMAR EXPLANATION

1. -Tai desu

To change verbs to mean "I want to _____," drop *masu* and add *tai desu*.

> ex. *Watashi-wa Tookyoo-ni ikimasu.*
> I go to Tokyo.

> *Watashi-wa Tookyoo-ni ikitai desu.*
> I want to go to Tokyo.

> *Watashi-wa tsugi-ni supeingo-o benkyoo shitai desu.*
> I want to study Spanish next.

When asking someone if they want to do something, Japanese people usually ask using a negative verb.

> ex. *Tookyoo-ni ikimasen-ka.*
> Don't you (want to) go to Tokyo?

2. Negative adjectives

To convert *i* adjectives into negative, drop the final *i* and add *-ku arimasen*.

> ex. *Kono kuruma-wa hayai desu.*
> This car is fast.

> *Kono kuruma-wa hayaku arimasen.*
> This car is not fast.

90

Kookoo-no benkyoo-wa muzukashii desu.
High school studies are difficult.

*Kookoo-no benkyoo-wa muzukashi**ku
arimasen**.*
High school studies are not difficult.

For informal speech, use *-ku nai*

ex. *Kono o-kashi-wa oishi**ku nai**.*
This snack is not delicious.

To change *na* adjectives into negative, add *dewa arimasen* after the adjective.

ex. *kirei **dewa arimasen***
not beautiful

*genki **dewa arimasen***
not healthy

For informal speech, use *ja nai* instead.

ex. *taihen **ja nai***
not tough

3. Adjectives to Adverbs

To change adjectives into adverbs:

For *i* adjectives, drop the final *i* and add *ku*

ex. *hayai*
*haya**ku** owarimashita*
finished quickly

osoi
*oso**ku** tabemasu*
eats slowly

Hajimeru and *hajimaru*, along with *oeru* and *owaru* are two examples of verbs that have the same meaning, but require different grammar structure. *Hajimeru* and *oeru* need to have objects preceeding them, while *hajimaru* and *owaru* are used without objects. *ex. Itsu owarimashita-ka.* When did you finish? *Itsu purojekuto-o oemashita-ka.* When did you finish the project?

91

koohai
one's junior

kookoo
high school

-kun
used instead
of -san at the
end of boys'
names

kurashikku
classical

nandemo
anything,
everything

oeru(-ru)
to finish
(requires
object)

ongakukai
concert

se-ga takai
tall

-sei
student
(suffix)

senmon
major

senpai
one's senior

shitte iru
to know

**sotsugyoo
suru**
to graduate

For *na* adjectives, drop the final *na* and add *ni*

> *ex. kirei**na***
> *kirei-**ni** nihongo-o hanashimasu*
> speaks Japanese beautifully

> *genki**na***
> *genki-**ni** narimasu*
> becomes healthy (better)

Adverbs can come either directly before the verb or the object:

> *ex. kuruma-o **hayaku** unten shimasu*
> ***hayaku** kuruma-o unten shimasu*
> drives the car quickly

> ***kirei-ni** nihongo-o hanashimasu*
> *nihongo-o **kirei-ni** hanashimasu*
> speaks Japanese beautifully

4. -Kamo shiremasen

To state that you are unsure about somthing, use a plain verb, then add *-kamo shiremasen.*

> *ex. Michiko-san-wa supeingo-o benkyoo suru **kamo shiremasen**.*
> I'm not sure, (but I think) Michiko studies Spanish.

> *Ashita ame-ga furu **kamo shiremasen**.*
> I'm not sure, (but I think) it will rain tomorrow.

EXERCISES

1. Shitai

Place these verbs into the following sentence:

ex. unten suru

➡️*Watashi-wa **unten shitai desu** kedo, moo yamemasu.*

kiku	*yaru*	*kaeru*
kaku	*kau*	*yomu*
kuru	*iku*	*aruku*
matsu	*asobu*	*miru*
narau	*dekakeru*	*nomu*
tsutomeru	*hairu*	*oshieru*
hanasu	*suru*	*hashiru*
taberu	*benkyoo suru*	

2. Negative Adjectives

Change the adjectives to negative, then place them in the following sentences:

ex. takai

➡️*Sore-wa **takai** desu-ka.*
*Iie, amari **takaku** arimasen.*

atsui	*hayai*	*osoi*
hiroi	*samui*	*muzukashii*
omoshiroi	*yasashii*	*oishii*
yasui	*kurai*	*furui*
taihen(na)	*kirei(na)*	*suki(na)*

-Kun
-Kun is used among male friends, when a male boss speaks to his male or female subordinate, or when talking to a male child.

Ga, Kedo
Ga is a little softer than *demo*, while *kedo* has the same meaning as *demo*. They are often used as sentence connectors. *Paatii-ni ikitai desu ga, shigoto-ni ikimasu.* I want to go to the party, but I will go to work. *Kuruma-o kaitai desu kedo, okane-ga tarimasen.* I want to buy a car, but I do not have enough money.

93

sukkari
completely

supeingo
Spanish

-tachi
plural suffix

**-to itte
imashita**
was saying

toshokan
library

tsugi-ni
next

**wasureru
(-ru)**
to forget

watashitachi
we

yameru(-ru)
to give up,
stop

zasshi
magazine

zuibun
very

3. Change the adjectives into adverbs when combining them with their paired word:

ex. *hayai, unten shimasu*
➡*hayaku unten shimasu*

hayai, hashirimasu	*osoi, narimasu*
yasashii, shimasu	*yoi, nemasu*
akarui, narimasu	*kireina, narimasu*

4. Substitute the following work places into the sentence:

Hanabusa-san-wa _____ -ni tsutomete imasu.

daigaku	*Toyota*	*yuubinkyoku*
biyooin	*depaato*	*Honda*
resutoran	*byooin*	*yakkyoku*

5. -Kamo shiremasen

Change the following sentences into the *-kamo shiremasen* phrase:

ex. *Geki-wa shichiji-han-ni hajimarimasu.*
➡*Geki-wa shichiji-han-ni hajimaru kamo shiremasen.*

Sensei-wa isogashiku arimasen.
Ninenkan nihongo-o benkyoo shite imasu.
Kare-wa watashi-no koohai desu.
Ano hito-no senmon-wa bijinesu desu.
Yagi-san-wa toshokan-ni tsutomete imasu.
Kyoo Morita-san-wa Tookyoo-ni ikimasen.
Ano hito-wa gakusei dewa arimasen.

SHORT DIALOGUES

1. *ex.* hon-o yomu

> A: *Nani-o shitai desu-ka.*
> B: *Nandemo ii desu. Anata-wa.*
> A: ***Hon-o yomitai*** *desu.*
> B: *Jaa, soo shimashoo.*

> 1. oishii tenpura-o tsukuru
> 2. kuruma-o unten suru
> 3. supeingo-o benkyoo suru
> 4. Tookyoo-ni iku
> 5. zubon-o kau
> 6. kurashikku-o kiku

Tachi
When *-tachi* is added to certain nouns, it changes those words to plural. *ex. kodomo + tachi*, children; *watashi + tachi*, we/us; *Yamada-san + tachi; Yamada* and the others.

2. *ex.* atarashii hon, yomu, omoshiroi

> A: *Sumimasen, osoku narimashite.*
> B: *Ii desu yo. Hirakawa-san-tachi-mo mada kite imasen yo.*
> A: *Tokorode,* ***atarashii hon****-o moo* ***yomimashita****-ka.*
> B: *Hai,* ***yomimashita****.*
> A: *Zuibun hayaku* ***yomimashita****, ne.*
> B: *Ee,* ***omoshirokatta*** *desu kara.*

> 1. atarashii zasshi, yomu, omoshiroi
> 2. atarashii purojekuto, oeru, yasashii
> 3. kippu, kau, yasui
> 4. atarashii bideo, miru, omoshiroi

3. *ex.* daigaku, muzukashii

> *Imai: Jonson-san-wa gakusei desu-ka.*
> *Jonson:Hai. Senshuu-kara **daigaku**-ni itte*
> *imasu.*
> *I: Soo desu-ka. **Muzukashii** desu-ka.*
> *J: Iie, amari **muzukashiku** arimasen. Kono*
> *goro-wa isogashii desu-ka.*
> *I: Iie, amari isogashiku arimasen.*

> 1. kookoo, yasashii
> 2. daigaku, isogashii
> 3. kookoo, muzukashii

SELF-TEST

Translate the following sentences into Japanese:

1. I want to go to Kyoto next week on Thursday.

2. I want to study Japanese three times a week.

3. Please come quickly.

4. I'm not sure, (but I think) he is ahead of me.

5. I'm not sure, (but I think) Mr. Tanaka is not going to the movie theater.

6. Today it is not very cold.

7. Grandfather is not healthy.

8. Do you want to go to a classical concert this evening?

9. That movie was not interesting.

10. I want to work for Fuji Bank.

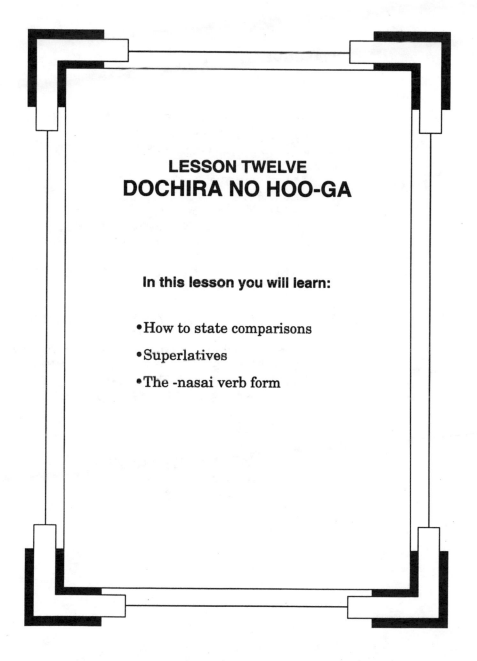

LESSON TWELVE
DOCHIRA NO HOO-GA

In this lesson you will learn:

- How to state comparisons
- Superlatives
- The -nasai verb form

DIALOGUE

I

A: いらっしゃいませ.　なにを　さしあげましょうか.

B: はな　もようの　ワンピースを　ください.

A: はい.　サイズは　いくつ　ですか.

B: きゅう　です.

A: いそいで　いますか.

B: ええ　まあ...

A: こちらは　どう　ですか.

B: もっと　あかるい　いろの　ものは　ありますか.

A: はい.　これと　これは　どう　ですか.　どちらが　すき
ですか.

B: こちらの　ほうが　きれい　です.　これを　ください.

A: はい　ありがとう　ございます.

II

A: けさ　ごはんを　たくさん　たべました.　でも　おなかが
すきました.　きっさてんに　いきましょう.

B: それは　いい　ですね.　わたしは　のどが　かわきました.
でも　その　きっさてんは　とても　こんで　いますよ.

A: ほんとうに　こんで　いますね.　じゃ　もっと　すいて
いる　ところを　さがしましょうか.

B: かまいませんよ.

A: つかれましたか.

B: そこし　つかれました.

A: わたしは　この　きっさてんが　いちばん　すき　です.

B: この　きっさてんは　たかい　ですか.

A: じつは　この　きっさてんは　ほかの　きっさてん　よりも
やすい　です.

B: それなら　はいりましょう.

I

A: *Irasshaimase, nani-o sashiagemashoo-ka.*

B: *Hana moyoo-no wanpiisu-o kudasai.*

A: *Hai. Saizu-wa ikutsu desu-ka.*

B: *Kyuu desu.*

A: *Isoide imasu-ka.*

B: *Ee, maa . . .*

A: *Kochira-wa doo desu-ka.*

B: *Motto akarui iro-no mono-wa arimasu-ka.*

A: *Hai. Kore-to kore-wa doo desu-ka. Dochira-ga suki desu-ka.*

B: *Kochira-no hoo-ga kirei desu. Kore-o kudasai.*

A: *Hai, arigatoo gozaimasu.*

II

A: *Kesa gohan-o takusan tabemashita, demo onaka-ga sukimashita. Kissaten-ni ikimashoo.*

B: *Sore-wa ii desu ne. Watashi-wa nodo-ga kawakimashita. Demo, sono kissaten-wa totemo konde imasu, yo.*

A: *Hontoo-ni konde imasu, ne. Jaa, motto suite iru tokoro-o sagashimashoo-ka.*

I

A: Welcome, may I help you?

B: I would like a floral dress, please.

A: Alright, what size do you wear?

B: I am a nine.

A: Are you in a hurry?

B: Yes, kind of.

A: How about this one?

B: Do you have a brighter colored one?

A: Yes. How about this one or this one? Which do you like?

B: This one is prettier. I'll take it.

A: Yes, thank you very much.

II

A: I ate a lot for breakfast, but I am hungry. Let's go to a cafe.

B: That sounds good. I'm thirsty. Oh, this one is very crowded.

A: Well, shall we find a place that's less crowded?

To state "I'm full," use *onaka-ga ippai desu.*

Although *ookii* and *chiisai* are *i* adjectives, when they are directly in front of the noun they modify, they can act as *na* adjectives as well. *ex. Ookii ringo, ookina ringo; chiisai tsukue, chiisana tsukue.* Either form is acceptable.

99

amai(i)
sweet

daijoobu
OK; all right

hana
flower

hontoo-ni
indeed,
really

ikutsu
how old

ippai(i)
full

**ippan teki-
ni ieba**
generally
speaking

irasshaimase
welcome

isogu(-u)
to be in a
hurry

jitsu-wa
actually

kaimono
shopping

kakeru(-ru)
to wear
(glasses)

kamaimasen
(I) don't mind

karui(i)
light (not
heavy)

B: *Kamaimasen, yo.*

A: *Tsukaremashita-ka.*

B: *Sukoshi tsukaremashita.*

A: *Watashi-wa kono kissaten-
ga ichiban suki desu.*

B: *Kono kissaten-wa takai
desu-ka.*

A: *Jitsu-wa, kono kissaten-
wa hoka-no kissaten yori-
mo yasui desu.*

B: *Sore nara hairimashoo.*

B: I don't mind.

A: Are you tired?

B: A little.

A: This cafe is my favorite!

B: Is this cafe expensive?

A: Actually, it's less expensive than other cafes.

B: In that case, let's go in.

GRAMMAR EXPLANATION
1. Comparisons

•When both objects of comparison are already known:

Motto

Item-*wa motto* adj. *desu.*

*ex. Kono tesuto-wa **motto** muzukashii desu.*
This test is more difficult.

To inquire:
Motto adj. *mono-ga arimasu-ka.*
Motto yasui mono-ga arimasu-ka.
Do you have a cheaper one?

Moo sukoshi

Item-*wa moo sukoshi* adj *desu.*

ex. Ippan teki-ni ieba kono gakkoo-no tesuto-

*wa **moo sukoshi** muzukashii desu.*
Generally speaking, this school's test is a little more difficult.

***Moo sukoshi** yasui mono-ga arimasu-ka.*
Do you have one that is a little cheaper?

No hoo-ga

Item ***no hoo-ga*** <u>adj</u> ***desu***.

*ex. Eigo **no hoo-ga** yasashii desu.*
English is easier.

*Sono kissaten **no hoo-ga** ii desu.*
That cafe is better.

• When both objects have yet to be stated:
Yori, yori mo (*yori mo* is a little stronger)

Item one-***wa*** <u>item two</u> ***yori*** (***mo***) <u>adj</u> ***desu***.

Item one is more + adj. than the second item.

*ex. Eigo-wa nihongo **yori mo** yasashii desu.*
English is easier than Japanese.

*Amerika-wa Nihon **yori** hiroi desu.*
America is more spacious than Japan.

2. Dochira no hoo-ga

To ask someone whether or not something is older, harder, more expensive, etc., use this sentence pattern:

Item one ***to*** <u>item two</u> ***dewa dochira***
(no hoo) -ga <u>adj.</u> ***desu-ka***.

kawaku(-u)
to be dry

kesa
this morning

kissaten
cafe

konde iru
to be
crowded

kono aida
the other
day

maa
kind of

megane
glasses

mono
thing

**moo
sukoshi**
a little more

motto
more

moyoo
print

ningyoo
doll

nodo
throat

**onaka-ga
suku(-u)**
to be hungry

sagasu(-u)
to look for

ex. *Kono hon-to sono hon dewa **dochira (no hoo)-ga** omoshiroi desu-ka.*
Which is more interesting, this book or that book?
*Sono ningyoo to ano ningyoo-wa **dochira (no hoo)-ga** kirei desu-ka.*
Which is more beautiful, that doll or that doll?

The subject phrase can be omitted if it is undestood.

ex. ***Dochira (no hoo)-ga** kirei desu-ka.*
Which is more beautiful?

If you are asked a *dochira (no hoo)-ga* question, you must answer in the *(no hoo)-ga* form.

If you are asked *dochira (no hoo)-ga hoshii desu-ka*, and it makes no difference to you, answer *dochira mo ii desu*, "either one is good."

3. Superlatives

To state that something is the biggest, most expensive, best, etc., use *ichiban*+ the adjective. As learned previously, *ichiban* means "number one;" therefore, when you state *ichiban ookii*, you are literally stating "number one big", or "biggest."

ex. ***ichiban** kirei*
prettiest
***ichiban** muzukashii*
most difficult
***ichiban** suki*
my favorite; what I like best

102

ichiban karui
lightest

4. -Nasai

To command or order someone to do something, only the verb needs to be changed. To do this, drop the ending *masu*, and add *nasai*.

ex. suwarimasu	sits
suwarinasai	sit down!
koko-ni kinasai	come here!

EXERCISES
1. No hoo-ga

Using the following combination of words, create questions and answers using the *no hoo-ga* phrase:

ex. daigaku, kookoo, taihen
➡ A: **Daigaku** to **kookoo**-dewa dochira
no hoo-ga **taihen** desu-ka.
B: **Daigaku** no hoo-ga **taihen** desu.

nihongo, eigo, muzukashii
sushi, tenpura, oishii
*Toyota-no kuruma, Nissan-no kuruma,
hayai*
Nihon, Amerika, hiroi
kono o-kashi, sono o-kashi, amai

saizu
size

sore nara
in that case

suite iru
not crowded;
to be empty

sunde iru
live

tanjoobi
birthday

tatsu(-u)
to stand

*tsukare-
mashita*
tired

uru(-u)
to sell

yakyuu
baseball

yori (mo)
more than

zutto
much

2. Substitute the given words into the following phrases based on your opinions:

___-*wa yori muzukashii desu.*___-*wa yori yasashii desu.*
    eigo, nihongo   *nihongo, supeingo*
    shigoto, benkyoo   *katakana, hiragana*

___-*wa motto omoshiroi desu.*
    kookoo, daigaku   *sakkaa, yakyuu*
    tanjoobi-no paatii, shigoto-no paatii
    eiga, ongakukai

___-*wa moo sukoshi takai desu.*
    ocha, koohii   *sushi, o-sashimi*
    akai budooshu, shiroi budooshu
    pan, gohan

3. Substitute the following verbs into the sentence using the -nasai form:

    ex. gohan-o tabemasu
  ➡ *Nobutaka-kun,* **gohan-o tabenasai**.

tomodachi-ni ageru	*gakkoo-ni iku*
aruku	*miru*
kiku	*benkyoo suru*
koko-de matsu	*dekakeru*
miruku-o nomu	*okiru*
uchi-ni hairu	*megane-o kakeru*
hanasu	*yomu*
isu-ni suwaru	*tatsu*
hashiru	*kaku*
baiten-de kippu-o kau	

SHORT DIALOGUES

1. *ex.* onaka-ga sukimashita, taberu, kudamono

   A: ***Onaka-ga sukimashita***, *ne.*
   B: *Watashi-mo soo desu yo.*
   A: *Nanika **tabemashoo**-ka.*
   B: *Hai. **Kudamono**-wa doo desu-ka.*
   A: ***Kudamono**-o **tabemashoo**.*

   1. nodo-ga kawakimashita, nomu, juusu
   2. onaka-ga sukimashita, taberu, o-kashi
   3. nodo-ga kawakimashita, nomu, biiru
   4. onaka-ga sukimashita, taberu, sushi

2. *ex.* takai

   A: *Anata-wa doko-ni sunde imasu-ka.*
   B: *Mae-ni Oosaka-ni sunde imashita.*
      Ima-wa Tookyoo-no apaato-ni sunde imasu.
   A: *Dochira no hoo-ga **takai** desu-ka.*
   B: *Tookyoo-no apaato no hoo-ga zutto **takai** desu.*
   A: *Soo desu-ka.*

   1. chiisai
   2. hiroi
   3. yasui
   4. suki

Although *shitte iru* means that one knows something, to state that one does **not** know something, *shirimasen* is always used. The Japanese do not say *shitte imasen.*

3. *ex.* chiisai, ookina

> Sumisu: *Sumimasen, kono kutsu-wa **chiisai** desu. Motto **ookina** kutsu-ga arimasu-ka.*
>
> Ten'in: *Chotto matte kudasai. Aa, arimashita.*
>
> Sumisu: *Kono kutsu no hoo-ga ii desu. Kore-o kudasai.*
>
> Ten'in: *Hai, arigatoo gozaimasu.*

1. takai, yasui
2. ookii, chiisai
3. iro-ga kurai, akarui iro-no
4. iro-ga akarui, kurai iro-no

SELF TEST

Unscramble the following sentences:

1. dewa dochira no Oosutoraria ka Nihon ga to desu hoo hiroi.

2. wa konde kissaten imasu totemo ne kono.

3. ano desu wa takai tatemono ichiban.

4. ookina hoshii seeta ga motto desu.

5. mo desu hiragana kantan yori.

Fill in the blanks with *wa, ga, de, o, ni, to, no, ka, ne,* or X:

6. Kono ningyoo ___ hoka ___ ningyoo ___ yori ___ takai desu.

7. Sono eiga ___ ano eiga ___ dochira ___ hoo ___ omoshiroi desu ___.

8. Kono saizu ___ hoo ___ ookii ___ desu.

9. Watashi ___ motto ___ ookina seetaa ___ kaitai desu.

10. Motto ___ akarui iro ___ mono ___ arimasu ___.

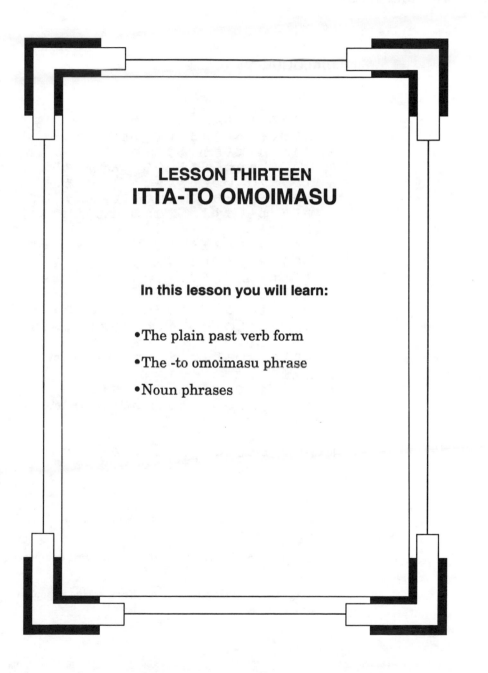

LESSON THIRTEEN
ITTA-TO OMOIMASU

In this lesson you will learn:

- The plain past verb form
- The -to omoimasu phrase
- Noun phrases

DIALOGUE

A: あなたの せんもんは なんですか。
B: こうがくを べんきゅう して います。
A: こうがくは にんきが ありますね。
B: はい。 じゅうねん まえ から にんきが あります。
A: エンジニアは いつも ざんぎょう しませんか。
B: いいえ ほとんどの にほんじんが ざんぎょう して
　 いると おもいますよ。 あなたの せんもんは
　 なんですか。
A: ほうりつを べんきょう して います。 それ から
　 しゅうしを とりたいと おもいます。
B: そう ですか。 あそこに すわって いる ひとも
　 ほうりつを べんきょう して います。
A: ああ。 あの ひとは もりさん ですね。 たぶん あの
　 ひとは わたしの せいじがくの クラスに はいって
　 いると おもいます。
B: もりさんと いっしょに すわって いる ひとが
　 みえますか。
A: コーヒーを のんで いる ひと ですか。
B: そう です。 あの ひとは だいがくいんの がくせい
　 ですよ。
A: そう ですか。
B: はい。 かのじょは きょうじゅに なると おもいます。
A: すごい ですね。

A: *Anata-no senmon-wa nandesu-ka.*

A: What's your major?

B: *Koogaku-o benkyoo shite imasu.*

B: I'm studying engineering.

A: *Koogaku-wa ninki-ga arimasu, ne.*

A: Engineering is popular, isn't it.

B: *Hai. Juunen mae kara, ninki-ga arimasu.*

B: Yes. It's been popular for (since) about ten years.

A: *Enjinia-wa itsumo zangyoo shimasen-ka.*

A: Don't engineers have to work a lot of overtime?

B: *Iie, hotondo-no nihonjin-ga zangyoo shite iru-to omoimasu yo. Anata-no senmon-wa nandesu-ka.*

B: I think almost all Japanese workers work overtime. What is your major?

A: *Hooritsu-o benkyoo shite imasu. Sore kara, shuushi-o toritai-to omoimasu.*

A: I'm studying law. After that, I think I want to get my master's degree.

B: *Soo desu-ka. Asoko-ni suwatte-iru hito-mo hooritsu-o benkyoo shite imasu.*

B: Really. That man sitting over there is also studying law.

A: *Aa. Ano hito-wa Mori-san desu, ne. Tabun ano hito-wa watashi-no seijigaku-no kurasu-ni haitte iru-to omoimasu.*

A: Oh, that's Mr. Mori, isn't it? I think he is in my political science class.

B: *Mori-san-to issho-ni suwatte iru hito-ga miemasu-ka.*

B: Do you see the person he's sitting with?

A: *Koohii-o nonde iru hito desu-ka.*

A: The person drinking coffee?

B: *Soo desu. Ano hito-wa dai-gakuin-no gakusei desu yo.*

B: Yes. She is a graduate student.

A: *Soo desu-ka.*

A: Really.

B: *Hai. Kanojo-wa kyooju-ni naru-to omoimasu.*

B: Yes. I think she will become a professor.

A: *Sugoi desu, ne.*

A: That is great.

Omoimasu
Many times when Japanese people state that they want to do something, they often add *-to omoimasu* at the end of the sentence. This is mainly done so that one does not appear to be stating his/her wants too strongly. Additionally, they often state *tabun* at the beginning of a sentence and *omoimasu* at the end to soften the statement.

109

anna
that kind of

chuugakkoo
middle
school

daigakuin
graduate
school

donna
what kind of

enjinia
engineer

hotondo
almost all

ima kara
from now

itsumo
always

jibiki, jisho
dictionary

kinmujikan
working
hours

konna
this kind of

kore kara
from here,
from now

kurasu
class

mieru(-ru)
can see

**ninki-ga
aru**
is popular

GRAMMAR EXPLANATION
1. Plain past verbs

To conjugate verbs into the plain past form, use the same rules as the *-te imasu* and *-te kudasai* forms, but add *-ta* or *-tta* instead of *-te* or *-tte*.

ex. ***itte** kudasai* please go
    itta went

    *hanashi**te** kudasai* please speak
    *hanashi**ta*** spoke

The plain past form of *desu* is *datta*.

2. -To omoimasu

To tell someone what you are thinking, change the verb in the sentence to the plain present or plain past form, and add *-to omoimasu*.

ex. *Morita-san-wa daigaku-ni ikimasu.*
Mr. Morita goes to the university.

*Morita-san-wa daigaku-ni **iku-to omoimasu.***
I think Mr. Morita goes to the university.

*Morita-san-wa daigaku-ni **ikanai-to omoimasu.***
I think Mr. Morita does not go to the university.

*Morita-san-wa daigaku-ni **itta-to omoimasu.***
I think Mr. Morita went to the university.

When using the *-tai* verb form, drop *desu* and add *-to omoimasu*.

    ex. *Konna daigaku-ni **hairitai-to omoimasu**.*
    I think I would like to enter this kind of
    university.

• *na* adjectives require a verb before *-to omoimasu*.
    ex. *Kono tanjoobi-no paatii-wa **nigiyaka da-
to omoimasu**.*
    I think this birthday party is lively.

    *Tanjoobi-no paatii-wa **nigiyaka datta-to
omoimasu**.*
    I think the birthday party was very lively.

• *i* adjectives do not require a verb before *-to omoimasu*.
    ex. *Watashi-wa rekishi-ga **omoshiroi-to
omoimasu**.*
    I think history is interesting.

    *Yamashita-san-no uchi-wa **hirokatta-to
omoimasu**.*
    I think Mr. Yamashita's home was spacious.

To summarize.

Kara
Kara also means "since." ex. *Nihon-ni kita toki **kara**, nihongo-o benkyoo shite imasu*; Since (the time) I came to Japan, I have been studying Japanese. When paired with *mae* to form *mae kara*, the meaning is "since that time." ex. *gonen **mae kara**,* since five years ago; *nishuukan **mae kara**,* since two weeks ago.

omou(-u)
to think

oyogu(-u)
to swim

raamen
noodles

**shitsurei
shimasu**
I am in your
way

shoogakkoo
elementary
school

sonna
that kind of

supootsu
sports

tabun
perhaps

toki
a certain
time

yuumei(na)
famous

zangyoo
overtime (at
work)

3. Noun Phrases:

Place-*no* preposition-*ni* plain verb noun

*ex. Onnanohito-wa watashitachi-no mae-ni
suwatte imasu.*
A woman is sitting in front of us.

***Watashitachi-no mae-ni suwatte iru
onnanohito-wa*** Yamashita-san-no oku-
san desu.
The woman sitting in front of us is Mr.
Yamashita's wife.

***Kuruma-no naka-ni iru hito*-**wa sensei
dewa nai-to omoimasu.*
I think the person in the car is not a teacher.

Object-*o* plain verb noun

ex. Otokonohito-wa megane-o kakete imashita.
A man was wearing glasses.

***Megane-o kakete ita otokonohito*-**wa
Sumisu-san deshita.*
The man who was wearing glasses was Mr.
Smith.

***Sushi-o tabete iru hito*-**wa akarui hito desu.*
The person eating sushi is a bright (fun) person.

4. Dare-mo kimasen

The interrogative nouns *nani, dare,* and *doko,*
used with *-mo* and verb+*masen* mean "not any," "no

one," and "nowhere."

> *ex. Watashi-wa nani-**mo** kai**masen** deshita.*
> I bought nothing.
>
> > *Dare-**mo** ki**masen**.*
> > No one comes.
> > *Doko-ni-**mo** iki**masen** deshita.*
> > I went nowhere.

EXERCISES

1. Plain past

Change the verbs in the following phrases to reflect plain past tense:

> *ex. Amerika-ni iku*
> ➡ *Amerika-ni itta*
>
> | | |
> |---|---|
> | *purojekuto-o oeru* | *tesuto-ga owaru* |
> | *Amerika-ni sunde iru* | *raamen-o taberu* |
> | *oyogu* | *shigoto-ni kuru* |
> | *jisho-o kau* | *kodomo-wa asobu* |
> | *kuruma-ni noru* | *watashitachi-wa yameru* |

2. -To omoimasu

Place the following sentences into the *-to omoimasu* pattern:

> *ex. Yamashita-san-wa daigaku-de yakyuu-o shimasu.*
> ➡ *Yamashita-san-wa daigaku-de yakyuu-o suru-to omoimasu.*

College Life
The four year period spent in college is usually the most enjoyable time in a Japanese person's life. The majority of Japanese students spend three to six years preparing for college entrance examinations. However, once they enter a university, they only need to spend a minimal amount of time studying in order to graduate. Japanese colleges are extremely difficult to enter, but easy to graduate from.

Plain verb-to omoimasu

Hanabusa-san-wa yuumeina hito desu.
Gakkoo-de iroirona supootsu-o shimasu.
Rekishi-no hon-o yonde iru hito-wa kyooju desu.
Kanojo-wa Nihon-ni kita toki kara, seijigaku-
  o benkyoo shite imasu.
Nihon-no shokuji-wa amari takaku arimasen.

Adjective -to omoimasu

Kono o-kashi-wa amai desu.
Karei-wa karakatta desu.
Raamen-wa oishikatta desu.
Kono hon-wa yuumei desu.
Juku-wa totemo taihen deshita.

-Tai-to omoimasu

Igaku-o benkyoo shitai desu.
Shuushi-o totta kara, Amerika-ni ikitai desu.
Uchi-de gohan-o tabetai desu.

Plain negative-to omoimasu

Konban-no paatii-ni dare-mo kimasen.
Tookyoo-de nani-mo kaimasen.
Yamashita-san-wa daigaku-de yakyuu-o shimasen.
Hirakawa-san-wa ocha-o iremasen.

3. Phrases

Substitute the given words into the following phrase:

ex. Tonari-ni suwaru

➡ ***Tonari-ni suwatte iru*** *hito-wa daigaku-*
de benkyoo shite imasu.

ningyoo-o kau   *koohii-o nomu*
yakyuu-o suru   *asoko-no mise-ni iru*
oyogu   *shinrigaku-no hon-o yomu*
Hara-san-no mae-ni suwaru

SHORT DIALOGUES

1. *ex.* benkyoo suru, bungaku

> A: *Anata-wa nani-o* **benkyoo shitai** *desu-ka.*
> B: **Bungaku**-*o* **benkyoo shitai**-*to omoimasu.*
> A: **Bungaku**-*wa muzukashii desu-ka.*
> B: *Iie, amari muzukashiku nai-to omoimasu.*

> 1. benkyoo suru, hooritsu
> 2. yomu, igaku-no hon
> 3. benkyoo suru, koogaku
> 4. yomu, seijigaku-no hon

2. *ex.* kippu-o kau, kyooju

> A: *Asoko-de* **Kippu-o katte iru** *hito-wa*
>   *Yamashita-san desu-ka.*
> B: *Ee, Yamashita-san desu.*
> A: *Yamashita-san-wa* **kyooju** *desu-ka.*
> B: *Ee,* **kyooju** *da-to omoimasu.*

> 1. shinbun-o yomu, Fuji ginkoo-no hito
> 2. ocha-o nomu, sensei
> 3. nanika kau, Mitsubishi ginkoo-no hito
> 4. isu-ni suwaru, Toyota-no hito
> 5. denwa-o kakeru, Honda-no hito

-Ni naru
If a person will become a teacher, a professor, a doctor, etc., use noun+*ni naru*. *ex. sensei-**ni naru***, become a teacher.

115

3. *ex.* kore kara, toshokan, rekishi

> A: ***Kore kara***, *dokoka-e ikimasu-ka.*
> B: *Kyooju-to hanashitai node, daigaku-ni ikimasu.*
> A: *Sore kara uchi-ni kaerimasu-ka.*
> B: *Hai. Uchi-ni kaeru-to omoimasu. Anata-wa.*
> A: ***Kore kara toshokan****-ni ikimasu. Asoko-de* ***rekishi****-no hon-o yomimasu. Sore kara, doko-ni mo ikimasen.*
> B: *Sore dewa, shitsurei shimasu.*
>
> > 1. kore kara, uchi, shakaigaku
> > 2. ima kara, toshokan, shinrigaku
> > 3. kore kara, kissaten, kagaku
> > 4. ima kara, uchi, seijigaku

SELF TEST

Translate the following sentences into Japanese:

1. I think Mr. Mori read the psychology book.

2. I thought he studied engineering.

3. The woman sitting behind me is eating rice.

4. The man reading a book is Mr. Johnson.

5. The woman driving the car is from Tokyo.

Fill in the blanks with *wa, ga, de, o, ni, to, no, ka, ne,* or X:

6. Isshuukan ___ ikkai ___ shinrigaku ___ kyooshitsu ___ ikimasu.

7. Sushi ___ tabete iru ___ hito ___ sensei ___ naru ___ omoimasu.

8. Yamada-san ___ ushiro ___ suwatte iru ___ hito ___ Mori-san desu.

9. Megane ___ kakete iru ___ hito ___ sensei desu.

10. Tanaka-san ___ daigaku ___ iroirona supootsu ___ shita ___ omoimasu.

LESSON FOURTEEN
MITA KOTO-GA ARIMASU-KA

In this lesson you will learn:

- The koto-ga aru phrase
- The -no desu verb form
- How to refer to a third person's wants
- Subject phrases

DIALOGUE

I
A: ジョギングを するのには いい ひ ですね.
B: そう ですね.
A: あそこの ちょうぞうは どんな ちょうぞう ですか.
B: だいぶつ です.
A: あの だいぶつは りっぱ です.
B: そう ですね. べつの だいぶつを みた ことが
ありますか.
A: しゃしんを みた だけ です.
B: わたしは もう やめます. きお つけて.
A: はい.
II
A: なんの しゃしんを みて いるの ですか.
B: せんしゅう きゅうかで なえばに いきました. その
ときの しゃしんを みて います. さっき できました.
みませんか.
A: はい. この しゃしんは スキーを して いる ところ
ですね. スキーを するのは あぶないと おもいますか.
B: いいえ スキーを するのは あぶなくないと おもいます.
あなたは スキーを したことが ありますか.
A: いいえ でも わたしの むすめは とても いきたがって
います.
B: おちゃを いかが ですか.
A: はい ありがとう ございます.

I

A: *Jogingu-o suru-no-ni-wa ii hi desu, ne.*

B: *Soo desu, ne.*

A: *Asoko-no choozoo-wa donna choozoo desu-ka.*

B: *Daibutsu desu.*

A: *Ano daibutsu-wa rippa desu.*

B: *Soo desu ne. Betsu-no daibutsu-o mita koto-ga arimasu-ka.*

A: *Shashin-o mita dake desu.*

B: *Watashi-wa moo yamemasu. Kio tsukete.*

A: *Hai.*

II

A: *Nanno shashin-o mite iru-no desu-ka.*

B: *Senshuu kyuuka-de Naeba-ni ikimashita. Sono toki-no shashin-o mite imasu. Sakki dekimashita. Mimasen-ka.*

A: *Hai. Kono shashin-wa sukii-o shite iru tokoro desu, ne. Sukii-o suru-no-wa abunai-to omoimasu-ka.*

B: *Iie, sukii-o suru-no-wa abunaku nai-to omoimasu. Anata-wa sukii-o shita koto-ga arimasu-ka.*

I

A: It's a nice day to jog, isn't it.

B: Yes, it is.

A: What kind of statue is that over there?

B: It's a Buddah statue.

A: That Buddah statue is impressive.

B: Yes, it is. Have you ever seen another Buddah statue?

A: I have only seen pictures.

B: I will quit now. Be careful.

A: OK.

II

A: What kind of pictures are you looking at?

B: Last week we went on vacation to Naeba. I'm looking at those pictures. I just got them developed. Would you like to look?

A: Yes. This picture is of a skiing place, isn't it. Do you think skiing is dangerous?

B: No, I think that skiing is not dangerous. Have you ever been skiing?

A plain verb followed by *dake desu* means "only." *ex. Fuirumu-o katta dake desu.* I only bought film.

Since Japan is a very small, crowded country, most people do not rely on cars for transportation. The mass transit system in Japan is excellent, so most people travel by bus or train.

abunai(i)
dangerous

anzen(na)
safe

benri(na)
convenient

betsu-no
other

boku
I (informal, male)

bun
sentence

chizu
map

chokoreeto
chocolate

(choo)zoo
statue

daibutsu
statue of buddah

dake
only

dekiru(-ru)
to turn out

densha
train

fasshon
fashion

fuirumu
film

hi
day

hoshigaru(u)
another person's wants

A: *Iie, demo watashi-no musume-wa totemo ikitagatte imasu.*

B: *Ocha-o ikaga desu-ka.*

A: *Hai, arigatoo gozaimasu.*

A: No, but my daughter really wants to go.

B: Would you like some tea?

A: Yes, thank you.

GRAMMAR EXPLANATION

1. Koto-ga(wa) arimasu-ka

To ask someone if they have ever done something, the sentence pattern is as follows:

> Subject-*wa* obj.+plain past verb+*koto-ga(wa)*
> *arimasu-ka.*

ex. Jonson-san-wa sushi-o tabeta **koto-ga arimasu-ka.**
Mr. Johnson, have you ever eaten sushi?

Two ways to answer affirmatively:
Hai, sushi-o tabeta koto-ga arimasu.
Hai, arimasu.
Yes, I have eaten sushi.

To answer negatively:
Iie, sushi-o tabeta koto-ga arimasen.
Iie, arimasen.
No, I have never eaten sushi.

ex. Sumisu-san-wa Nihon-ni itta **koto-wa arimasu-ka.**
Mr. Smith, have you ever been to Japan?

Hai, Nihon-ni itta koto-ga arimasu.
Hai, arimasu.

Iie, Nihon-ni itta koto-wa arimasen.
Iie, arimasen.

2. -No desu

To use this form, use a plain verb+*no desu.*

> ex. *taberu-**no desu***   eat, will eat
> *tabeta-**no desu***   ate
>
> *bun-o **kaite iru-no desu***
> is writing a sentence
> *bun-o **kaite ita-no desu***
> was writing a sentence

In less formal situations, -*n desu* can be used instead:

> ex. *taberu-**n desu***   *tabeta-**n desu***

Da, the plain form of *desu*, changes into *na* when preceding -*no desu* or -*n desu.*

> ex. *Akachan-wa onnanoko da.*
> *Akachan-wa onnanoko **na-no desu.***
> The baby is a girl!
>
> *Sugoi o-tera **na-no desu.***
> It is a great temple!

Adjectives

For *i* adjectives, use the adjective+-*no desu* or -*n desu.*

> ex. *sugoi desu*   is great
> *sugoi-**no desu***   is great!
> *sugoi-**n desu***   is great!
> *sugokatta-**no desu***   was great!
> *sugokatta-**n desu***   was great!
> *sugoku nai-**no desu***   was NOT great
> *sugoku nai-**n desu***   was NOT great

The -*no desu* form of verbs is the same in meaning as the *masu* form, but it is more expressive. When used as a statement, the speaker may be surprised, excited, etc. The one who uses it as a question often wants an explanation. For example, if a mother saw her child going out after she told him not to, she would say *doko-ni iku-no desu-ka*, instead of *doko-ni ikimasu-ka.*

hoshii
want

ikaga desu-ka
How about that? Do you like that?

iyahoon
earphones

jogingu suru
to jog

kamera
camera

kio tsukete
be careful, use good judgement, take care

kotoba
word

kyuuka
vacation

moderu
model

Naeba
a ski resort in Japan

nanno
what kind of

(o)tera
temple

rippa(na)
impressive

saa
well

Na adjectives require *na* before *-no desu* or *-n desu*, except when they are past tense or negative.

ex. *genki desu*	is healthy
genkina-no desu	is healthy!
genkina-n desu	is healthy!
genki datta-no desu	was healthy!
genki datta-n desu	was healthy!
genki dewa nai-no desu	is NOT healthy
genki ja nai-n desu	is NOT healthy

3. -Gatte imasu

When referring to a third person's wants, drop the *i* from *-tai desu* and add *-gatte imasu*. However, if you are asking the person directly, use the negative verb form.

ex. *Anata-wa rajio-o kikimasen-ka.*
Do you want to listen to the radio?

Kare-wa rajio-o kikitagatte imasu.
He wants to listen to the radio.

Watashi-wa chizu-o mitai desu.
I want to look at the map.

Kitamura-san-wa chizu-o mitagatte imasu.
Mrs. Kitamura wants to look at the map.

In phrases, it comes directly before the noun it modifies:

ex *Tanaka-san-ga shashin-o toritagatte iru moderu-wa asoko-ni imasu.*
The model that Mrs. Tanaka wants to take a picture of is over there.

*Sumisu-san-ga **yomitagatte ita** zasshi-wa kore desu-ka.*

Is this the magazine that Mr. Smith wanted to read?

4. Subject Phrases

When using a verb as a subject phrase use:

> object+plain verb **no-wa**

ex. nihongo-no kotoba-o narau
Nihongo-no kotoba-o narau no-wa *muzukashii desu.*
Learning Japanese words is difficult.

*Amerika-de **shuushi-o toru no-wa** ninki-ga arimasu.*
In America, getting a master's degree is popular.

Another way to say that you want something is object+*ga hoshii desu.* ex. *iyahoon-**ga hoshii desu.*** I want earphones.

EXERCISES

1. Koto-ga arimasu

Substitute the given words into the following sentences to form the *koto-ga arimasu* phrase:

ex. daibutsu-o miru
➡*Sumusi-san-wa **daibutsu-o mita** koto-ga arimasu-ka.*
➡*Hai, **daibutsu-o mita** koto-ga arimasu.*
➡*Iie, **daibutsu-o mita** koto-ga arimasen.*

> o-tera-ni iku   o-kashi-o tsukuru
> shashin-o toru   sukii-o suru
> shinrigaku-no hon-o yomu
> Nihon-no fasshon zasshi-o yomu

In English, we say "listen to ear phones," but the Japanese use *suru* with *iyahoon*, not *kiku*.

sakki
a short time
ago

shashin
picture

shukudai
homework

**sukii-o
suru**
to ski

toru(-u)
to take; get

tsukau(-u)
to use

zenzen
(not) at all

2. -Gatte imasu

Substitute the phrases into the following sentence:

ex. Nihon-ni kitai desu

➡*Sumisu-san-wa **Nihon-ni kitagatte iru**-to
omoimasu.*

> *sukii-o naraitai desu*
> *shashin-o toritai desu*
> *densha-ni noritai desu*
> *kagaku-o benkyoo shitai desu*
> *raamen-o tabetai desu*
> *shuushi-o toritai desu*
> *shoogakkoo-ni tsutometai desu*
> *baiten-de kippu-o kaitai desu*
> *asagohan-o tabetai desu*

3. Match the following phrases:

1. *Kono kamera-de*
2. *Anata-wa jogingu shita*
3. *Boku-wa omoshiroi zasshi-o*
4. *Kare-wa rajio-o*
5. *Anata-wa hooritsu-o*
6. *Sono ongakukai-wa*
7. *Daigaku-wa amari*

a. *koto-ga arimasu-ka.*
b. *taihen ja nai-no desu.*
c. *shashin-o toru-no desu-ka.*
d. *benkyoo shinai-no desu-ka.*
e. *kiku-no desu.*
f. *omoshiroi-no desu.*
g. *yomu-n desu, yo.*

4. Subject Phrases

Change the following verbs into subject phrases:

> *ex. Jogingu suru, taihen*
>
> ➡ ***Jogingu suru** no-wa **taihen** desu, ne.*

> *juku-de benkyoo suru, muzukashii*
> *chizu-o miru, yasashii*
> *shashin-o toru, omoshiroi ie-o kau, taihen*

apaato-ni sunde iru, benri
geki-o miru, omoshiroi
shukudai-o suru, taihen

SHORT DIALOGUES

1. *ex.* sushi-o tsukuru, muzukashii, kantan da

    Yagi: Buraun-san-wa, **sushi-o tsukutta** koto-ga arimasu-ka.
    Buraun: Hai. **Sushi-o tsukutta** koto-ga arimasu.
    Yagi: **Muzukashikatta** desu-ka.
    Buraun: Iie. **Sushi-o tsukuru**-no-wa **kantan da**-to omoimasu.

    1. seijigaku-o benkyoo suru, muzukashii, yasashii
    2. sukii-o suru, yasashii, taihen da
    3. daigakuin-de nihongo-o narau, muzukashii, yasashii

2. *ex.* zubon, zubon-ga hoshii

    Okaa-san: Murasaki iro-no **zubon**-to akai **zubon** dewa dochira no hoo-ga **hoshii** desu-ka.
    Jun: Boku-wa akai **zubon-ga hoshii** desu.
    Okaa-san (ten'in-ni): Sore dewa akai **zubon**-o kudasai.
    Ten'in: Hai, arigatoo gozaimasu.

    1. kutsu, kutsu-o kaitai
    2. kami, kami-ga hoshii
    3. kooto, kooto-o kaitai
    4. shatsu, shatsu-ga hoshii

When in Japan, you may be surprised by the layout of the towns and cities. Since Japan is such an old country, its streets and roads were not logically planned out ahead of time. If you are in an unfamiliar area, it is very easy to become lost because the roads twist around in many directions, and many roads do not have names. Additionally, when a person gives directions in Japan, he/she will not use road names (*ex.* go to Main Street and turn right), but instead use landmarks (go past the very large tree).

3. *ex.* doko-ni iku, gakkoo-ni iku

> Tomoe: Jun-san, ***doko-ni iku**-no desu-ka.*
> Jun: ***Gakkoo-ni iku**-no desu.*
> Tomoe: *Isogu-no desu-ka.*
> Jun: *Iie, isoide imasen, yo.*

  1. nani-o taberu, chokoreeto-o taberu
  2. nani-o suru, shukudai-o suru
  3. nani-o nomu, juusu-o nomu
  4. nani-o yomu, shakaigaku-no hon-o yomu
  5. dare-to hanasu, tomodachi-to hanasu
  6. nani-o suru, shashin-o toru

SELF TEST

Translate the following sentences into Japanese:

1. Have you ever read a Japanese magazine?

2. Have you ever taken a picture?

3. That statue of Buddah is very impressive.

4. Please be careful.

5. The baby is walking!

6. What kind of map is that?

7. He is skiing!

8. Have you ever used this kind of camera?

9. A short time ago, she graduated with a four year degree.

10. Kanji is more difficult than hiragana.

LESSON FIFTEEN
DOITSU-NI ITTA TOKI

In this lesson you will learn:

- The toki noun phrase
- The shinagara verb phrase
- How to express the statements of others
- Subject phrases

DIALOGUE

I

スミス： もりたさんは ほうえき がいしゃに つとめて
いると ききました。

もりた： そう です。 いろいろな ものを ゆしゅつ して
います。 ヨーロッパや アメリカに たくさん
ゆしゅつ して います。

スミス： ほかの くにへ よく しゅっちょう しますか。

もりた： ええ． きょねん ドイツへ いきました。

スミス： どの くらい たいざい したの ですか。

もりた： さんしゅうかん です． ドイツに いった とき
えいごで せつめい しながら せいひんを
しょうかい しました． えいごが へたな ので
とても たいへん でした。

スミス： さいきん しゅっちょう しましたか。

もりた： いいえ しばらく して いません． でも ちかい
うちに アメリカへ いくと ききました。

スミス： えいごを べんきょう して いるの ですか。

もりた： はい じつは しごとの あとで えいかいわ
きょうしつが あります。

スミス： はたらきながら えいごを べんきょう するのは
たいへん でしょうね。

もりた： ええ すこし たいへん です。

スミス： じゃ がんばって ください。

もりた： はい ありがとう ございます。

II

A： すみませんが しつもんが あります． いまは つごうが
わるい ですか。

B： いいえ ラジオを ききながら しんぶんを よんで いる
だけ です。

A： これを せつめい して ほしいの ですが． わたしの
せんせい が 「きょうじゅうに これを おえなさい」
と いいました． いい ですか。

B： もちろん。

I

Sumisu: *Morita-san-wa booeki gaisha-ni tsutomete iru-to kikimashita.*

Morita: *Soo desu. Iroirona mono-o yushutsu shite imasu. Yooroppa-ya Amerika-ni takusan yushutsu shite imasu.*

S: *Hoka-no kuni-e yoku shucchoo shimasu-ka.*

M: *Ee. Kyonen Doitsu-e ikimashita.*

S: *Dono kurai taizai shita-no desu-ka.*

M: *Sanshuukan desu. Doitsu-ni itta toki eigo-de setsumei shinagara seihin-o shookai shimashita. Eigo-ga heta-na node, totemo taihen deshita.*

S: *Saikin shucchoo shimashita-ka.*

M: *Iie, shibaraku shite imasen, demo chikai uchi-ni Amerika-e iku-to kikimashita.*

S: *Eigo-o benkyoo shite iru-no desu-ka.*

M: *Hai, jitsu-wa shigoto-no ato de eikaiwa kyooshitsu-ga arimasu.*

I

Smith: I heard you work for a trading company, Mr. Morita.

Morita: That's right. We export various products. We export a lot to Europe and America.

S: Do you often travel to other countries?

M: Yes, last year I went to Germany.

S: How long were you there?

M: For three weeks. When I was in Germany, I explained things in English while I showed products. Because my English is terrible, it was very tough.

S: Have you recently been on a trip?

M: No, I have not for a long time, but I heard that I will go to America in the near future.

S: Are you studying English?

M: Yes, actually I have an English conversation class after work.

Quotes
Quotation marks are written differently in Japanese than in English. At the beginning of a quote, 「 is used. At the end of a quote, 」 is used.

-Shite hoshii
To state that you want another person to do something, use the *-shite kudasai* form learned before or *-shite hoshii desu*. ex. *Kaita hon-o* **misete hoshii desu**. I want you to show me the book you wrote. Exercises for this grammar pattern will be in chapter 19.

129

ato de
after

booeki gaisha
trading company

booeki suru
to trade

chikai uchi-ni
in the near future

dame
not good

Doitsu
Germany

eikaiwa
English conversation

ganbaru(u)
to do one's best

hataraku(-u)
to work

heta(na)
poor at

itsu made
until when

kuni
country

kyonen
last year

kyoojuu-ni
by the end of today

---

benkyoo suru-no-wa taihen deshoo, ne.

English must be very difficult.

M: *Ee, sukoshi taihen desu.*

M: Yes, it is a little difficult.

S: *Jaa, ganbatte kudasai.*

S: Well, do your best.

M: *Hai, arigatoo gozaimasu.*

M: Thank you.

II

II

A: *Sumimasen-ga, shitsumon-ga arimasu. Ima-wa tsugoo-ga warui desu-ka.*

A: Excuse me, I have a question. Is now a bad time?

B: *Iie, rajio-o kikinagara shinbun-o yonde iru dake desu.*

B: No, I am only listening to the radio and (while) reading the paper.

A: *Kore-o setsumei shite hoshii-no desu ga. Watashi-no sensei-ga⌐kyoojuu-ni kore-o oenasai⌐ -to iimashita. Ii desu-ka.*

A: I would like you to explain this to me. My teacher said, "finish this by the end of the day." Is it alright?

B: *Mochiron.*

B: Of course.

GRAMMAR EXPLANATION
1. Toki

To state "when I was a child," or "when I was (something)," the grammar structure is as follows:

> noun-***no***
> subject-***wa*** verb phrase ***toki***

ex. ***Watashi-wa gakusei-no toki*** *takusan benkyoo shimashita.*
When I was a student, I studied a lot.

Watashi-wa kodomo-no toki, iroirona
hon-o yomimashita.

When I was a child, I read various books.

Sumisu-san-wa Nihon-ni itta toki,
kamera-o motte ikimashita.

When Mr. Smith went to Japan, he took a
camera.

Tanaka-san-wa daigaku-ni ita toki,
hotondo-no supootsu-o shimashita.

When Miss Tanaka was in college, she
played almost all of the sports.

Hara-san-wa hirugohan-o taberu toki,
taitei resutoran-ni ikimasu.

When Mr. Hara eats lunch, he usually goes
to a restaurant.

2. -Nagara

To state that one is doing two things at the same
time, like eating while watching TV, or listening to the
radio while studying, the following pattern is used:

| verb+*nagara* | main object | main verb |

When using the *nagara* pattern, the verb that is the
easiest to do, or the one that is routine, is paired with
nagara. The action that is unusual or special comes last.
When both actions are considered equal, it does not
matter which is used with *nagara*.

> ex. iyahoon-o **shinagara** jogingu shite imasu
> using (doing) earphones while jogging

mina-san all of you	*Sumisu-san-wa koohii-o nominagara shinbun-o yonde imasu.* Mr. Smith drinks coffee while reading the newspaper.
minna all	
miseru(-ru) to show	
mochiron of course	*Sumisu-san-wa o-kashi-o tabenagara terebi-o mite imasu.* Mr. Smith eats snacks while watching TV.
omoi(i) heavy	To form this pattern, drop *masu* and add *nagara*.
ryokoo suru to travel	*ex. benkyoo shimasu* *benkyoo shinagara*
saikin recently	
seihin products	*mimasu* *minagara*
setsumei suru to explain	*tabemasu* *tabenagara*

3. -To iimasu

When quoting someone, or expressing what a person said, use the same grammar pattern as for *-to omoimasu*, but substitute *-to iimasu* instead. If you use quotes, you must say exactly what the person said. If you do not use quotes, you do not have to say their exact words, but still use *-to iimashita*.

ex. Kare-wa nihonjin da-to omoimasu.
I think he is Japanese.

Kare-wa ⌈nihonjin da ⌋-to iimashita.
He said he is Japanese.

Mitsumura-san-wa ⌈watashi-no kaisha-wa kamera-o yushutsu suru ⌋-to iimashita.

shibaraku for a long time	
shitsumon question	
shookai suru to show, recommend	
shucchoo suru to take a business trip	
suu(-u) to inhale	
tabako cigarettes	

Mrs. Mitsumura said, "my company exports cameras."

Additionally, when stating that someone asked a question, use *-ka-to kikimashita*.

ex. *Sumisu-san-wa* ⌈*booeki gaisha-ni tsutomete iru-ka*⌋-*to kikimashita*.
Mr. Smith asked, "Do you work for a trading company?"

Mitsutake-san-wa ⌈*sono hon-ga omoi-ka* ⌋ *to kikimashita*.
Mrs. Mitsutake asked "Is that book heavy?"

Kikimasu also means hear:

ex. *Watashi-wa Matsumoto-san-ga kyoo Kyooto-ni iku-to kikimashita*.
I heard that Mr. Matsumoto will go to Kyoto today.

4. Phrases

Another way to create noun phrases is to use:

> **ga**
> (Noun-*no*), (place or time), plain verb, object

ex. *Watashi-wa uchi-de hon-o yomimashita*.
I read a book at home.
Watashi-no uchi-de yonda hon-*wa hooritsu-no hon deshita*.
The book I read at home was a law book.

chuugakkoo-de eigo-o benkyoo shimashita
studied English at middle school

taizai
stay for a
period of
time

tazuneru(-ru)
to visit

tsugoo-ga
warui
a bad time

warui(i)
bad

ya
etc.

yoku
often

Yooroppa
Europe

yunyuu
suru
import

yushutsu
suru
export

***Chuugakkoo-de benkyoo shita eigo**-wa kantan deshita.*
The English studied at middle school was simple.

Watashitachi-wa yuube eiga-o mimashita.
We saw a movie last night.
***Watashitachi-ga yuube mita eiga**-wa totemo yokatta desu.*
The movie we saw last night was very good.

Watashi-wa kuruma-o unten shimashita.
I drove a car.
***Watashi-no unten shita kuruma**-wa Toyota-no kuruma deshita.*
The car I drove was a Toyota.

Yamada-san-wa hon-o kakimashita.
Mrs. Yamada wrote a book.
*Watashi-wa **Yamada-san-ga kaita hon**-ga suki desu.*
I like the book that Mrs. Yamada wrote.

EXERCISES
1. -Toki

Substitute the following phrases into this sentence:

ex. Yooroppa-ni iku
➡*Sumisu-san-wa **Yooroppa-ni itta** toki, iroirona hito-ni aimashita.*

> *Tookyoo-ni kuru*
> *Oosutoraria-o ryokoo suru*
> *daigaku-ni hairu*
> *toshokan-ni tsutomete iru*

2. -Nagara

Combine the following phrases using -*nagara*:

> *ex. tabako-o suu, shinbun-o yomu*
> ➡*tabako-o suinagara shinbun-o yonde imasu.*
>
> > *iyahoon-o suru, jogingu suru*
> > *suwaru, denwa-o kakeru*
> > *rajio-o kiku, kuruma-o unten suru*
> > *eigo-o benkyoo suru, hataraku*
> > *terebi-o miru, gohan-o taberu*
> > *hon-o yomu, o-kashi-o taberu*

3. -To iimasu, -to kikimasu

Place the sentences into the -*to iimasu* phrase:

> *ex. Konban eiga-o mitai desu.*
> ➡*Tanaka-san-wa* ⌜***konban eiga-o mitai***⌟ *-to iimashita.*
>
> > *Kaisha-wa iroirona seihin-o yunyuu shite imasu.*
> > *Hara-san-wa booeki gaisha-ni tsutomete imasu.*
> > *Uchi-de tsukutta karei wa karakatta desu.*
> > *Senshuu katta tsukue-wa omokatta desu.*
> > *Tabako-o suu-no-wa dame desu.*
> > *Amerika-ni itta koto-ga arimasu.*
>
> *ex. Sumisu-san-wa nihongo-ga wakarimasu-ka.*
> ➡*Tanaka-san-wa* ⌜***Sumisu-san-wa nihongo-ga wakaru-ku***⌟ *-to kikimashita.*
>
> > *Mouri-san-wa ginkoo-ni tsutometa koto-ga arimasu-ka.*

Tazuneru is preceded by *o*.
ex. Yamori-san-wa Doitsu-o ***tazunemashita***. Mrs. Yamori visited Germany.

Ya
Ya can be used in place of *to* to mean "etc." It usually comes after the first noun when listing objects or things.
ex. Ryokoo suru toki kamera-ya, okane, chiizu-o motte ikimasu. When I travel, I take a camera, money, a map, etc.

*Hara-san-ga yomitagatte ita hon-wa sore
    deshita-ka.*

*Buraun-san-no tabetagatte ita shokuji-wa
    kore desu-ka.*

*Harada-san-no oku-san-ga tsukutta sushi-
    o tabeta koto-ga arimasu-ka.*

Yuube mita eiga-wa omoshirokatta desu-ka.

4. Phrases

Change the given sentences into noun phrases:

ex. Oosutoraria-de tomodachi-ni aimashita.
➡*Oosutoraria-de atta tomodachi*

Baiten-de kippu-o kaimashita.
Suupaamaaketto-de ringo-o kaimashita.
Eigakan-de eiga-o mimashita.
Kissaten-de ocha-o nomimashita.
*Tanaka-san-no uchi-de sakana-o
    tabemashita.*

ex. Watashi-wa ocha-o iremashita.
➡*Watashi-no ireta ocha*
➡*Watashi-ga ireta ocha*

Hara-san-wa karei-o tsukurimashita.
Oku-san-wa tegami-o kakimashita.
Watashi-wa sake-o nomimashita.
Hanabusa-san-wa paatii-ni ikimashita.
*Watashi-wa daigaku-de nihongo-o
    naraimashita.*

Ano hito-wa asoko-de hon-o yomimasu.

SHORT DIALOGUES

1. *ex.* ocha-o nomu, terebi-o miru, kissaten-ni iku

> Azusa:*Michiko-san-wa nani-o shite iru-no desu-ka.*
> Emiko:*Michiko-san-wa* **ocha-o nominagara terebi-o mite** *imasu.*
> Azusa: *Kanojo-wa mise-ni ikitagatte imasu-ka.*
> Emiko:*Iie,* ⌈**kissaten-ni ikitai** ⌋*-to iimashita.*

> 1. ringo-o taberu, rajio-o kiku, resutoran-ni iku
> 2. juusu-o nomu, zasshi-o yomu, ginkoo
> 3. tabako-o suu, denwa-o kakeru, kusuriya
> 4. niku-o taberu, terebi-o miru, biyooin
> 5. isu-ni suwaru, bideo-o miru, kissaten

2. *ex.* daigaku-ni iru, eigo

> Hirakawa: **Daigaku-ni ita** *toki, nani-o benkyoo shimashita-ka.*
> Nishiyama: **Daigaku-ni ita** *toki,* **eigo**-*o benkyoo shimashita.*
> H: *Soo desu-ka.* **Eigo**-*o benkyoo shinagara supootsu-mo shimashita-ka.*
> N: *Hai, shimashita.*
> H: *Taihen deshita, ne.*

> 1. kodomo-no, eigo
> 2. Amerika-ni iru, bungaku
> 3. kookoo-ni iru, kagaku
> 4. shoogakkoo-ni iru, rekishi
> 5. Yooroppa-ni sunde iru, supeingo

De
To say that someone speaks in English, writes in *Hiragana*, etc., use *de. ex. Eigo-de hanashite kudasai.* Please say it in English. *Kanji-de kakimashita.* I wrote in *kanji.*

3. *ex.* Uchi-de bideo-o miru, omoshiroi

A: *Yuube shigoto-no ato de nani-o shimashita-ka.*
B: ***Uchi-de bideo-o mimashita.***
A: ***Uchi-de mita bideo***-*wa* ***omoshirokatta*** *desu-ka.*
B: *Ee,* ***omoshirokatta*** *desu.*

1. resutoran-de shokuji-o suru, oishii
2. gakkoo-de supeingo-o benkyoo suru, muzukashii
3. gekijoo-de geki-o miru, yoi
4. mise-de ningyoo-o kau, takai

SELF TEST

Unscramble the following sentences:

1. o daigaku shimashita ni ita toki rekishi benkyoo o.
2. de Tanaka-san iimashita wa no ato sake o nomitai to shigoto.
3. ano jogingu o shinagara iyahoon shite hito wa o imasu.
4. nai zenzen iimashita wa zasshi ga to Yamada-san.
5. tachinagara shite Hara-san wa hanashi-o imasu.

Fill in the blanks with *wa, ga, de, o, ni, to, no, ka, ne,* or *X:*

6. Toyota ＿＿ tsutomete ita ＿＿ toki ＿＿ iroirona seihin ＿＿＿ shookai shimashita.
7. Harada-san ＿＿「 anata ＿＿ kono hon ＿＿ yonda ＿＿」＿＿ kikimashita.
8. Yamada-san ＿＿ tsukutta ＿＿ gohan ＿＿ totemo ＿＿ oishikatta desu.
9. Watashitachi ＿＿ kinoo ＿＿ mita bideo ＿＿ sugokatta-n desu, ＿＿.
10. Hara-san ＿＿「 anata ＿＿ katta seetaa ＿＿ kirei da」＿＿ iimashita.

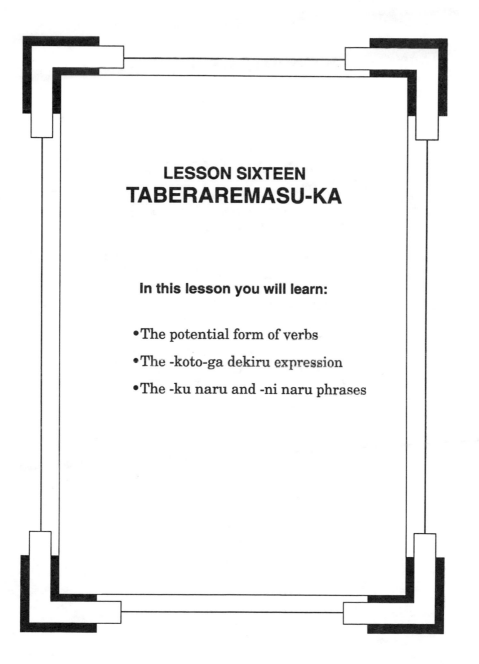

LESSON SIXTEEN
TABERAREMASU-KA

In this lesson you will learn:

- The potential form of verbs
- The -koto-ga dekiru expression
- The -ku naru and -ni naru phrases

DIALOGUE

I

A: いやな てんき ですね.

B: ほんとうに そう ですね. きょうは さむくて あめが
ふって いますが あしたは てんきに なりますよ.

A: おちゃ でも のみましょうか.

B: はい. どこに いきましょうか.

A: ちかくに きっさてんが ありますよ.

B: そこで ケーキも たべられますか.

A: ええ. ケーキも おいて ありますよ.

II ひらかわさんの むすめの けっこん しき

A: ジョンソンさん こちらは ひらかわさん です.

ひらかわ: はじめまして. よく いらっしゃいました.

ジョンソン: どうぞ よろしく. おめに かかれて
こうえい です. きょうのけっこん しきは
すばらしかった ですね. にほんの けっこん
しきに でたのはこれが はじめて です.

ひらかわ: ほんとう ですか. にほんごが じょうずに
はなせますね. はつおんが とても いい
です.

ジョンソン: いいえ そんな ことは ありませんよ.

ひらかわ: どこで にほんごを べんきょう しましたか.

ジョンソン: はじめは ひとりで べんきょう しましたが
それ から にほんに きて にほんごの
がっこうで べんきょう しました.

ひらかわ: もじは かけますか.

ジョンソン: はい. ひらがなと かたかなは かけますが
かんじは ぜんぜん しりません.

ひらかわ: ああ. かんじは にほんじん でも
むずかしい ですよ.

I

A: *Iyana tenki desu, ne.*

B: *Hontoo-ni soo desu ne. Kyoo-wa samukute ame-ga futte imasu ga, ashita-wa tenki-ni narimasu, yo.*

A: *Ocha demo nomimashoo-ka.*

B: *Hai. Doko-ni ikimashoo-ka.*

A: *Chikaku-ni kissaten-ga arimasu, yo.*

B: *Soko-de keeki-mo taberaremasu-ka.*

A: *Ee. Keeki-mo oite arimasu, yo.*

II Hirakawa-san-no mu-sume-no kekkon shiki

A: *Jonson-san, kochira-wa Hirakawa-san desu.*

Hirakawa: *Hajimemashite, yoku irrashaimashita.*

Jonson: *Doozo yoroshiku. Ome-ni kakarete kooei desu. Kyoo-no kekkon shiki-wa subarashikatta desu, ne. Nihon-no kekkon shiki-ni deta-no-wa kore-ga hajimete desu.*

H: *Hontoo desu-ka. Nihongo-ga joozu-ni hanasemasu, ne. Hatsuon-ga totemo ii desu.*

I

A: The weather is unpleasant today, isn't it.

B: It really is. It is cold and rainy today, but tomorrow will be nice.

A: Shall we drink some (thing such as) tea?

B: Yes. Where shall we go?

A: There is a cafe nearby.

B: Can we also eat cake there?

A: Yes, they have (display) cake there.

II At Hirakawa's daughter's wedding

A: Ms. Johnson, this is Mrs. Hirakawa.

Hirakawa: Nice to meet you; welcome.

Johnson: It is a pleasure to meet you. Today's wedding ceremony was wonderful, wasn't it. This is the first time I have been to a Japanese wedding.

H: Really. You can speak Japanese very well. Your pronunciation is very good.

aki
autumn

asatte
the day after
tomorrow

atatakai(i)
warm

(o)bentoo
box lunch

bukka
commodity
price(s)

chikaku
close, near

demo
such as;
even for

deru(-ru)
to attend

fuyu
winter

gaikoku
foreign
(country)

gakuhi
school
tuition

hajime
at first

hare
clear

haru
spring

hatsuon
pronuncia-
tion

J: *Iie, sonna koto-wa arimasen, yo.*

H: *Doko-de nihongo-o benkyoo shimashita-ka.*

J: *Hajime-wa hitori-de benkyoo shimashita ga, sore kara Nihon-ni kite nihongo-no gakkoo-de benkyoo shimashita.*

H: *Moji-wa kakemasu-ka.*

J: *Hai. Hiragana-to kata-kana-wa kakemasu ga, kan-ji-wa zenzen shirimasen.*

H: *Aa, kanji-wa nihonjin demo muzukashii desu, yo.*

J: No, not really.

H: Where did you study Japanese?

J: At first, I studied by myself, but then I came to Japan and studied at a Japanese language school.

H: Can you write Japanese letters?

J: Yes, I can write in hiragana and katakana, but I don't know any kanji at all.

H: Oh, kanji is difficult even for Japanese people.

GRAMMAR EXPLANATION

1. Potential Form of Verbs (I can _____)

• If the verb is a-*ru* verb, replace *ru* with *rareru*.

ex. ageru	age**(ra)**reru	can give
miru	mi**(ra)**reru, (mieru)	can see
kaeru	kae**(ra)**reru	can change

• If the verb is an -*u* verb, replace the final *u* with *eru* (*tsu* with *teru*).

ex. hanasu	hanas**eru**	can speak
kaku	kak**eru**	can write
iku	ik**eru**	can go
uru	ur**eru**	can sell
motsu	mo**teru**	can hold
matsu	ma**teru**	can wait

Exceptions: *kuru*   *ko(**ra**)reru* can come
               iu   ***ieru***   can say

• No potential form of *suru* exists, instead use *dekiru*

To conjugate these verbs into the plain negative form, drop the final *ru* and add *nai*.

    *ex. mi(ra)reru mi(ra)re**nai**, (mie**nai**)*   can't see
        ikeru   *ike**nai***   can't go

To change these verbs into the *masu* form, drop the final *ru* and add *masu*.

    *ex. age(ra)reru age(ra)re**masu***   can give
        *kae(ra)reru kae(ra)re**masu*** can change

2. Koto-ga dekimasu

Another way to express potential verbs is the *koto-ga dekimasu* form. The formation of this phrase is very similar to the *koto-ga arimasu* phrase.

> Subject-***wa*** noun-***o*** plain verb+***koto-ga dekimasu***.

    *ex. Tanaka-san-wa tenisu-o suru **koto-ga dekimasu**-ka.*
    Mrs. Tanaka, can you play tennis?

    *Sumisu-san-wa hitori-de moji-o kaku**koto-ga dekimasu**-ka.*
    Mr. Smith, can you write Japanese letters by yourself?

To answer: *Hai, dekimasu.*
             Iie, dekimasen.

The Japanese language is changing, and younger people sometimes drop the middle *ra* from potential *-ru* verbs. *ex. kaereru* instead of *kaerareru*

Miru
The potential of *miru* is sometimes *mieru*, sometimes *mirareru*. *Mieru* means that one can see an object easily, whereas *mirareru* means that one can see an object that is not in plain sight.

143

hitori-de
by oneself;
alone

iya(na)
unpleasant

jibun-de
by oneself

joozu(na)
skillful

kaisei
very nice
weather

kasa
umbrella

keeki
cake

**kekkon
shiki**
wedding
ceremony

**kekkon
suru**
to marry

kumori
cloudy

moji
Japanese
letters

natsu
summer

-nin
counter for
people

niwa
garden

3. -Ku narimasu, ni narimasu

To state that "It is becoming cold," "It is getting better," or "I am (becoming) late," etc., for *i* adjectives, drop the final *i* and add *ku naru*.

> *ex. ookii*
>
> *ooki**ku narimasu***
> becomes big
> *Kodomo-wa ooki**ku natte imasu***.
> The child is becoming bigger.
>
> *Soto-wa samu**ku narimashita***.
> It became cold outside.

• For *na* adjectives, drop the final *na*, and add *ni naru*.

> *ex. Kare-wa nihongo-ga joozu-**ni natte imasu***.
> He is getting better (skillful) at Japanese.
>
> *Niwa-ga kirei-**ni narimashita***.
> The garden became beautiful.

EXERCISES
1. Potential verbs

Subsititute the given verbs into the sentences:

> *ex. koko-de matsu*
>
> ➡*A: Sumisu-san-wa **koko-de matemasu**-ka?*
> *B: Hai, matemasu.*
> *Iie, matemasen.*
>
> *kekkon shiki-ni deru*   *rokuji-ni okiru*
> *kissaten-ni hairu*   *gaikoku-ni iku*
> *ima kara uchi-ni kaeru*   *jibun-de densha-*
> *ni noru*

2. -O + verb, -ga + potential verb

Change the following phrases as shown in the example:

ex. rajio-o kiku
➡*rajio-ga kikemasu*

sake-o nomu	*eigo-o oshieru*
nihongo-o hanasu	*sushi-o taberu*
ocha-o ireru	*kuruma-o kau*
kasa-o kau	*moji-o yomu*
kyuuka-o toru	*kippu-o sagasu*
yakyuu-o suru	*shashin-o toru*
jisho-o tsukau	*o-bentoo-o taberu*
kuruma-o unten suru	
shakaigaku-o benkyoo suru	

O and ga
As learned previously, objects are followed by *o* in a sentence. However, when the verb is changed into its potential form, change the *o* to *ga*. *ex. Eigo-o hanashimasu.* I speak English. *Eigo-ga hanasemasu.* I can speak English.

3. Negative potential verbs

Place the phrases and negative potential verbs into the following sentence:

ex. oku-san-no hoshigatte iru kuruma, kaenai
➡*Yamada-san-wa* **oku-san-no hoshigatte iru kuruma**-ga **kaemasen**.

kodomo-ga kaita kanji, yomenai
shujin-no tsukutta sushi, taberarenai
kodomo-no hairitagatte iru daigaku-no
gakuhi, haraenai
kodomo-ga hoshigatte ita omocha-no
namae, oboerarenai

oboeru(-ru)
to remember,
memorize

oku(-u)
to display,
put out for
sale

**ome-ni
kakarete
kooei desu**
very pleased
to meet you
(polite)

omocha
toy

**renshuu
suru**
to practice

-sama
polite form
of *-san*

subarashii(i)
great,
wonderful

tashika(na)
certain, sure

tenisu
tennis

tenki
weather;
nice weather

watakushi
I (formal)

4. Koto-ga dekiru

Place the given phrases into the *koto-ga dekimasu* phrase:

ex. sushi-o tsukuru

➡️A: **Sushi-o tsukuru** *koto-ga dekimasu-ka.*

B: *Ee, dekiru-to omoimasu.*

nihongo-de booeki-o setsumei suru
Nihon-no chizu-o yomu
Tanaka-san-no tanjoobi-no paatii-ni iku
geki-no kippu-o kau
supeingo-o hanasu
kanji-o yomu

5. -Ku narimasu, -ni narimasu

Match the following phrases:

1. *Kono goro-wa bukku-ga*   a.*takaku narimashita.*
2. *Akachan-wa*   b.*waruku narimasu.*
3. *Hara-san-wa eigo-ga*   c.*osoku narimashita.*
4. *Asatte tenki-ga*   d.*ookiku natte imasu.*
5. *Sumimasen,*   e.*joozu-ni natte imasu.*

6. Memorize the counters for people:

1 person	*hitori*	7 people	*shichi / nana-nin*
2 people	*futari*	8 people	*hachi-nin*
3 people	*san-nin*	9 people	*kyuu-nin*
4 people	*yo-nin*	10 people	*juu-nin*
5 people	*go-nin*	11 people	*juuichi-nin*
6 people	*roku-nin*	12 people	*juuni-nin*

•The pattern continues regularly, number + *nin*

146

SHORT DIALOGUES

1. *ex.* koko-ni kuru, san-nin

   Satoshi: *Kyoo-wa ii o-tenki desu, ne.*
   Takashi: *Soo desu ne. Kaisei desu, ne.*
   Satoshi: *Nan-nin **koko-ni kimasu**-ka.*
   Takashi: ***San-nin koko-ni kuru**-to omoimasu.*

   1. jogingu-o suru, futari-de
   2. kekkon shiki-ni deru, hyaku-nin
   3. shashin-o toru, hitori-de
   4. yakyuu-no geimu-o suru, juuni-nin

2. *ex.* sukii, dekiru, suru, iku

   Sumisu: *Anata-wa **sukii**-ga **dekimasu**-ka.*
   Imai: *Ee, watashi-wa sukoshii **sukii**-ga **dekiru**-to omoimasu.*
   Sumisu: *Subarashii desu, ne.*
   Imai: *Demo, joozu-ni **dekimasen**.*
   Sumisu: *Boku-wa zenzen **sukii**-ga **dekimasen**. **Sukii-o suru**-no-wa muzukashii desu-ka.*
   Imai: *Sukoshi muzukashii-to omoimasu Juu, kondo issho-ni **ikimashoo**.*
   Sumisu: *Watashi-ni oshieraremasu-ka.*
   Imai: *Mochiron.*
   Sumisu: *Arigatoo.*

   1. tenpura, tsukuru, tsukuru
   2. kanji, kaku, benkyoo suru
   3. tenisu, dekiru, iku
   4. moji, yomu, benkyoo suru
   5. kuruma, unten dekiru, renshuu suru

People+de
When stating that one person does something, or a number of people do something together, use *de*. *Hitori-de unten shite imasu.* One person is driving. *San-nin-de ikimashita.* Three people went.

147

3. *ex.* fuyu, sukii-o dekiru, atatakai

> Urabe: **Fuyu** yasumi Tanaka-san-wa **sukii-**
> **o suru** koto-ga dekimasu-ka.
> Tanaka: **Atatakaku** natta kara dekimasen.
> Urabe: Zannen desu, ne.
> Tanaka: Daijoobu desu. Kyooto-ni ikimasu.
> Asoko-de iroirona koto-ga dekimasu.
> Urabe: Sore-wa ii desu, ne.

1. natsu, oyogu, samui
2. fuyu, Hokkaido-ni iku, tenki-ga warui
3. haru, sakkaa-o suru, samui
4. aki, tenisu-o suru, samui

SELF-TEST

Translate the following sentences into Japanese:

1. The baby can walk by herself!

2. Grandmother can speak English.

3. Mrs. Hara can play tennis.

4. The weather is becoming cold.

5. Four people can sit down.

Unscramble the following sentences:

6. wa iku natsu watashi dekimasu ga Sapporo koto yasumi ni

7. Tanaka imasu wa ni sukii joozu natte ga san

8. ni koraremasu de ka uchi hitori

9. shiki omoimasu subarashikatta to wa kekkon

10. de wa desu o-bentoo o tabeta futari gakkoo no

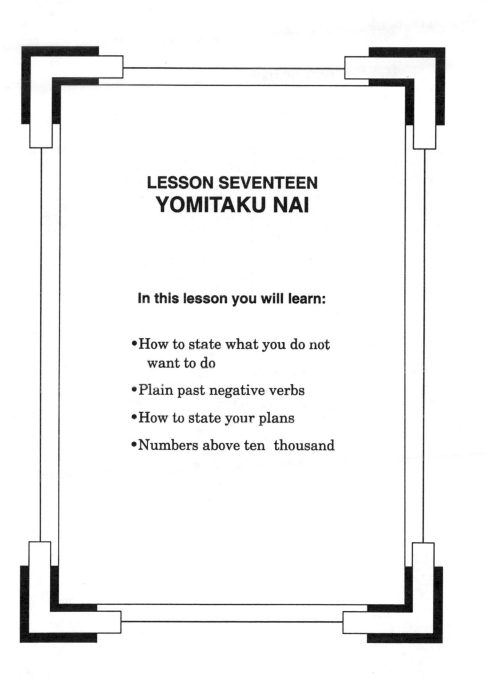

LESSON SEVENTEEN
YOMITAKU NAI

In this lesson you will learn:

- How to state what you do not want to do
- Plain past negative verbs
- How to state your plans
- Numbers above ten thousand

DIALOGUE

I

あや： こうすけくん ゆうべ えいごを べんきょう
した の.

こうすけ： いや べんきょう しなかった.

あや： どうして あなたは べんきょう しなかったの.

こうすけ： じかんが なかった. あやちゃんは.

あや： すこし べんきょう したよ. この ほんも
よんだの.

こうすけ： ぼくは よまなかったよ.

あや： これ から よみたい.

こうすけ： いや よみたくない.

II

A: この しゅうまつは よていが ありますか.

B: ええ. ともだちが アメリカから たずねて きます.
くうこうへ かれを むかえに いきます.

A: おともだちは ホテルに とまるの ですか.

B: いいえ にほんごが はなせない ので ホテルには
とまりたくないと いって いました.

A: ところで かりた テープを いつ かえしましょうか.

B: あしたで いい ですよ. わたしは でかけて いますが
わたしの おとうとに わたして ください.
たのしかった ですか.

A: ええ. おんがくが とても すばらしかった です.

B: また いつでも どうぞ.

150

I

Aya: *Koosuke-kun, yuube eigo-o benkyoo shita-no.*

Koosuke: *Iya, benkyoo shinakatta.*

A: *Dooshite anata-wa benkyoo shinakatta-no.*

K: *Jikan-ga nakatta. Aya-chan-wa.*

A: *Sukoshi benkyoo shita yo. Kono hon-mo yonda-no.*

K: *Boku-wa yomanakatta, yo.*

A: *Kore kara yomitai.*

K: *Iya, yomitaku nai.*

II

A: *Kono shuumatsu-wa yotei-ga arimasu-ka.*

B: *Ee. Tomodachi-ga Amerika-kara tazunete kimasu. Kuukoo-e kare-o mukae-ni ikimasu.*

A: *O-tomodachi wa hoteru-ni tomaru-no desu-ka.*

B: *Iie, nihongo-ga hanasenai node, hoteru-ni-wa tomari-taku nai-to itte imashita.*

A: *Tokorode, karita teepu-o itsu kaeshimashoo-ka.*

B: *Ashita-de ii desu, yo. Watashi-wa dekakete*

I

Aya: Kosuke, did you study English last night?

Kosuke: No, I didn't.

A: Why didn't you study?

K: I didn't have time. What about you?

A: I studied a little. Did you read this book already?

K: No, I did not read it.

A: Do you want to read it?

K: No, I don't want to read it.

II

A: Do you have plans for this weekend?

B: Yes, my friend is visiting from America. I will go pick him up at the airport.

A: Will your friend stay in a hotel?

B: No, he cannot speak Japanese, so he doesn't want to stay in a hotel.

A: By the way, when should I return the tape you lent me?

B: Tomorrow is fine. I will be out, but you can give it

151

-chan
used insted of *-san* at the end of small children's names, and girls' names

daibu
very

deru(-ru)
to leave

dooshite
why

heya
room

hikooki
airplane

hiku(-u)
to look up in a dictionary

hora
here, look

irassharu(-u)
to go, come, be (honorific)

iya
no (informal)

jaa mata
see you later

kaesu(-u)
to return something

imasu ga, watashi-no otooto-ni watashite kudasai. Tanoshikatta desu-ka.

A: *Ee. Ongaku-ga totemo subarashikatta desu.*

B: *Mata itsudemo doozo.*

to my brother. Did you enjoy it?

A: Yes. The music was wonderful.

B: (Borrow it) again anytime.

GRAMMAR EXPLANATION
1. -Taku nai

You learned in lesson 11 how to state that you want to do something by changing *masu* to *tai* and adding *desu*. If you do **not** want to do something, drop the *i desu* and add *-ku arimasen*. For the plain form, use *nai* instead of *arimasen*.

> *ex. Niku-o tabe**tai desu**.*
> I want to eat meat.
>
> *Niku-o tabe**taku arimasen**.*
> I don't want to eat meat.
>
> *Iyahoon-o shi**taku nai**-to omoimasu.*
> I do not think I want to listen to earphones.

2. -Nakatta

To change a plain negative verb into past form, drop the final *i* and add *nakatta*.

> *ex. yame**nai***   does not give up
> *yame**nakatta***   did not give up

152

*wakara**nai***	does not understand
*wakara**nakatta***	did not understand

• For *i* adjectives, use the *ku* form and add *nakatta*.

   ex. kowaku arimasen deshita
   was not frightening
   *kowa**ku nakatta***
   was not frightening (plain)

   *tanoshi**ku nakatta***
   was not enjoyable

Deru
When *deru* is
used to mean "to
leave," -*o*
precedes it, not
-*ni*.

• When using *desu*, or a *na* adjective, drop *dewa arimasen deshita* and add *ja nakatta*.

   ex. sensei dewa arimasen deshita
   was not a teacher

*sensei **ja nakatta***	was not a teacher
*jisho **ja nakatta***	was not a dictionary
*yuumei **ja nakatta***	was not famous

Hora
Hora is used
when giving an
object to
someone. It is
like saying,
"Here you are."

• The plain past negative adjectives and verbs can modifiy nouns when directly preceding them.

   ex. Teeburu-wa ookikunakatta.
   The table was not big.
   *ookiku**nakatta** teeburu*
   the table that was not big

   Kodomo-wa asobanakatta.
   The child did not play.
   *asoba**nakatta** kodomo*
   the child that did not play

kai
ka (informal)

kariru(-ru)
to borrow

kasu(-u)
to lend, rent

katarogu
catalogue,
brochure

kimi
you (informal)

kiro
kilo

kowai(i)
frightening

kuukoo
airport

(o)kyaku
visitor

maa maa
so-so

meshiagaru(u)
to eat
(polite)

mukae-ni iku
go to pick
someone up

Narita
airport near
Tokyo

3. Chigaimasu

To express that two things are different, use the following sentence pattern:

> Item one-*wa* item two-*to* **chigaimasu**.

ex. Nihon-wa Amerika-to zuibun **chigaimasu**.
Japan is very different from America.

*Kore-wa Emiko-san-no sunde ita apaato-***to***
chigaimasu**.
This is different from Emiko's apartment; or this is not Emiko's apartment.

4. Yotei desu

To state that you have plans to do something, use a plain verb + *yotei desu*.

ex. Okurimono-o **kau yotei desu**.
I plan to buy a present.

Yamada-san-ni katarogu-o **miseru yotei deshita**.
I planned to show the catalogue to Mr. Yamada.

It is good to use *yotei* when talking about what you will do in the future so that you do not appear to be presumptuous.

EXERCISES

1. -Taku arimasen

Conjugate the following verbs to the *-taku arimasen* form:

> *ex. rekishi-o benkyoo suru*
> ➥ *Shu: Azusa-san-wa* **rekishi-o benkyoo shitai** *desu-ka.*
> *Azusa: Iie,* **rekishi-o benkyoo shitaku** *arimasen.*

toranpu-de asobu	*terebi-o miru*
teipu-o kiku	*hikooki-ni noru*
zasshi-o yomu	*kuukoo-ni iku*
koohii-o ireru	*jisho-o kau*
kanji-o kaku	*tenisu-o suru*

2. Plain negative past

Change the following into plain negative past tense:

> *ex. teipurekoodaa dewa arimasen deshita*
> ➥ *teipurekoodaa ja nakatta*

> *hikooki dewa arimasen deshita*
> *kyooju dewa arimasen deshita*
> *okurimono dewa arimasen deshita*
> *o-bentoo dewa arimasen deshita*
> *gaikokujin dewa arimasen deshita*

Irasshaimasu
Irasshaimasu is the polite word for *imasu, ikimasu,* and *kimasu.* When speaking to someone who is of a higher position than you, or someone you wish to show respect to, use *irasshaimasu* instead of *imasu, ikimasu,* or *kimasu. ex. Tanaka-san-wa ginkoo-ni* **irasshaimashita**-*ka.* Mr. Tanaka, did you go to the bank? *Okaa-san-wa* **irasshaimasu**-*ka.* Is your mother there?

okurimono
present

oru(-ru)
iru (humble)

ototoi
the day
before
yesterday

rusu(-u)
to be out or
away from
home

shuumatsu
weekend

tanoshii(i)
enjoyable

teepu
tape

teepurekoodaa
tape
recorder

tomaru(-u)
to come to a
stop, sleep over

tsukeru(-ru)
to attach,
stick on

un
yes (informal)

watasu(-u)
to hand over,
deliver

yotei
plans,
schedule

zenbu
all

ex. oishiku arimasen deshita
➡ *oishiku nakatta*

sugoku arimasen deshita
ookiku arimasen deshita
subarashiku arimasen deshita
atarashiku arimasen deshita
furuku arimasen deshita

ex. watasanai
➡*watasanakatta*

shinai   *misenai*
tsukawanai   *awanai*
toranai

3. Plain negative past

Place the following phrases into the given sentences using the plain negative past tense form:

ex. Nobu-kun-wa kuru .
➡A: **_Nobu-kun-wa kita_**-no.
  B: Iie, **_Nobu-kun-wa konakatta_**-to
    omoimasu.

Shu-kun-wa matte iru .
Yuki-chan-wa shoogakkoo-de eigo-o
    narau.
Hiroko-chan-wa neru.
Kare-wa shichiji-ni uchi-o deru.
Kyooto-de shashin-o toru.
Tomoe-chan-wa teipu-o kikeru.

Jun-kun-wa chuugakkoo ni iku.
Satoshi-kun-wa ie-ni haireru.
Kinoo ame-ga furu.
Takashi-kun-wa eigo-ga wakaru.
Geki-no kippu-wa takai.
Shu-kun-ga hanashita eigo-wa joozu da.
Yuube atta hito-wa kyooju da.

4. Memorize the following numbers:

10,000 *ichiman*

100,000 *juuman*

1,000,000 - *hyakuman*

10,000,000 - *senman*

100,000,000 - *ichioku*

1,000,000,000 - *juuoku*

10,000,000,000 - *hyakuoku*

100,000,000,000 - *senoku*

1,000,000,000,000 - *itchoo*

5. Say the following numbers:

ex. 2,941,008,357

➡*nijuu kyuu oku | yonsen hyaku man |*
hassen | sanbyaku gojuushichi

1,000,892,000

9,296,460

2,169,292,845

562,728,500

329,000,227,451

1,947,091,253,008

45,728,134,978

Orimasu
Orimasu, the humble word for *imasu*, should be used when referring to yourself or someone from your group when you are trying to show humility. *ex. Imooto-wa Amerika-ni sunde orimasu.* My younger sister lives in America. **Never** use *orimasu* to refer to someone that you are speaking to.

157

SHORT DIALOGUES

1. *ex.* san-nen, Kyooto-ni irassharu, iku

> *Sumisu:* Tanaka-sama-wa dochira-ni tsutomete
> irasshaimasu-ka.
> *Tanaka:* Mitsubushi ginkoo-ni tsutomete orimasu.
> Hara-san-wa ⌐Sumisu-sama-wa Toyota-
> ni tsutomete inagara nihongo-mo
> benkyoo shite irassharu ⌐to itte imashita.
> *Sumisu:* Soo desu.
> *Tanaka:* Nihon-ni moo dono kurai
> irasshaimasu-ka.
> *Sumisu:* **San-nen** gurai Nihon-ni sunde orimasu.
> *Tanaka:* Sumisu-sama-wa **Kyooto-ni**
> **irasshatta** koto-ga arimasu-ka.
> *Sumisu:* Iie, **Kyooto-ni itta** koto-wa arimasen.
> Totemo **ikitai**-to omoimasu.

   1. ichinen, Hokkaido-ni irassharu, iku
   2. hachikagetsu, Oosaka-ni irassharu, iku
   3. ikkagetsu, sushi-o meshiagaru, taberu
   4. rokkagetsu, tenpura meshiagaru, taberu

2. *ex.* resutoran-ni iku, sukoshi tsukarete iru

> *Tanaka:* *Shigoto-no ato de kimi-wa*
> **resutoran-ni ikanai**-*kai.*
> *Sumisu:* *Iya,* **Ikitaku** *nai, yo.* **Sukoshi**
> **tsukarete iru** *kara. Ashita-no hoo-*
> *ga ii yo.*
> *Tanaka:* *Un, wakatta. Katarogu-o moo yonda-*
> *kai.*
> *Sumisu:* *Un, zenbu yonda, yo. Hora, koko da yo.*

> 1. kissaten-ni iku, isogashii
> 2. sake-o nomu, sukoshi tsukarete iru
> 3. eiga-o miru, purojekuto-o shite iru
> 4. jogingu-o suru, isogashii

3. *ex.* mise-ni itta, jikan, iku

> *Morita:* *Ototoi* **mise-ni ikimashita**-*ka.*
> *Jonson:* *Iie,* **mise-ni ikimasen deshita**.
> *Morita:* *Dooshite* **ikanakatta**-*no desu-ka.*
> *Jonson:* **Jikan**-*ga nakatta-no desu.*
> *Morita:* *Zannen deshita ne.*
> *Jonson:* *Soo desu ne. Demo, sugu-ni* **iku** *yotei*
> *desu kara.*

> 1. teipurekoodaa-o katta, okane, kau
> 2. resutoran-de tabeta, okane, taberu
> 3. Hirakawa-san to hanashita, jikan, hanasu
> 4. jisho-o katta, okane, kau
> 5. resutoran-de sake-o nonda, jikan, nomu

SELF-TEST

Translate the following sentences into Japanese:

1. I did not buy a present last night (plain).

2. Here you are.

3. I did not have enough time.

4. I think I do not want to go to the temple.

5. Do you work at Honda, Mr. Hara (honorific)?

6. This weekend, I do not want to ski.

7. I am living in Tokyo (humble).

8. The airport was not large (plain form).

9. Japanese magazines and American magazines are different.

10. Tomorrow, I plan to go to Australia.

LESSON NINETEEN
TSURETE ITTE KUREMASHITA

In this lesson you will learn:

- Giving verbs
- How to say a favor was given
- The plain -mashoo verb form
- How to state that you would like another person to do something

DIALOGUE

I

ジョンソン： はらださんの　おたく　ですか。

はらだ：　　はい　そう　です。　ああ　ジョンソンさん
　　　　　　どうぞ　あがって　ください。

ジョンソン： おじゃま　します。　これ　つまらない　もの
　　　　　　です　けど。　めしあがって　ください。

はらだ：　　どうも　ありがとう　ございます。いただきます。
　　　　　　ジョンソンさんは　ごきょうだい
　　　　　　いらっしゃいますか。

ジョンソン： はい　おとうとが　おります。

はらだ：　　おとうとさんは　おいくつ　ですか。

ジョンソン： じゅうろくさい　です。

はらだ：　　おとうとさんは　にほんに　いらっしゃった
　　　　　　ことが　ありますか。

ジョンソン： まだ　ありません。　でも　おとうとは　とても
　　　　　　にほんに　きたがっています。　すてきな
　　　　　　かびん　ですね。

はらだ：　　ありがとう　ございます。　これは　けっこん
　　　　　　いわいに　ともだち　から　いただいた　もの
　　　　　　です。

II

ジョンソン： ごちそうさま　でした。

はらだ：　　もう　いいの　ですか。　ビールを　もっと
　　　　　　いかが　ですか。

ジョンソン： いいえ　もう　けっこう　です。　ありがとう
　　　　　　ございました。

はらだ：　　おへやを　おんないしましょう。　ふとんで
　　　　　　ねた　ことが　ありますか。

ジョンソン： まだ　ありません。　ごしんせつ　ありがとう
　　　　　　ございます。

I

Jonson. *Harada-san-no o-taku desu-ka.*

Harada: *Hai, soo desu. Aa, Jonson-san doozo agatte kudasai.*

J: *Ojama shimasu. Kore tsumaranai mono desu kedo. Meshiagatte kudasai.*

H: *Doomo arigatoo gozaimasu. Itadakimasu. Jonson-san-wa go-kyoodai irasshaimasu-ka.*

J: *Hai, otooto-ga orimasu.*

H: *Otooto-san-wa o-ikutsu desu-ka.*

J: *Juuroku-sai desu.*

H: *Otooto-san-wa Nihon-ni irasshatta koto-ga arimasu-ka.*

J: *Mada arimasen. Demo, otooto-wa totemo Nihon-ni kitagatte imasu. Sutekina kabin desu, ne.*

II: *Arigatoo gozaimasu. Kore-wa kekkon iwai-ni tomoda-chi-kara itadaita mono desu.*

II

J: *Gochisoo-sama deshita.*

H: *Moo ii-no desu-ka. Biiru-o motto ikaga desu-ka.*

I

Johnson: Is this the Harada residence?

Harada: Yes, that's correct. Oh, Mr. Johnson, please come in.

J: I'm interrupting you. Here is a small gift. Please enjoy it (please eat).

H: Thank you very much. Mr. Johnson, do you have any brothers or sisters?

J: Yes, I have a little brother.

H: How old is your brother?

J: He is sixteen years old.

H: Has he ever been to Japan?

J: Not yet. However, he really wants to come to Japan. That is a sharp vase.

H: Thank you. It was a wedding gift from a friend.

II

J: It was a feast!

H: Would you like more? Would you like more beer?

Tsumaranai mono

Tsumaranai mono desu kedo, doozo, is a common expression when giving someone a small gift. It literally means "this is junk, but please accept it," and it is a humble form of asking someone to accept your gift. Whenever you are invited to a Japanese home, it is polite to bring a small gift to express appreciation for their hospitality. A souvenir from your home country is a good idea.

annai suru
to take and show

buchoo
boss

futon
Japanese bed

genkin
cash

gochisoo-sama deshita
it was a feast; thanks for the meal

iie, kekkoo desu
no thank you

ikutsu
how old

itadakimasu
the word of thanks uttered before eating

itadaku(-u)
to receive

iwai
celebration

kabin
vase

kagi
key

kekkoo(na)
fine

J: *Iie, moo kekkoo desu. Arigatoo gozaimashita.*

H: *O-heya-o annai shimashoo. Futon-de neta koto-ga arimasu-ka.*

J: *Mada arimasen. Go-shin-setsu arigatoo gozaimasu.*

J: No, I'm fine. Thank you very much.

H: I shall show you your room. Have you ever slept on a futon bed?

J: Not yet. Thank you for your kindness.

GRAMAR EXPLANATION

1. Giving and receiving from another person

Different words are used when talking about giving and receiving, depending on the position of both the giver and receiver.

kuremasu

To be given a gift from an **equal.** The giver is the subject, receiver is the indirect object.

Sentence structure:

Giver-***ga*** receiver-***ni*** object-***o kuremashita***.

ex. *Tanaka-san-ga (watashi-ni) ningyoo-o* ***kuremashita***.
Mrs. Tanaka gave me a Japanese doll.

Tanjoobi-no iwai-ni imooto-ga watashi-ni kono moofu-o ***kuremashita***.
For my birthday, my sister gave me this blanket.

kudasaimasu

To be given a gift from a **superior.** The giver is the subject, receiver the indirect object.

Sentence structure:

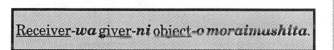

Giver-*ga* receiver-*ni* object-*o* **kudasaimashita.**

ex. Morita-sensei-ga watashi-ni jisho-o **kudasaimashita.**
My teacher, Mr. Morita, gave me a dictionary.

Sensei-ga Hara-san-ni hon-o kudasaimashita.
The teacher gave Mr. Hara a book.

moraimasu

To receive a gift from an **equal.** The receiver is the subject, giver the indirect object.

Sentence structure:

Receiver-*wa* giver-*ni* object-*o* *moraimashita.*

ex. Watashi-wa haha-ni saifu-o **moraimashita.**
I received a wallet from my mother.

Tanaka-san-wa Sumisu-san-ni omiyage-o **moraimashita.**
Ms. Tanaka received a souvenir from Mr. Smith.

165

konpyuutaa
computer

kudasaru(u)
to be given

kureru(-ru)
to be given

kyaku
visitor

makura
pillow

moofu
blanket

morau(-u)
to receive

omiyage
souvenir

omiyageya
souvenir
shop

otaku
residence

*rokku
konsaato*
rock concert

-sai
added to a
number to
indicate how
old someone is

saifu
wallet

itadakimasu

To receive a gift from a **superior.** The receiver is the subject, giver is the indirect object.

Sentence structure:

> Receiver-*wa* giver-*ni* object-*o itadakimashita.*

ex. Imai-san-wa Yamada-san-ni kabin-o
itadakimashita.
Mrs. Imai received a vase from Mr. Yamada.

*Watashi-wa Hara-san-no okaa-san-ni rokku
konsaato-no kippu-o* ***itadakimashita.***
I received a rock concert ticket from Mrs.
Hara's mother.

To summarize:

>   ***itadakimashita.***
> Receiver-*wa* giver-*ni* object-*o*
>   ***moraimashita.***

>   ***kudasaimashita.***
> Giver-*ga* receiver-*ni* object-*o*
>   ***kuremashita.***

EXERCISES

1. Family terms

Memorize the following chart; use polite words when referring to another's family, and humble terms when speaking of your own:

Agatte kudasai
The reason why most Japanese people will invite a visitor to "step up" to their house is because there usually are one or two steps in front of the main entrances to most Japanese homes.

	Polite	**Humble**
Family	*go-kazoku*	*kazoku*
Mother	*okaa-san*	*haha*
Father	*otoo-san*	*chichi*
Parent	*oyago-san*	*oya*
Parents	*go-ryooshin*	*ryooshin*
Wife	*oku-san*	*kanai/tsuma*
Husband	*go-shujin*	*shujin*
Child	*kodomo-san*	*kodomo*
Son	*musuko-san/bottchan*	*musuko*
Daughter	*musume-san/ojoo-san*	*musume*
Sibling(s)	*go-kyoodai*	*kyoodai*
Older sister	*onee-san*	*ane*
Younger sister	*imooto-san*	*imooto*
Older brother	*onii-san*	*ani*
Younger brother	*otooto-san*	*otooto*
Aunt	*oba-san*	*oba*
Uncle	*oji-san*	*oji*
Cousin	*o-itoko-san*	*itoko*
Grandmother	*obaa-san*	*sobo*
Grandfather	*ojii-san*	*sofu*

shikibuton
mattress

shikifu
sheet

shinsetsu(na)
kindness

suteki(na)
tasteful,
looks sharp

taoru
towel

tatami
a reed mat
covering the
floor

teinei(na)
polite

tsumaranai mono
this small
gift

yoku nemure-mashita
good night's
sleep (lit.
slept well)

zabuton
floor cushion

2. Family terms

Use each term to convey respect and humility:

ex. okaa-san, haha

➠ A: ___Okaa-san___-*wa irasshaimasu-ka.*
B: *Iie.* ___Haha___-*wa orimasen.*

otoo-san, chichi	*imooto-san, imooto*
onee-san, ane	*go-shujin, shujin*
onii-san, ani	*otooto-san, otooto*
oku-san, kanai	

3. Giving and Receiving

Substitute the given words into the following sentences:

___Subject___-*ga watashi-ni* ___object___-*o kuremashita.*

Subjects	Objects
haha	*konpyuutaa*
ane	*shatsu*
Hirakawa-san	*kagi*
Mouri-san	*moofu*

Watashi-wa ___giver___-*ni* ___object___-*o moraimashita.*

Givers	Objects
imooto	*makura*
Hanabusa-san	*taoru*
Kitamura-san	*kippu*
otooto	*genkin*

___Subject___-*ga watashi-ni* ___object___-*o kudasaimashita.*

Subjects	Objects
Morita-sensei	*jisho*
Yamashita-san	*okurimono*

buchoo hon

sensei kaban

Watashi-wa **giver**-*ni* **object**-*o itadakimashita.*

Givers	Objects
Yagi-san-no oku-san	*kutsu*
Tanaka-san	*megane*
Nishiyama-san	*taoru*
Hara-san-no okaa-san	*kutsushita*

4. Counter for long, thin objects like pencils, bottles, etc:

1	*ippon*	6	*roppon*
2	*nihon*	7	*nanahon*
3	*sanbon*	8	*happon / hachihon*
4	*yonhon*	9	*kyuuhon*
5	*gohon*	10	*jippon*

5. Ages:

1	*issai*	11	*juuissai*
2	*nissai*	12	*juunissai*
3	*san-sai*	13	*juusan-sai*
4	*yon-sai*	14	*juuyon-sai*
5	*go-sai*	15	*juugo-sai*
6	*roku-sai*	16	*juuroku-sai*
7	*nana / shichi-sai*	17	*juunana / juushichi-sai*
8	*hassai*	18	*juuhassai*
9	*kyuu-sai*	19	*juukyuu-sai*
10	*jussai*	20	*nijussai*

•This pattern continues regularly, just change *jussai* to *sanjussai, yonjussai,* etc.

Souvenirs
In Japan, souvenirs include food from another country as well as small gifts.

Slippers
Whenever entering a Japanese house, always remove your shoes. Slippers can be found just inside the entrance. Additionally, be sure to remove slippers when walking on a *tatami* mat.

SHORT DIALOGUES

1. *ex.* ane, onee-san, juuhassai

> *Tanaka:* *Buraun-san, go-kyoodai-wa*
> *irasshaimasu-ka.*
> *Buran:* *Ee, **ane**-ga imasu.*
> *Tanaka:* ***Onee-san**-wa Nihon-ni irasshatta*
> *koto-ga arimasu-ka.*
> *Buran:* *Iie, demo **ane**-wa hayaku Nihon-ni*
> *ikitai-to itte imashita.*
> *Tanaka:* *Soo desu-ka. **Onee-san**-wa o-ikutsu*
> *desu-ka.*
> *Buran:* ***Juuhassai** desu.*

>> 1. ani, onii-san, juukyuu-sai
>> 2. otooto, otooto-san, nijuugo-sai
>> 3. imooto, imooto-san, sanjuuissai

2. *ex.* wanpiisu, chichi, yomitagatte ita hon

> *Morita:* *Sutekina **wanpiisu** desu ne. Nihon-*
> *de katta-no desu-ka.*
> *Sumisu:* *Iie, kore-wa kyonen **chichi**-ga*
> *kuremashita.*
> *Morita:* *Soo desu-ka. Tokorode, Anata-ga*
> ***yomitagatte ita hon**-o go-shujin-ni*
> *moraimashita-ka.*
> *Sumisu:* *Hai. Kinoo shujin-ni moraimashita.*

>> 1. tokei, haha, kaitagatte ita wanpiisu
>> 2. seetaa, Tanaka-san, mitagatte ita bideo
>> 3. booshi, imooto, kaitagatte ita kasa
>> 4. kabin, Yamada-san, hoshigatte ita zabuton

3. *ex.* nekutai, Hanabusa-san, Kitamura-san-no
   okaa-san

> *Morita:* Ii **_nekutai_** *desu ne. Atarashii-no*
> *desu-ka.*
> *Sumisu:* *Jitsu-wa furui* **_nekutai_** *desu, yo.*
> *Sannen mae-ni* **_Hanabusa-san_***-ga*
> *kureta-no desu.*
> *Morita:* *Soo desu-ka. Sono tokei-mo soo*
> *desu-ka.*
> *Sumisu:* *Iie, kono tokei-wa* **_Kitamura-san-_**
> **_no okaa-san_***-ni itadakimashita.*

1. kabin, Hara-san, Hanabusa-san
2. seetaa, Yagi-san, sensei
3. booshi, Kitamura-san-no otoo-san, sensei
4. hon, Mouri-san-no oku-san, Ishihara-san

SELF TEST

Translate the following sentences into Japanese:

1. My father gave me this clock.

2. I received a clock from my younger brother.

3. My teacher gave me a dictionary.

4. I recieved a pen from my teacher.

5. My mother lives in America (humble).

6. I have been in your way.

7. Please don't bother.

8. My younger sister is fourteen years old.

9. I think my older brother wants to come to Japan.

10. The teacher, Mr. Morita, went to my father's house.

LESSON EIGHTEEN
TSURETE ITTE KUREMASHITA

In this lesson you will learn:

- Giving verbs

- How to say a favor was given

- The plain -mashoo verb form

- How to state that you would like
  another person to do something

DIALOGUE

A: あなたが かった にほんの おみやげは だれに
あげるの ですか.

B: らいげつ わたしの ははの たんじょうび な ので
ははに あげようと おもいます.

A: どこで かいましたか.

B: にほんの おみやげやで かいました. たなかさんが
つれて いって くれました.

A: いつ おくるの ですか.

B: きょう ゆうびんきょくに もって いきたいの ですが
じかんが ないの です.

A: ああ それ なら わたしが ゆうびんきょくの ちかくに
いく ので かわりに もって いって あげましょう.

B: ごめいわく では ありませんか.

A: かまいませんよ. こうくうびんと ふなべんの どちらで
おくりたいの ですか.

B: たんじょうび までに まにあわせたい ので
こうくうべんで おくりたい です.

A: はい わかりました.

B: ついでに この えはがきも だして もらえますか.

A: もちろん. きっては ありますか.

B: はい. ごしんせつ ありがとう ございます.

A: どう いたしました.

A: *Anata-ga katta Nihon-no omiyage-wa dare-ni ageru-no desu-ka.*

A: To whom will you give the souvenir that you bought?

B: *Raigetsu watashi-no haha-no tanjoobi na node, haha-ni ageyoo-to omoimasu.*

B: Next month is my mother's birthday, so I think I will give it to her.

A: *Doko-de kaimashita-ka.*

A: Where did you buy it?

B: *Nihon-no omiyageya-de kaimashita. Tanaka-san-ga tsurete itte kuremashita.*

B: At a Japanese souvenir shop. Mr. Tanaka did me the favor of taking me.

A: *Itsu okuru-no desu-ka.*

A: When will you send it?

B: *Kyoo yuubinkyoku-ni motte ikitai-no desu ga, jikan-ga nai-no desu.*

B: I want to take it to the post office today, but I do not have enough time.

A: *Aa, sore nara, watashi-ga yuubinkyoku-no chikaku-ni iku node, kawari-ni motte itte agemashoo.*

A: Well, I will be near the post office, so I can take it instead of you.

B: *Gomeiwaku dewa arimasen-ka.*

B: But wouldn't that be troublesome?

A: *Kamaimasen, yo. Kookuu-bin-to funabin-no dochira-de okuritai-no desu-ka.*

A: I do not mind. Do you want to send it by air or by sea?

B: *Tanjoobi made-ni mania-wasetai node, kookuubin-de okuritai desu.*

B: Well, I want it to reach her in time for her birthday, so I want to send it by air.

A: *Hai, wakarimashita.*

A: All right.

B: *Tsuide-ni kono ehagaki-mo dashite moraemasu-ka.*

B: While you are doing that, could you also mail this postcard for me?

A: *Mochiron. Kitte-wa*

A: Of course. Do you have a

When a plain verb is followed by *node*, it means "because . . ." ex. *Raishuu chichi-no tanjoobi na node, okurimono-o kaimasu.* Because my father's birthday is next week, I will buy a gift.

175

atena
return
address

dasu(-u)
to mail

e
picture

ehagaki
picture post
card

funabin
sea mail

fuutoo
envelope

gomeiwaku
troublesome

hagaki
postcard

harau(-u)
to pay

inu
dog

juusho
address

kawari-ni
instead of

kitte
stamp

**kookuu
shokan**
air letter

kookuubin
airmail

kowaremono
fragile item

arimasu-ka.

B: *Hai. Go-shinsetsu
arigatoo gozaimasu.*

A: *Doo itashimashite.*

stamp?

B: Yes. Thank you so much
for doing me this favor.

A: It's no trouble.

GRAMMAR EXPLANATION
1. Giving

For giving, three verbs may be used: *sashiagemasu*,
agemasu, and *yarimasu*. The sentence pattern is:

> | | | | *sashiagemasu.* |
> | *(Giver-wa)* | receiver-*ni* | object-*o* | *agemasu.* |
> | | | | *yarimasu.* |

sashiagemasu

to give to someone of a *higher* position:

> *ex. Yagi-san-wa okurimono-o sensei-ni*
> ***sashiagemashita.***
> Mr. Yagi gave a present to the teacher.

agemasu

to give to someone of an *equal* position:

> *ex. Watashi-wa teipu-o tomodachi-ni*
> ***agemashita.***
> I gave a tape to my friend.

yarimasu

to give to someone of a *lower* position, or someone
from your family:

> *ex. Watashi-wa imooto-ni kitte-o **yarimashita.***
> I gave a stamp to my sister.

2. Favors

When describing that someone did you a favor, or asking someone for a favor, use the *-te* form of the verb plus the giving and receiving verbs previously learned.

> ***kudasaimashita.***
> Favor giver-***ga*** receiver-***ni*** object -*te* verb
> ***kuremashita.***

> ***itadakimashita.***
> Receiver-***wa*** favor giver-***ni*** object -*te* verb
> ***moraimashita.***

> *ex. Sensei-ga (watashi-ni) tegami-o **katte kudasaimashita.***
> The teacher did (gave) me the favor of writing a letter.
>
> *Haha-ga (watashi-ni) jisho-o **katte kuremashita.***
> My mother did the favor of buying me a dictionary.
>
> *(Watashi-wa) kyooju-ni nihongo-o **oshiete itadakimashita.***
> I received a favor from my professor (which was) teaching me Japanese.
>
> *(Watashi-wa) Hanabusa-san-ni kozutsumi-o **okutte moraimashita.***
> I received a favor from Mrs. Hanabusa (which was) sending the package.

Kondo
Kondo can be used to either mean "next time" or "this time." To determine which meaning is being used, pay attention to the context of the sentence.

177

kozutsumi
package, parcel

made-ni
in time

**maniawa-
seru**
to make it ready by

matsuri
festival

okuru(-u)
to send

omaneki
invitation

posuto
mail box, mail drop

saigo
the end

saisho
the beginning

sashiageru(-ru)
to give

shoosetsu
novel

sokutatsu
special delivery

tetsudau(-u)
to help

tsuide-ni
while you are at it

3. Plain -mashoo

To change -*mashoo* verbs into the plain form:

•For -*ru* verbs: drop the final *masu* and add *yoo*

tabemasu	tabe**yoo**
oshiemasu	oshie**yoo**
shimasu	shi**yoo**
agemasu	age**yoo**

•For -*u* verbs: drop the final *u* and add *oo*
Exceptions: ending in *tsu*, drop *tsu* and add *too*

harau	hara**oo**
au	a**oo**
kau	ka**oo**
asobu	asob**oo**
iku	ik**oo**
yomu	yom**oo**
hashiru	hashir**oo**
sagasu	sagas**oo**
matsu	mat**oo**
tatsu	tat**oo**

Exceptions: *kuru*   ko**yoo**
       suru   **shiyoo**

4. -Te hoshii

When you want another person to do something, use:

> person-***ni*** object -*te* verb ***hoshii desu.***

*ex. Haha-ni kitte-o ka**tte hoshii desu.***
I want my mother to buy a stamp.

*Anata-ni watashi-to issho-ni paatii-ni **itte***
hoshii desu.

I want you to go to the party with me.

EXERCISES
1. Giving

Substitute the given words into the sentence:

Sashiagemasu

*Watashi-wa **object**-o **receiver**-ni sashiagemashita.*

Objects	Receiver
shoosetsu	Morita-san-no okaa-san
fuutoo	buchoo
moofu	Hara-san-no oku-san
jisho	sensei

Agemasu

*Watashi-wa **object**-o **receiver**-ni agemashita.*

Object	Receiver
tokei	Yagi-san
kagi	tomodachi
okane	Watanabe-san
teipu	kyaku

Yarimasu

*Watashi-wa **object**-o **receiver**-ni yarimashita.*

Object	Receiver
gohan	inu
zubon	imooto
seetaa	ane
iyahoon	otooto

Yaru
The verb *yarimasu* means "to give to someone of a lower position." It is not used frequently in Japanese, unless one is talking about giving something to an animal. If you are talking about a superior giving a gift to a subordinate, or giving within your family, *ageru* is all right to use.

tsurete iku
to take and
show

yaru(-u)
to give

**yorokonde
iru**
be happy to

**FOREIGN
COUNTRIES**
Chuugoku
China

Furansu
France

Igirisu
England

Itaria
Italy

Kanada
Canada

Kankoku
Korea

**Kita-
Choosen**
North Korea

Oranda
Holland

2. Receiving favors

Choose the appropriate terms for each of the following sentences:

Imai-san-wa **giver**-*ni* **obj.,-te verb** *itadakimashita.*
Imai-san-wa **giver**-*ni* **obj.,-te verb** *moraimashita.*

Giver	Object, verb
imooto	*matsuri-ni tsurete iku*
Yamamoto sensei	*nihongo-no hon-o kau*
Hara sensei-no oku-san	*shashin-o toru*
Yamada-san	*hagaki-o okuru*
watashi-no chichi	*shoosetsu-o kau*

Giver-*ga Hara-san-ni* **obj.,-te verb** *kudasaimashita.*
Giver-*ga Hara-san-ni* **obj.,-te verb** *kuremashita.*

Giver	Object, verb
buchoo	*teipu-o kau*
Kitamura-san	*jisho-o hiku*
sensei	*oshieru*
Yoosuke-kun	*kuukoo-e mukae-ni iku*
Koosuke-kun	*katarogu-o watasu*

3. Plain -mashoo

Conjugate the following verbs into the plain *mashoo* form and substitute them into the following sentences:

> *ex. jisho-o hiku*
> ➡ A: ***Jisho-o hikimashoo**-ka.*
>   B: *Ee, **hikoo**-to omoimasu.*

tsuku	*watasu*
asobu	*okuru*
sake-o nomu	*matsu*
benkyoo suru	*omaneki-o suru*
itadaku	*uru*
miru	*kiku*
oeru	*isu-ni suwaru*
ageru	*shoosetsu-o kau*

4. -Te hoshii

Change the following sentences into the -te hoshii form:

> *ex. Kono hagaki-o yuubinkyoku-ni motte ikitai desu.*
> ➡ *Anata-ni **kono hagaki-o yuubinkyoku-ni motte itte** hoshii desu.*
>
> *Tanjoobi-no paatii-ni ikitai desu.*
> *Fuutoo-ni juusho-o ikitai desu.*
> *Kaita kanji-o naoshitai desu.*
> *Kono tegami-o okuritai desu.*
> *Hara-san-o kuukoo-ni mukae-ni ikitai desu.*

When Japanese people point to themselves, they point to their noses, not their chests like American people do.

SHORT DIALOGUES
1. *ex.* sensei, sashiageru

> *Tokuichiro:* Nobushige-san, anata-wa moo **sensei**-ni shoosetsu-o **sashiagemashita**-ka.
>
> *Nobushige:* Iie, **sensei**-ni shoosetsu-o **sashiagemasen** deshita.
>
> *Tokuichiro:* Jaa, ashita **sensei**-ni shoosetsu-o **sashiageru** hoo-ga ii-to omoimasu, yo.
>
> *Nobushige:* Hai, soo shimashoo.

    1. tomodachi, ageru
    2. Kankoku-no kata, ageru
    3. Yamashita-san, sashiageru
    4. buchoo, sashiageru

2. *ex.* ehagaki, okuru, morau

> *Hiroko:* Anata-wa **ehagaki**-o moo **okurimashita**-ka.
>
> *Sachiko:* Jikan-ga nakatta node, Yamashita-san-ni **okutte moraimashita**.
>
> *Hiroko:* Soo desu-ka. Itsumo Yamashita-san-ni iroirona koto-o shite **moratte iru**-no desu, ne.
>
> *Sachiko:* Ee, honto-ni soo desu. Yamashita-san-wa shinsetsuna hito desu.

1. kozutsumi, kookuubin-ni suru, itadaku
2. tegami, dasu, morau
3. kitte, kau, itadaku
4. kozutsumi, funabin-ni suru, morau

3. *ex.* tegami, kaku, sensei, kudasaru

Hirakawa: **Tegami**-o moo **kakimashita**-ka.
Sumisu: Hai, **kakimashita**.
Hirakawa: Jibun-de **kakemashita**-ka.
Sumisu: Saisho jibun-de **kakimashita**
kedo, totemo muzukashikatta
desu; soshite, saigo-ni **sensei**-ga
tetsudatte **kudasaimashita**.
Hirakawa: Itsumo **sensei**-ga tetsudatte
kudasaimasu-ka.
Sumisu: Iie. Jibun-de yaru hoo-ga ii-no
desu-ga, wakaranai toki-wa,
sensei-ga tetsudatte
kudasaimasu.

1. kanji-o yomu, Hirakawa sensei, kudasaru
2. shinbun-o yomu, Yamada-san, kureru
3. tegami-o kaku, tomodachi, kureru
4. hanashi-o suru, Hara-san, kudasaru

SELF-TEST

Translate the following sentences into Japanese:

1. The teacher helped me write the speech.

2. Mr. Matsumoto did the favor of taking me to the post office.

3. I gave a novel to my teacher, Mrs. Morimoto.

4. I gave a Japanese book to my younger sister.

5. I want Mr. Morita to mail this postcard.

Fill in the blanks with *wa, ni, o, ga, o, to,* or X:

6. Watashi ___ haha ___ bideo ___ agemashita.

7. Watashi ___ sensei ___ jishoo ___ sashiagemashita.

8. Chichi ___ watashi ___ hon ___ kaite ___ kuremashita.

9. Anata ___ kore ___ mite ___ hoshii desu.

10. Kyoo ___ Mitsutake-san ___ koko ___ kuru ___ omoimasu.

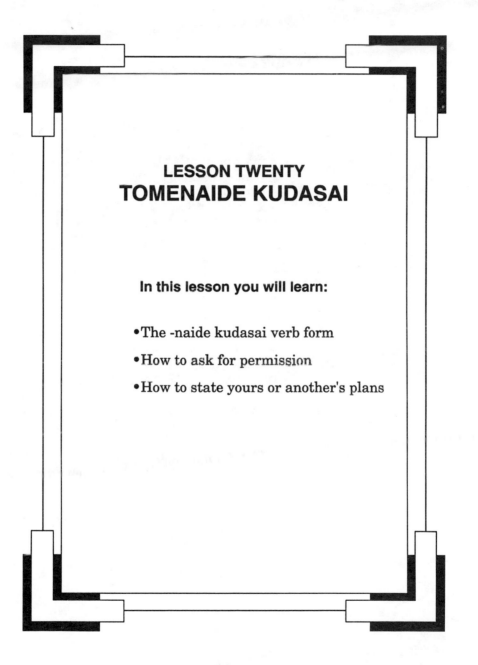

LESSON TWENTY
TOMENAIDE KUDASAI

In this lesson you will learn:

- The -naide kudasai verb form
- How to ask for permission
- How to state yours or another's plans

DIALOGUE

I
スミス： とうきょう　きょうと　かんの　おうふく　きっぷを
　　　　 いちまい　ください。　いきは　あしたの
　　　　 とうきょう　はつ　よじ　そして　かえりは
　　　　 あさっての　きょうと　はつ　にじは　ありますか。
B： とうきょう　はつ　ごじ　でも　いい　ですか。
スミス： ええ　いい　です。
B： はい。　いちまん　ごせん　えん　です。
　　　 しんかんせんの　ほうむは　じゅうごばん　せん
　　　 です。
スミス： はい　わかりました。
つぎのひ
いまい： きょうは　どこに　いくの　ですか。
スミス： きょうとに　いく　つもり　です。
いまい： なんじに　でますか。
スミス： ごじ　はつの　しんかんせん　です。
いまい： じかんは　どの　ぐらい　かかりますか。
スミス： いちじかん　はんで　つく　はず　です。
II
スミス： 　うんてんしゅさん　きょうと　ホテル　まで
　　　　 おねがい　します。
うんてんしゅさん： はい。
　　　　 この　こうさてんの　てまえでも　いい　ですか。
　　　　 ホテルは　この　みぎ　がわに　あります　から。
スミス： 　そんな　ところで　とめないで　ください。
　　　　 どこかで　ユーターン　して　ホテルの
　　　　 ちゅうしゃじょう　まで　いって　ください。
うんてんしゅさん： はい　わかりました。

I

Sumisu: *Tookyoo Kyooto kan-no oofuku kippu-o ichimai kudasai. Iki-wa ashita-no Tookyoo hatsu yoji, soshite kaeri-wa asatte-no Kyooto hatsu niji-wa arimasu-ka.*

B: *Tookyoo hatsu goji demo ii desu-ka.*

S: *Ee, ii desu.*

B: *Hai. Ichiman gosen en desu. Shinkansen-no hoomu-wa juugoban sen desu.*

S: *Hai, wakarimashita.*

Tsugi-no hi

Imai: *Kyoo-wa doko-ni iku-no desu-ka.*

S: *Kyooto-ni iku tsumori desu.*

I: *Nanji-ni demasu-ka.*

S: *Goji hatsu-no shinkansen desu.*

I: *Jikan-wa dono gurai kakurimasu-ka.*

S: *Ichijikan han-de tsuku hazu desu.*

II

Sumisu: *Untenshu-san, Kyooto hoteru made onegai shimasu.*

Untenshu-san: *Hai.*

I

Smith: I would like to buy a round trip ticket from Tokyo to Kyoto please; do you have one that leaves Tokyo tomorrow at 4:00 and returns from Kyoto the day after tomorrow at 2:00?

B: Would 5:00 from Tokyo be all right?

S: Yes, that's fine.

B: All right. It is 15,000 yen. The bullet train's platform line is number 15.

S: O.K.

The next day

Imai: Where are you going today?

S: I'm planning to go to Kyoto.

I: What time will you leave?

S: On the 5:00 bullet train.

I: How long will it take?

S: It's expected to take one and a half hours.

II

Smith: Driver, please take me to the Kyoto Hotel.

Driver: Of course.

Addresses
Addresses are made up of the city, *shi*, place name, *machi* or *choo*, then *choome* (divisions of *machi* or *choo*) + *banchi* (sections of *choome*) + *goo* (house number). ex. *Tachikawa-shi, Ogawa-choo, san-choome, go-banchi, hyakunana-goo.*

arubaito
part-time job

**chuusha
kinshi**
no parking

chuushajoo
parking lot

deguchi
exit

hatsu
departure
time

hazu
it's expected

**hidari
gawa**
left side

hidari
left

hoomu
platform

kado
corner

kochiragawa
this side

koosaten
intersection

kotoshi
this year

kure
the end of
the year

*Kono koosaten-no temae-
de mo ii desu-ka. Hoteru-
wa kono migi gawa-ni
arimasu kara.*

S: *Sonna tokoro-de tomenaide
kudasai. Dokoka-de yuu
taan shite hoteru-no chuushajoo made itte kudasai.*

U: *Hai, wakarimashita.*

May I stop just before
this intersection? The
hotel is on the right side
of the street.

S: Please do not stop there.
Please do a u-turn
somewhere and go to the
parking lot of the hotel.

D: Yes, I understand.

GRAMMAR EXPLANATION
1. -Naide kudasai

The negative form of *kudasai* is *-naide kudasai*.
It is formed by using the *nai* form of plain verbs and
adding *-de kudasai*.

> *ex. takushii-o tomenai*
> the taxi does not stop
> *takushii-o tome**naide kudasai***
> please do not stop the taxi
>
> *sashiagenai*
> does not give
> *sashiage**naide kudasai***
> please do not give

2. -Te mo ii desu-ka

To ask someone if it is alright to do something, use

-te verb + *mo ii desu-ka.*

ex. Itte mo ii desu-ka.
Is it all right to go?

Tabete mo ii desu-ka.
Is it all right to eat?

Common ways to answer are:
1. The *-te* verb form + *mo ii desu.*
Itte mo ii desu.
It is all right to go.

Tabete mo ii desu.
It is all right to eat.

2. *Hai, kamaimasen.*
Yes, I do not mind.

3. The *-naide kudasai* phrase.
ikanaide kudasai
Please do not go.

tabenaide kudasai
Please do not eat.

4. The *-te* verb + *-wa ikemasen* means an
action is prohibited or impossible.
itte-wa ikemasen.
not allowed to go

tabete-wa ikemasen.
not allowed to eat

magaru(-u)
to turn

-mai
counter for
papers,
tickets, plates

massugu
straight
ahead

migi
right
(direction)

mukoogawa
across the
street

noriba
boarding
place

oofuku
round trip

otsuri
change
(money)

ryoori
cuisine

shingoo
traffic light

shokudoo
cafeteria

temae
just before

tomaru(-u)
to stop at (no
object)

tomeru(-ru)
to stop, park
(needs object)

3. Tsumori, yotei, hazu

To state that **you** plan to do something, use

> ## plain verb + *tsumori desu*

*ex. Ashita watashi-wa Igirisu-ni kono
kozutsumi-o okuru **tsumori desu**.*
Tomorrow, I plan to send this package to
England.

*Kyoo watashi-wa koko-o rokuji-ni deru
tsumori desu.*
Today I plan to leave from here at 6:00.

To state **yours** or **another's** plans, use

> ## plain verb + *yotei desu*

*ex. Raigetsu-no kokonoka-wa Sumisu-san-no
imooto-san-no tanjoobi desu kara, hon-o
kau **yotei desu**.*
Because Ms. Smith's sister's birthday is
next month on the ninth, (I) plan to buy
(her) a book.

*Tanaka-san-wa Chuugoku-de chuugokugo-
o benkyoo suru **yotei desu**.*
Mr. Tanaka plans to study Chinese in China.

To say that something is expected, use

> ## plain verb + *hazu desu*

*ex. Hikooki-wa sanji gojuppun-ni koko-ni tsuku
hazu desu.*

The plane is expected to arrive here at 3:50.

*Eiga-wa goji-ni hajimaru **hazu desu.***
The movie is expected to begin at 5:00.

Yotei
To ask someone
if they have any
plans, use
*nanika yotei-ga
arimasu-ka.* "Do
you have any
particular
plans?"

4. -Te . . .

Another way to connect sentences is to use the *-te* form for the verb in the first sentence, then state the second sentence.

> *ex. Anata-no namae-o **kaite**, suwatte kudasai.*
> Write you name, and please sit down.
>
> *Watashi-wa kitte-o **katte**, hagaki-o okurimashita.*
> I bought a stamp, and mailed the postcard.

EXERCISES

1. -Te mo ii desu-ka, -naide kudasai

Place the following phrases into the given sentences:

> *ex. densha-no naka-de o-bentoo-o taberu*
> ➡A: ___Densha-no naka-de o-bentoo-o tabete___
>   *mo ii desu-ka.*
>   B: *Au, **tabenaide** kudasai.*
>
>   *koko-de tabako-o suu*
>   *kono ehagaki-o okuru*
>   *kono taoru-o tsukau*
>   *ano kado-de tomaru*
>   *ano koosaten-de hidari-ni magaru*

tsuku(-u)
to arrive

tsumori
plan

umi
sea

*untenshu-
san*
driver

yama
mountain

yukkuri
slowly,
leisurely

yuu taan
u-turn

nagai(i)
long

**MODES OF
TRANSPOR-
TATION:**
basu
bus

chikatetsu
subway

michi
road, street

shinkansen
bullet train

takushii
taxi

tetsudoo
railway

2. -Te mo ii desu

Place the following phrases into the given sentences:

ex. basu-de yama-ni iku
➡ A: **Basu-de yama-ni itte** *mo ii desu-ka.*
B: *Ee,* **itte** *mo ii desu.*

umi-de oyogu
buchoo-san, kyoo hachiji-ni uchi-ni kaeru
kono hagaki-o Kanada-ni okuru
Tanaka-san-no nooto-ni kaku
sono deguchi kara deru
*o-kyaku-san, asoko-no chuushajoo-de
    tomaru*

3. Tsumori, yotei, hazu

Change the sentences into the *hazu desu* form:

ex. Basu-wa kuji-ni kimasu.
➡ *Basu-wa kuji-ni kuru hazu desu.*

*Sumisu-san-wa kokonoka-ni Oosaka-ni
    ikimasu.*
*Purojekuto-wa raishuu-no getsuyoobi-
    ni owarimasu.*
Asatte haha-ga tazunete kimasu.
Hiruton hoteru-de paatii-o shimasu.

Place the following phrases into both sentences:

> *ex. Nihon-ni ikimasu*
> ➡ *Watashi-wa **Nihon-ni iku** tsumori desu.*
> ➡ *Tanaka-san-wa **Nihon-ni iku** yotei desu.*

> *Sumisu-san-ga yuube mita eiga-o mimasu.*
> *Hara-san-ga hoshigatte ita teipu-o*
> *kaimasu.*
> *Sensei-no kaita hon-o yomimasu.*
> *Rekishi-o benkyoo shimasu.*
> *Chikatetsu-de Tookyoo-ni ikimasu.*

-de
Use *de* as the
particle when
explaining how
you went or
came. *ex. Basu-
de kimashita;*
came by bus.
*Takushii-de
uchi-ni
kaerimashita;*
came home by
taxi.

4. -Te . . .

Combine the given sentences into one sentence
using the -te . . . form:

> *ex. E-o kaimasu. Uchi-ni kaerimasu.*
> ➡ *E-o katte, uchi-ni kaerimasu.*

> *Mise-ni ikimasu. Yamada-san-ni aimasu.*
> *Omiyageya-ni ikimasu. Omiyage-o*
> *kaimasu.*
> *Gorufu-o shimasu. Tenisu-o shimasu.*
> *Taoru-o kaimasu. Tomodachi-ni sono*
> *taoru-o agemasu.*
> *Hara-san-no ie-ni ikimasu. Hara-san-*
> *to iroirona koto-o hanashimasu.*

SHORT DIALOGUES

1. *ex.* densha, oishii resutoran, resutoran-ni iku

A: *Nagai aida machimashita-ka.*
B: *Iie, sakki tsukimashita.*
A: *Basu-de kimashita-ka.*
B: *Iie, **densha**-de kimashita.*
A: *Mukoogawa-ni **oishii resutoran**-ga arimasu ne. Sono **resutoran-ni itte** mo ii desu-ka.*
B: *Hai, sono **resutoran**-ga ii desu.*

1. takushii, ii eigakan, eiga-o miru
2. kuruma, subarashii resutoran, resutoran-de taberu
3. densha, sugoi kissaten, kissaten-ni iku
4. takushii, ii depaato, depaato-ni iku

2. *ex.* kanji-o benkyoo suru, nihongo-no gakkoo-ni iku

I: *Sumisu-san-wa itsu made Nihon-ni imasu-ka.*
S: *Kotoshi-no kure made iru tsumori desu.*
I: *Sono-aida-ni nanika yotei-ga arimasu-ka.*
S: ***Kanji-o benkyoo suru** yotei desu.*
I: *Ii desu ne. Hajimete Nihon-ni kita toki **nihongo-no gakkoo-ni iku**-no-wa taihen deshita-ka.*
S: *Sukoshi taihen deshita, sorede tomodachi-ga tetsudatte kuremashita.*

1. Nihongo-o benkyoo suru, apaato-o kariru
2. Eigo-o oshieru, densha-ni noru
3. Iroirona yuumeina tokoro-o tazuneru,
   nihongo-o hanasu
4. Mitsubishi ginkoo-ni tsutomeru,
   arubaito-o sagasu
5. Tanaka-san-no ie-ni sumu, nihongo-o
   hanasu

3. *ex.* kado, magaru, kissaten-no mae-de, tomaru

> *Jonson:*   *Doko-de takushii-ni noremasu-ka.*
> *Hara:*   *Asoko-no takushii noriba-de*
>   *takushii-ni noremasu yo.*
> *Jonson:*   *Arigatoo gozaimasu.*
>   *Kono juusho made tsurete itte kudasai.*
> *Untenshu-san:*   *Hai, wakarimashita.*
> *Jonson:*   *Motto yukkuri unten shite kudasai.*
> *Untenshu-san:*   *Hai.*
>   *O-kyaku-san, ano **kado**-de **magatte***
>   *mo ii desu-ka.*
> *Jonson:*   *Aa. **Magaranaide** kudasai. Ano*
>   ***kissaten-no mae-de** **tomaru** hoo-*
>   *ga ii desu yo.*
> *Untenshu-san:*   *Hai, wakarimashita.*

1. shingoo, tomaru, koosaten-de hidari-ni
   magaru
2. kado, tomaru, chuushajoo-de tomaru
3. kado, magaru, shokudoo-no mae-de tomaru
4. koosaten, magaru, mise-no mae-de tomaru

SELF-TEST

Translate the following sentences into Japanese:

1. Please do not turn at that corner.

2. The bus is expected to stop here at 3:00.

3. Is it alright if I eat the food you made?

4. The day after tomorrow, I plan to go skiing, and play tennis (use -te...).

5. You cannot turn right at this corner.

Unscramble the following sentences:

6. kono ka no temae de ii yuu taan koosaten desu shite mo.

7. desu Kyooto mo ni itte de densha ii ka.

8. oeru desu wa kyoo ni o watashi tsumori hachiji shigoto.

9. kudasai san kochiraga wa untenshu tomaranaide de.

10. ni itte Tookyoo o kaimasu tokei.

LESSON TWENTY ONE
HIRAKANAKUTE-WA IKEMASEN

In this lesson you will learn:

- •The tari/dari expression
- •The nakute-wa ikemasen verb form
- •The -te mimasu verb phrase

DIALOGUE

I

ジョンソン： いま いそがしい ですか.

いまい： いいえ ただ ほんを よんだり テレビを
みたり して いる だけ です. なにか
てつだいましょうか.

ジョンソン： ええ じつは ぎんこうへ いって ドルを
えんに りょうがえ しなければ なりません.
それ から こうざを ひらかなくては
いけません. てつだって くださいますか.

いまい： もちろん. いま から いきましょうか.

ジョンソン： そう して くれますか. にほんでは
ふつうよきん にも りしが つきますか.

いまい： すこし. でも たしか では ありません.
いって みましょう.

II

ジョンソン： この ドルを えんに りょうがえ したいの
ですが.

B： わかりました. かわせ レートは いち ドル
ひゃく じゅう えん で てすうりょうが ご
パーセント です. はい どうぞ.

ジョンソン： ありがとう ございます.

ジョンソン： あのう こうざを ひらきたいの ですが.

B： わかりました. この かみに きにゅう して
ください. これが あなたの よきん
つうちょう です. あなたの キャッシュ
カードを あとで おくります. げんきんを
ひきだしたり にゅうきん したり する とき
その カードを つかってください.

ジョンソン： はい わかりました.

B： いっかげつに いちど あなたの ざんだかを
きにゅう した けいさんしょを おくります.
それで おかねの だしいれと おりしの
めいさいが わかります.

I

Jonson: *Ima isogashii desu-ka.*

Imai: *Iie, tada hon-o yondari terebi-o mitari shite iru dake desu. Nanika tetsudaimashoo-ka.*

J: *Ee, jitsu-wa ginkoo-e itte doru-o en-ni ryoogae shinakereba narimasen. Sore kara kooza-o hiraka-nakute-wa ikemasen. Tetsudatte kudasaimasu-ka.*

I: *Mochiron. Ima kara ikimashoo-ka.*

J: *Soo shite kuremasu-ka. Nihon-dewa futsuu yokin ni-mo rishi-ga tsukimasu-ka.*

I: *Sukoshi, demo tashika dewa arimasen. Itte mimashoo.*

II

J: *Kono doru-o en-ni ryoogae shitai-no desu ga.*

B: *Wakarimashita. Kawase reeto-wa ichi doru hyaku juu en de tesuuryoo-ga go paasento desu. Hai, doozo.*

J: *Arigatoo gozaimasu.*

J: *Anoo, kooza-o hirakitai-no desu ga.*

B: *Wakarimashita. Kono*

I

Johnson: Are you busy now?

Imai: No, I'm just reading a book and watching TV. Do you want me to help you with something?

J: Yes, actually I need to go to a bank and change my dollars into yen, and then I need to open an account. Could you help me?

I: Of course. Shall we go now?

J: You will do me this favor? In Japan, do banks also pay you interest when you have an account?

I: A little, but I'm not certain. Let's go and see.

II

J: I would like to change these dollars into yen.

B: I understand. The exchange rate is one hundred ten yen for one dollar, plus there is a five percent charge. Here you are.

J: Thank you.

J: I would like to open an account.

B: All right, please fill out

ano(o)
well . . .

arau(-u)
to wash

betsu betsu ni
separately

dashiire
deposit and withdraw

de
is...and

denki
light, electricity

doru
dollar

futsuu yokin
savings account

(go) yoo
something one needs to do

hikidasu(-u)
to withdraw

hiraku(-u)
to open

ka
or

kaado
card

kami-ni ki'nyuu shite kudasai. Kore-ga anata-no yokin tsuuchoo desu. Anata-no kyasshu kaado-o ato de okurimasu. Genkin-o hikidashitari nyuukin shitari suru toki sono kaado-o tsukatte kudasai.

J: *Hai, wakarimashita.*

B: *Ikkagetsu-ni ichi-do anata-no zandaka-o ki'nyuu shita keisansho-o okurimasu. Sorede okane-no dashiire-to o-rishi-no meisai-ga wakarimasu.*

these papers. This is your bank book. Your money card will be sent to you later. When you need to withdraw cash or make a deposit, please use that card.

J: All right.

B: Once a month (we) will send you a statement that will show your balance. Also, it will show all your transactions and the details of your interest.

GRAMMAR EXPLANATION

1. Tari/dari

When a verb+*tari/dari*, with another verb+*tari/dari* +*shite imasu* are used in a sentence, it means that one has been doing these things back and forth for a while. To form this pattern, add *ri* to the plain past verb.

> ex. *Kyoo-wa keiki-o tsukutta**ri** hon-o yonda**ri** shite imasu.*
> Today I've been making a cake, reading a book, making a cake, and reading a book.

> *Sono kaisha-wa iroirona seihin-o yunyuu shita**ri** yushutsu shita**ri** shite imasu.*
> That company imports and exports various products.

2. Nakute, nakereba

There are two different expressions to state that one has to do something. They differ from the *nasai* verb form studied previously in that *nasai* is a command given, whereas this verb form is not necessarily ordered.

Nakute-wa ikemasen

To form this pattern, use the plain negative form of verbs, and instead of using *nai* as the ending, use *nakute-wa ikemasen*.

> *ex. ikanai*
> *ginkoo-ni ika**nakute-wa ikemasen***
> have to go to the bank

> > *orosanai*
> > *genkin-o orosa**nakute-wa ikemasen***
> > have to withdraw cash

> > *tsukawanai*
> > *toraberaazu chekku-o tsukawa**nakute-wa
> > ikemasen***
> > have to use traveler's checks

Nakereba narimasen

The meaning and grammar structure for this expression are exactly the same as for *nakute-wa ikemasen*. Use *nakereba narimasen* after dropping *nai*.

> *ex. hanasanai*
> > *sensei-to hanasa**nakereba narimasen***
> > have to talk with the teacher

When using *nakereba narimasen* or *nakute-wa ikemasen*, you are stating that you have to do something. Literally, it means that if you do not do it, you will be in a bad situation.

kawase reeto
exchange rate

keisansho
statement

kesu(-u)
to turn off

kimatte iru
it has been decided

ki'nyuu suru
to fill out

koo yuu
that kind of

kooza
account

kyasshu kaado
money card

meisai
details

modoru(-u)
to return

nyuukin
deposit

orosu(-u)
to withdraw

paasento
percent

peeji
page

harawanai
zeikin-o harawanakereba narimasen
have to pay taxes

shinai
en-o doru-ni ryoogae shinakereba narimasen
have to change yen into dollars

3. -Te mimasu

When the *-te* verb is used with *mimasu*, the meaning becomes "try _____ and see."

> *ex. Juppeeji made yonde mimasu.*
> I will read to page 10 and see (if I like it).

When used with *mimashoo*, the nuance changes to "let's try _____ and see."

> *ex. Sono kissaten-de tabete mimashoo.*
> Let's try eating at that cafe and see (if we like it, if it's good, etc.).

EXERCISES
1. Tari/dari

Combine the following verbs and place them into the given sentence:

> *ex. supeingo-o benkyoo suru, rajio-o kiku*
> ➡*Boku-wa __supeingo-o benkyoo shitari rajio-o kiitari__ shite imasu.*
>
> *shinbun-o yomu, rajio-o kiku*
> *o-kashi-o taberu, miruku-o nomu*

tegami-o kaku, jisho-o hiku
takushii-ni noru, basu-ni noru
gohan-o tsukuru, sooji-o suru

2. Nakute-wa ikemasen, nakereba naranai

Change the following phrases into the *nakute-wa ikemasen* and *nakereba narimasen* forms:

ex. sooji-o suru
➡ *sooji-o shikanakute-wa ikemasen*
➡ *sooji-o shinakereba narimasen*

      denki-o kesu
      kozutsumi-o okuru
      megane-o kakeru
      doa-o shimeru
      kuruma-o arau
      isoide imasu kara sugu-ni dekakeru
      toshokan-ni hon-o kaesu
      ane-o kuukoo-e mukae-ni iku

3. Matching

Match the following phrases:

1. *Akaruku narimashita kara denki-o*   A. *shimenakereba narimasen*
2. *Samuku narimashita kara doa-o*   B. *tsukenakute-wa ikemasen*
3. *Asatte tesuto-ga arimasu kara*   C. *kesanakereba narimasen*
4. *Nodo-ga kawakimashita kara mizu-o* D. *nomanakute-wa ikemasen*
5. *Samuku narimashita kara sutoobu-o* E. *benkyoo shinakereba narimasen*
6. *Gaikoku-ni iku node*   F. *jogingu-o shinakute-wa ikemasen*
7. *Takusan tabemashita kara*   G. *toraaberazu chekku-o kawanakute-wa ikemasen*

To convert one currency into another, use: Currency 1-*o* currency 2-*ni* *ryoogae shite kudasai.* ex. *En-o doru-ni* **ryoogae shite kudasai.** Please change the yen to dollars.

rishi
interest

**-ryo,
ryookin**
charge, fee

**ryoogae
suru**
to exchange,
change
money

shimeru(-ru)
to close

sooji suru
to clean

sutoobu
wood-
burning
stove,
furnace

tada
just

teiki yokin
fixed time
deposit

tesuuryoo
service fee

toiiru
put in and
take out

tooza yokin
checking
account

**toraberaazu
chekku**
traveler's
checks

tsuku(-u)
to pay

4. -Te mimasu

Change the following sentences into the -te mimashoo form:

> ex. kanji-o kaku
> ➡ kanji-o kaite mimashoo
>
> Michiko-san-ga suki datta ongakukai-ni iku
> Nihon ryoori-o tsukuru
> Hara-san-no tsukutta ryoori-o taberu
> Mitsubishi-no kuruma-no katarogu-o yomu

SHORT DIALOGUES

1. ex. bun-o kaku

A: *Ima o-isogashii desu-ka.*

B: *Sukoshi isogashii desu. Kyoo-wa o-kyaku-san-ga kuru node, sooji-o shitari gohan-o tsukuttari shite imasu, yo. Nanika go-yoo desu-ka.*

A: *Anoo, jitsu-wa nihongo-de **bun-o kaite** imasu node, chotto naoshite kudasaimasu-ka.*

B: *Ii desu yo. Kono **bun**-wa joozu desu, yo. Nagai aida **kaite** ita-no desu-ka.*

A: *Hai. Kyoo ichinichijuu **bun-o kaitari** jisho-o hitari shite imashita. Arigatoo gozaimashita.*

B: *Doo itashimashite.*

1. kanji-o kaku
2. shukudai-o suru
3. tegami-o kaku
4. taipu-o utsu

2. *ex.* yuugata haha-ga kuru, kuukoo-e mukae-ni iku,
denki-o kesu

A: *Ima kara o-hima desu-ka.*

B: *Iie.* **Yuugata haha-ga kimasu** *node,*
Kuukoo-e mukai-ni ikanakereba
narimasen.

A: *Soo desu-ka. Watashi-mo issho-ni*
ikimashoo-ka.

B: *Demo gomeiwaku deshoo . . .*

A: *Ii desu yo. Ima iku hoo-ga ii desu-ka.*

B: *Chotto matte kudasai.* **Denki-o**
kesanakute*-wa ikemasen kara.*

1. senshuu hon-o karita, Yagi-san-no ie-ni
iku, doa-o shimeru
2. ototoi katta saifu-o kaesu, mise-ni iku,
terebi-o kesu
3. raigetsu chichi-no tanjoobi desu,
okurimono-o kau, denki-o kesu
4. konban haha-ga kuru, eki-e mukae-ni iku,
mado-o shimeru

tsumetai(i)
cool (when touched)

tsutsumu(-u)
to wrap

yokin
savings, deposit

yokin tsuuchoo
bank book

zandaka
balance

zeikin
tax

3. *ex.* ongakukai-no kippu, iku, ongakukai-ni iku

A: ***Ongakukai-no kippu**-ga aru-no desu ga. Issho-ni **ikimasen**-ka.*

B: *Soo desu ne. Koo yuu **ongakukai-ni itta** koto-ga arimasen.*

A: *Watashi-mo soo desu yo. **Itte** mimashoo-ka.*

B: *Soo shimashoo.*

A: *Anata-ni okane-o harawanakereba narimasen.*

B: *Kekkoo desu. Harawanakute-mo ii desu.*

A: *Hontoo desu-ka.*

B: *Mochiron.*

1. kowai eiga-no kippu, miru, eiga-o miru
2. Furansu-no keiki, taberu, keiki-o taberu
3. geki-no kippu, iku, geki-ni iku
4. rokku konsaato-no kippu, iku, konsaato-ni iku

SELF-TEST

Translate the following sentences into Japanese:

1. Today, I've been reading the paper and making sushi.
2. To withdraw cash, I have to use this cash card.
3. I have to buy a gift for my mother.
4. I have to read to page 40.
5. Please change the yen into dollars.
6. Let's try going to the restaurant Mr. Morita liked.
7. Let's try eating the food my husband made.
8. The baby eats and sleeps, eats and sleeps.
9. It has become hot, so I must open the window.
10. I have to open an account.

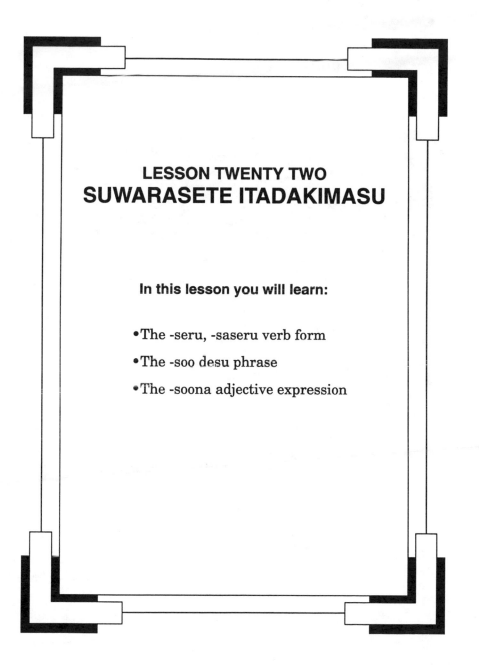

LESSON TWENTY TWO
SUWARASETE ITADAKIMASU

In this lesson you will learn:

- The -seru, -saseru verb form
- The -soo desu phrase
- The -soona adjective expression

DIALOGUE

I
ジョンソン： こんにちは．　わたしは　アイビーエムの
　　　　　　ジョンソン　です．　はなぶささんと　にじに
　　　　　　おやくそく　して　いるの　ですが．
さくらい： 　いらっしゃいませ．　はなぶさは　ただいま
　　　　　　かいぎ　ちゅうで　ございます．
ジョンソン： つごうが　わるいの　でしょうか．
さくらい： 　いいえ．　にじ　すぎには　おわると　もうして
　　　　　　おりました．　どうぞ　おかけに　なって
　　　　　　ください．
ジョンソン： はい　すわらせて　いただきます．
さくらい： 　コーヒーは　いかが　ですか．
ジョンソン： ありがとう　ございます．
さくらい： 　カタログを　どうぞ．
ジョンソン： ありがとう　ございます．　おもしろそうな
　　　　　　カタログ　ですね．　あなたの　かいしゃは
　　　　　　さいきん　きゅうせいちょう　して　いる　そう
　　　　　　ですね．
さくらい： 　おかげさまで．
II
A： しごとの　あとで　みんなで　しょくじに　でかけようか．
B： いい　ですね．
A： レストランで　きょう　みた　スライドの　しつもんに
　　こたえよう．　それに　ボーナスに　ついても　はなそう．
B： かちょうの　いった　こと　きいたかい．
C： いや　きかなかった．
B： しごとの　あとで　しょくじに　でかけよう　と
　　いってたよ．　きみも　いくかい．
C： もちろん．

I

Jonson:*Konnichi-wa.
Watashi-wa Ai-Bii-Emu-
no Jonson desu. Hanabusa-
san-to niji-ni oyakusoku
shite iru-no desu ga.*

Sakurai: *Irasshaimase.
Hanabusa-wa tadaima
kaigi chuu de gozaimasu.*

J: *Tsugoo-ga warui-no
deshoo-ka.*

S: *Iie. Niji sugi-ni-wa owaru-to
mooshite orimashita. Doozo
o-kake-ni natte kudasai.*

J: *Hai, suwarasete
itadakimasu.*

S: *Koohii-wa ikaga desu-ka.*

J: *Arigatoo gozaimasu.*

S: *Katarogu-o doozo.*

J: *Arigatoo gozaimasu.
Omoshirosoona katarogu
desu, ne. Anata-no kai-
sha-wa saikin kyuu-sei-
choo shite iru soo desu ne.*

S: *Okagesamade.*

II

A: *Shigoto-no ato de minna-
de shokuji-ni dekakeyoo-ka.*

B: *Ii desu ne.*

A: *Resutoran-de kyoo mita
suraido-no shitsumon-ni*

I

Johnson: Hello, I am Mr.
Johnson from IBM. I
have a 2:00 appointment
with Mr. Hanabusa.

Sakurai: Welcome. Mr.
Hanabusa is in a confer-
ence right now.

J: Then it is a bad time?

S: No, he said he would be
finished soon after 2:00.
Please take a seat.

J: With your permission, I
will.

S: Would you care for coffee?

J: Yes, thank you.

S: Please have our catalogue.

J: Thank you. This is an
interesting looking
catalogue. I understand
recently your company
has been growing rapidly.

S: Thank goodness.

II

A: After work, would all of
you like to go out to eat?

B: Yes.

A: While we are at the restaurant, I will answer your

**Company
Name**
To state which
company you are
from, say
Watashi-wa
company's
name-*no,* your
name *desu. ex.
Watashi-wa
Mitsubishi-no
Jonson desu.* I
am Miss
Johnson from
Mitsubishi.

Ai-Bii-Emu
IBM

atsumeru(-ru)
to gather

bikkuri suru
to be
surprised

boonasu
bonus

gorufu
golf

hazukashii(i)
embarrased,
shy

honsha
headquarters

itteta
said

joobu(na)
strong

kaigi chuu de
in a confer-
ence

kaigi shitsu
conference
room

kaigi suru
to have a
conference

katazukeru(ru)
to finish up,
clean up

kawaii(i)
cute

keesu
showcase

kotaeyoo. Sore-ni
boonasu-ni tsuite-mo
hanasoo.

B: *Kachoo-no itta koto kiita -
kai.*

C: *Iya, kikanakatta.*

B: *Shigoto-no ato de shokuji-
ni dekakeyoo to itteta yo.
Kimi-mo ikukai.*

C: *Mochiron.*

questions about the slides
we saw today. We will also
talk about your bonuses.

B: Did you hear what the
section chief said?

C: No, I did not.

B: He said that after work
we will go out to eat. Will
you come with us?

C: Of course.

GRAMMAR EXPLANATION

1. -Seru, -saseru

When this verb form is used, it means that someone makes or forces another to do something. To form
this pattern use plain negative verbs:

- For *-ru* verbs, drop the final *nai* and add *saseru*

  ex. *tabenai*

*tabe**saseru***	makes one eat
irenai	
*ire**saseru***	makes one pour
konai	
*ko**saseru***	makes one come

- For *-u* verbs, drop the final *nai* and add *seru*

  ex. *asobanai*

*asoba**seru***	makes one play
kakanai	
*kaka**seru***	makes one write

yomanai

yomaseru   makes one read

hanasanai

hanasaseru   makes one speak

awanai

awaseru   makes one meet

Exceptions: *shinai*   *saseru*

             minai   *miseru*

Grammar pattern for using -*seru*, -*saseru* verbs:

Subject-*wa* indirect object-*ni* object-*o*-*seru*, -*saseru* verb

   ex. Gakusei-wa eigo-o benkyoo shimasu.
   The student studies English.
   Sensei-wa gakusei-ni eigo-o benkyoo
   sasemasu.
   The teacher makes the student study English.

-Seru, -saseru itadakimasu

When you use the *seru*, *saseru* verb form with *itadakimasu*, you are saying, "With your permission, I will ____." In Japanese, it literally means "given the favor of being allowed to____."

   *ex. ika**sete itadakimasu***
   with your permission, (I) will go

   *mata**sete itadakimasu***
   with your permission, (I) will wait

The -*seru, saseru* form of verbs usually implies that the person who makes another do something is a superior, like a boss making an employee do something, a teacher making a student do something, etc. It also can mean an older person makes a younger person do something, or that someone has been tricked or bribed into doing something.

keisan suru
to calculate

kikai
machine

koofuku(na)
happy

koosu
course

kotaeru(-ru)
to answer

kotoshi
this year

kyuu
suddenly,
rapidly

*Midori-ga
oka*
a golf course

moosu(-u)
to say
(humble)

nemui(i)
sleepy

Nippon
Japan
(formal)

Nyuu Yooku
New York

*o-kake-ni
natte
kudasai*
please take a
seat (polite)

-Seru, -saseru kudasai

When this verb form is used with *kudasai*, it means, "Please allow me the favor of _____."

> *ex. ika**sete kudasai***
> please allow (me) to go
>
> *mata**sete kudasai***
> please allow (me) to wait

2. Soo desu

When *soo desu* is used at the end of a sentence, it means that the speaker heard the information from somewhere, or understands that to be the case.

The following patterns can be used:

1. plain verb + *soo desu*

> *ex. Sumisu-san-wa paatii-no toki bikkuri shita **soo desu.***
> I heard Ms. Smith was surprised during the party.
>
> *Tanaka-san-wa kitte-o atsumete iru **soo desu.***
> I understand that Mr. Tanaka is collecting stamps.

2. *i* adjective + *soo desu*

> *ex. Sono eiga-wa omoshiroi **soo desu.***
> I heard that movie is interesting.
>
> *Mitsutake-san-no kodomo-wa kawaii **soo desu.***
> I heard that Mrs. Mitsutake's child is cute.

3. *na* adjective + *da* or *datta* + *soo desu*
   ex. *Matsumoto-san-wa genki datta **soo desu.***
   I heard Mrs. Matsumoto is healthy.

   *Tanaka-san-to kekkon shita onnanohito-wa totemo kirei da **soo desu.***
   I heard the woman who Mr. Tanaka married is very beautiful.

-soo can also be combined with adjectives to state that something looks _____. For *i* adjectives, drop the final *i* before *soo desu*; when using *na* adjectives, drop the *na*.

ex. *oishi**soo***	looks delicious
*joobu**soo***	looks strong
*nemu**soo***	looks sleepy
*joozu**soo***	looks skillful
*koofuku**soo***	looks happy
Exception: *yoi / ii*	*yosa**soo***

3. Adjective + soona

To use the adjective + *soo* form to directly modify a noun, and add *na* to both *i* and *na* adjectives.

ex. *oishisoo*	looks delicious
*oishisoo**na** sakana*	delicious looking fish
nemusoo	looks tired
*nemusoo**na** okaa-san*	tired looking mother
genkisoo	looks healthy
*genkisoo**na** kodomo*	healthy looking child
koofukusoo	looks happy
*koofukusoo**na** hito*	happy looking person

(o)yakusoku
suru
to make an
appointment
or reservation

okagesa-
made
thank
heavens;
thank all
that is good

sabishii(i)
lonely

seichoo
suru
to grow

semai(i)
narrow,
small

shigoto-no
ato de
after work

shinjiru
(-ru)
to believe

sugi
(soon) after

suraido
slide

tadaima
just now

(o)tetsudai-
san
maid

tsugoo
convenience

tsuite
concerning

EXERCISES

1. -Seru, -saseru

Change the following sentences into the *-seru*, *-saseru* form:

> *ex. O-tetsudai-san-wa gohan-o tsukurimasu.*
> ➡ *O-tetsudai-san-ni gohan-o tsukurasemasu.*
>
> > *Gakusei-wa nihongo-o hanashimasu.*
> > *Onnanoko-wa kusuri-o nomimasu.*
> > *Gakusei-wa eigo-no hon-o yomimasu.*
> > *Otokonoko-wa eki-de machimasu.*
> > *Kodomotachi-wa yasai-o tabemasu.*
> > *Hirashain-wa purojekuto-o*
> > *katazukemasu.*

2. -Sete, -sasete itadakimasu

Change the following sentences into the *-sete, -sasete itadakimasu* form:

> *ex. Hara-san-no tsukutta gohan-o taberu.*
> ➡ *Hara-san-no tsukutta gohan-o tabesasete itadakimasu.*
>
> > *Hara-san-ga ireta ocha-o nomu*
> > *Isu-ni suwaru*
> > *Kaichoo-no kaita tegami-o yomu*
> > *Kaigi-shitsu-de hanashi-o suru*
> > *Kono kikai-no setsumei-o suru*
> > *Jisho-o tsukau*

3. -Sete, -sasete kudasai

Using the given words, conjugate them into the

-sete, -sasete form and fill in the blank spaces:

matsu   tsukau   unten suru   kaeru   tetsudau

1. *Michiko-san-wa sugu-ni kuru deshoo kara,
   koko-de watashi-ni ____ kudasai.*
2. *Kono purojekuto-wa muzukashii desu kara,
   watashi-ni ____ kudasai.*
3. *Watashi-no kuruma-ga aru node, ____ kudasai.*
4. *Anata-no denwa-o ____ kudasai.*
5. *Juugofun hayaku shigoto-kara ____ kudasai.*

4. Soo desu
Match the following phrases:

1. *Asatte Yamada-san-wa koko-ni*   A. *kuru soo desu.*
2. *Yagi-san-wa booeki-no purojekuto-o*   B. *takai soo desu.*
3. *Konban shachoo-wa Nyuu Yooku-ni*   C. *taihen da soo desu.*
4. *Senshuu totta shashin-ga*   D. *iku soo desu.*
5. *Kotoshi-no boonasu-wa*   E. *dekiru soo desu.*
6. *Doitsugo-o joozu-ni hanasu-no-wa*   F. *hanasu soo desu.*
7. *Buchoo-wa shigoto-no*   G. *shite iru soo desu.*
   ato-de boonasu-ni tsuite

5. Combine the adjectives with their paired nouns to form the *-soona* phrase:

ex. *rippa, o-tera*
➡*rippasoona o-tera*

hayai, kuruma   *nigiyaka, paatii*
omoshiroi, hon   *wakai, onnanohito*
akarui, e   *muzukashii, tesuto*
samui, tenki   *oishii, kudamono*
sabishii, obaa-san *hazukashii, onnanoko*

215

tsumara-
nai(i)
boring

yasai
vegetables

SHORT DIALOGUES

1. *ex.* buchoo, kachoo

Harada: **Buchoo**-*kara kikimashita-ga Sumisu-*
san-no hanashi-wa yokkatta soo desu, ne.
Sumisu: *Hontoo desu-ka.*
Harada: *Ee. Shigoto-no ato de dokoka-e*
ikimashoo-ka.
Sumisu: *Sore-wa ii desu, ne.*
Harada: **Kachoo**-*mo iku-ka kikimashoo-ka.*
Sumisu: *Mochiron. Soo shimashoo.*

   1. shachoo, shihainin
   2. fuku shihainin, buchoo
   3. kachoo, jichoo
   4. shachoo, kaichoo

2. *ex.* ie, hiroi, semai

Sumisu: *Suwatte-mo ii desu-ka.*
Tanaka: *Hai, doozo suwatte kudasai.*
Sumisu: *Tanaka-san-no **ie**-wa totemo ii desu,*
*ne. **Hirosoona ie** desu ne.*
Tanaka: **Hirosoo** *desu kedo, jitsu-wa totemo*
semai *desu.*
Sumisu: *Soo desu-ka. Shinjiraremasen, ne.*

   1. seetaa, takai, yasui
   2. teeburu, atarashii, furui
   3. tsukutta ryoori, taihen, kantan
   4. kabin, omoi, karui
   5. ryoori, amai, karai

3. *ex.* asatte Yamamoto-san-no soobetsukai-ga aru,
ano hoteru-ni iku

Japanese people
are uncomfort-
able introducing
themselves to
other people for
the first time.
They like to
have a third
party that
knows both
groups or
individuals
introduce them
to each other.
Try to avoid
introducing
yourself to a
Japanese person
that you have
never met
before. Have
another intro-
duce you; if you
know no one
familiar to the
group you want
to do business
with, there are
Japanese
companies that
specialize in
introductions, or
you can send a
letter of intro-
duction.

> *Buraun:* *Konshuu-wa taihen deshita ne.*
> *Buchoo-wa Hara-san-ni kikaku-*
> *shitsu-no purojekuto-o*
> *tetsudawasete iru soo desu ne.*
> *Hara:* *Daijoobu desu, yo. Kyoojuu-ni owaru-*
> *to omoimasu yo.*
> *Buraun:* *Tokorode **asatte Yamamoto-san-no***
> ***soobetsukai-ga aru** soo desu ne.*
> *Hara:* *Hai. Watashitachi-wa **ano hoteru-***
> ***ni ikimasu**.*
> *Buraun:* *Itsu buchoo-wa sono setsumei-o suru-*
> *no desu-ka.*
> *Hara:* *Hirugohan-no ato de suru soo desu.*

1. asatte o-kyaku-san-ga kuru, ano
resutoran-ni iku
2. ashita gorufu-o suru, midori-ga oka
gorufu koosu-ni iku
3. raishuu kaigi-ga aru, honsha-ni iku
4. raishuu-no doyoobi sukii-o suru, Naeba-
ni iku

JOB LEVELS

kaichoo
chairperson

shachoo
president

fuku-shachoo
vice president

joomu torishi-mariyaku
executive director

senmu torishi-mariyaku
sr. managing director

buchoo
boss of section chief; general manager

jichoo
assistant general manager

kachoo
section chief

shihainin
manager

fuku shihainin
assistant manager

juugyooin
employee

4. *ex.* Morita, yuube, yaru

> *Buchoo: Dareka-ni kono purojekuto-o tetsudatte moraitai-n da ga.*
>
> *Imai: Boku-ni o-tetsudai sasete kudasai.*
>
> *B: Isogashii-n ja nai-ka, **Morita**-kun-ga yatte-iru shigoto-no hoo-o shite iru-n ja nai-no.*
>
> *I: Iie, **yuube** moo katazukemashita.*
>
> *B: Soo-ka.*
>
> *I: Hai.*
>
> *B: Sore nara kore-o **yatte** kureru-kai.*
>
> *I: Hai. **Yarasete** itadakimasu.*

1. Hara, kesa, suru
2. Watanabe, kinoo, kaku
3. Yagi, kyoo, katazukeru
4. Tanaka, senshuu, keisan suru

SELF-TEST

Fill in the blanks with *wa, ga, de, o, ni, to, no, ka, ne,* or X:

1. Sensei ___ gakusei ___ iroirona ___ hon ___ yomasemasu.

2. Kachoo ___ juugyooin ___ gorufu ___ ikasemasu.

3. Yamada-san ___ aitai hito ___ Ai Bi Emu ___ tsutomete iru ___ soo desu.

4. Hara-san ___ hoshigatte ___ ita bideo ___ omoshirosoo desu.

5. Yagi-san ___ musume ___ akarusoona ___ kodomo desu.

Translate the following sentences into Japanese:

6. With your permission, I will leave early.

7. I understand the chairperson is in the middle of a conference.

8. Please allow me to wait.

9. That is an expensive looking vase.

10. I understand the manager will finish up the project today.

218

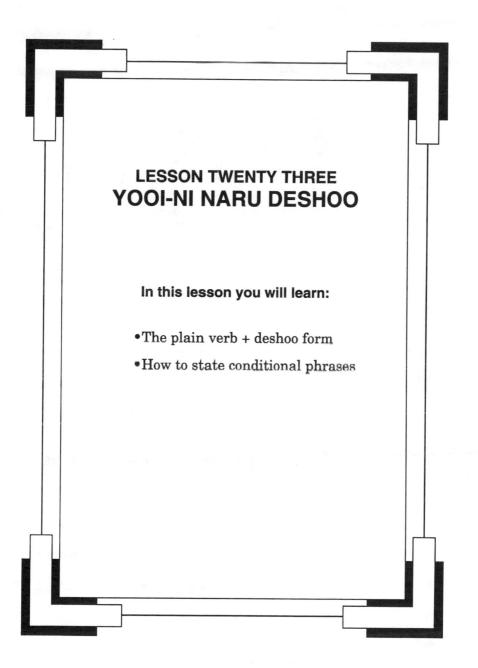

LESSON TWENTY THREE
YOOI-NI NARU DESHOO

In this lesson you will learn:

• The plain verb + deshoo form

• How to state conditional phrases

DIALOGUE

はなぶさ：　　とおい　ところを　ありがとう　ございます.

ジョンソン：　どう　いたしまして.

はなぶさ：　　おまちに　なりましたか.

ジョンソン：　いいえ　わたしが　すこし　ばかり　はやく
　　　　　　　　きた　もの　です　から　カタログを　みせて
　　　　　　　　いただきました.　すばらしい　ですね.

はなぶさ：　　ありがとう　ございます.

ジョンソン：　わがしゃの　あたらしい　コンピューター
　　　　　　　　システムに　ついて　すこし　ばかり　おはなし
　　　　　　　　させて　いただきたいの　ですが.　よろしい
　　　　　　　　でしょうか.

はなぶさ：　　もちろん　です.

ジョンソン：　あなたの　かいしゃが　かいがいへ　の
　　　　　　　　しんしゅつを　つづける　おつもり　でしたら
　　　　　　　　この　さいしん　ぎじゅつの　ネットワークが
　　　　　　　　あれば　さいこう　でしょう.　かいがい
　　　　　　　　ししゃとの　コミュニケーションが　よういに
　　　　　　　　かのう　でしょう.

はなぶさ：　　そう　ですね.　わがしゃは　すでに　きかく
　　　　　　　　しつの　ごういを　えて　にねん　いないに
　　　　　　　　とうなん　アジアと　きた　アメリカに
　　　　　　　　しんしゅつ　する　ことに　なって　います.

ジョンソン：　もし　わがしゃの　コンピューター　システムを
　　　　　　　　とりいれれば　かいがい　しんしゅつが
　　　　　　　　よういに　なる　でしょう.

はなぶさ：　　なかなか　よさそうな　コンピューター
　　　　　　　　システム　ですね.

ジョンソン：　カタログを　さしあげましょうか.

はなぶさ：　　はい　ありがとう　ございます.

ジョンソン：　おじかんを　いただきまして　ありがとう
　　　　　　　　ございました.

はなぶさ：　　いいえ　わざわざ　ありがとう　ございました.

Hanabusa: *Tooi tokoro-o,
arigatoo gozaimasu.*

Jonson: *Doo itashimashite.*

H: *O-machi-ni narimashita-ka.*

J: *Iie, watashi-ga sukoshi
bakari hayaku kita mono
desu kara, katarogu-o
misete itadakimashita.
Subarashii desu, ne.*

H: *Arigatoo gozaimasu.*

J: *Wagasha-no atarashii
konpyuutaa shisutemu-ni
tsuite sukoshi bakari o-
hanashi sasete itadakitai-
no desu ga. Yoroshii
deshoo-ka.*

H: *Mochiron desu.*

J: *Anata-no kaisha-ga
kaigai-e no shinshutsu-o
tsuzukeru o-tsumori
deshitara, kono saishin
gijutsu-no nettowaaku-ga
areba saikoo deshoo.
Kaigai shisha-to-no
komyunikeeshon-ga yooi-
ni kanoo deshoo.*

H: *Soo desu ne. Wagasha-wa
sudeni kikaku shitsu-no
gooi-o ete, ninen inai-ni
Toonan Ajia to Kita
Amerika-ni shinshutsu
suru koto-ni natte imasu.*

J: *Moshi wagasha-no
konpyuutaa shisutemu-o*

Hanabusa: You (came) from
a far place, thank you.

Johnson: It was nothing.

H: Did you wait for me?

J: No, I came a little early,
so I was given the favor
of seeing your catalogue.
It was excellent.

H: Thank you.

J: I would like the favor
of being allowed to
speak a little about my
company's new com-
puter system. Is that
alright?

H: Of course it is.

J: If your company plans to
continue expanding
overseas, and you had this
network, you would have
the latest technology. It
would enable you to
communicate easily (lit.
smoothly) with your
company's branches.

H: I see. Our corporate planning has already reached a
consensus, and it was
decided that within the next
two years we will expand
into Southeast Asia and
North America.

J: If you used our computer
system, it would help

"Time is money,"
is not a popular
phrase in Japan.
Instead,
business people
spend a great
amount of time
with each other
in order to
develop a
friendship and a
sense of trust
before proceed-
ing to company
matters.

bakari
just

bengoshi
lawyer

byooki
sick

ete
get...and

gijutsu
technology

gooi
consensus

ima mada
for now

inai-ni
within

kaigai
overseas

kanoo(na)
enabled

kaze-o hiku
to catch a cold

Kita Amerika
North
America

**komyuni-
keeshon**
communication

kusuri
medicine

meishi
name or
business card

mitsukeru(ru)
to find

*toriirereba kaigai
shinshutsu-ga yooi-ni
naru deshoo.*

H: *Nakanaka yosasoona
konpyuutaa shisutemu
desu, ne.*

J: *Katarogu-o
sashiagemashoo-ka.*

H: *Hai, arigatoo gozaimasu.*

J: *O-jikan-o itadakimashite,
arigatoo gozaimashita.*

H: *Iie, wazawaza arigatoo
gozaimashita.*

your expansion to be very
smooth.

H: That sounds like a very
good computer system.

J: Shall I leave some
information for you?

H: Yes, thank you.

J: Thank you so much for
your time.

H: No, thank you for all your
trouble.

GRAMMAR EXPLANATION

1. Plain verb + deshoo

When a plain verb is added to *deshoo*, the meaning
becomes "probably _____."

> *ex. kuru deshoo*   probably come
> *kau deshoo*   probably buy

> *Zaimu-bu-no hito-wa kaigai-ni **iku deshoo**.*
> The people in the finance department will
> probably go to the meeting.

2. -Eba

Verbs

When verbs end in *eba*, they show condition. To
create this verb form, drop the final *u* and add *eba*.

> *ex. toriireru*
> *toriire**eba***   if (you) get and use

222

miru

mireba   if (you) see

kesu

keseba   if (you) turn it off

magaru

magareba   if (you) turn

For *-u* verbs ending in *tsu*, drop the *su*:

ex. *matsu*

mateba   if (you) wait

Ii-no desu often follows these verbs to mean, "If you _____ it will be good."

ex. *benkyoo sureba **ii-no desu***

If (you) study, it will be good, or all (you) need to do is study.

*Anata-wa byooki-no toki, kusuri-o nom**eba** **ii-no desu**.*

When you get sick, if you take medicine, it will be good.

Adjectives

When *i* adjectives end in *kereba*, they show condition. The meaning becomes "If it is adj+*kereba*, I will verb." For *i* adjectives, drop the final *i* and add *kereba*.

ex. *omoshiroi*   *omoshiro**kereba***

takai   *taka**kereba***

*Eiga-ga omoshiro**kereba**, mimashoo.*

If the movie is interesting, let's see it.

*Rishi-ga taka**kereba**, okane-o ginkoo-ni iremashoo*

If rates are high, I'll put my money in the bank.

When negotiating with the Japanese, keep in mind at all times that they prefer not to be direct - try to pick up on their subtle language and body language. Never back a Japanese person into a corner - chances are that they will give you the answer you are looking for just to avoid an unpleasant situation, while having no intention of following through.

223

mono desu kara because	To use *na* adjectives to show condition, add *naraba*
moshi if	ex. *taihen*
	taihennaraba
nakanaka quite good; or (not) easily	*kirai*
	kirainaraba
nettowaaku network	*Boeki purojekuto-ga taihennaraba,*
-ni tsuite concerning, about	*Buchoo-ga tetsudatte kudasaru soo desu.* If the trading project is difficult, I understand my boss will help me.
o-machi shimasu to wait (polite)	*Kanojo-ga amai tabemono-ga kirainaraba, keiki-wa agenai hoo-ga ii desu.* If she dislikes sweet food, it is better not to give her the cake.
pondo pound	
saikoo best	**3. -Ra**
saishin the latest	A final way to show condition is to add *-ra* to a plain past verb.
shinshutsu expand	ex. *datta*
shisha branch office	***dattara*** *Yamashita-san-ga rusu* ***dattara*** *oku-san-ni agete kudasai.*
shisutemu system	If Mr. Yamashita is out, please give it to his wife.
soobetsukai farewell party	*kita* ***kitara*** *Konban Hirakawa-san-ga* ***kitara***, *bideo-o mimashoo.*
sudeni already	If Mrs. Hirakawa comes tonight, let's watch the video.
todokeru(-ru) to deliver	

A plain past verb+*ra doo desu-ka* means "how about ___?"

> ex. *Jogingu-o shita**ra doo desu-ka**.*
> How about jogging?

> *Kono konpyuutaa shisutemu-o katta**ra doo desu-ka**.*
> How about buying this computer system?

EXERCISES

1. -Eba

Answer the questions using the given words:

> ex. *Anata-wa samuku natta toki, doo sureba ii deshoo-ka.*
> *sutoobu-o tsukeru*
> ➡ *Sutoobu-o tsukereba ii-no desu.*

> *Anata-wa onaka-ga suite iru toki, doo sureba ii deshoo-ka.   gohan-o taberu*
> *Anata-wa muzukashii tesuto-ga aru toki, doo sureba ii deshoo-ka. benkyoo suru*
> *Anata-wa kaze-o hiite iru toki, doo sureba ii deshoo-ka. kusuri-o nomu*
> *Okane-ga tarinai toki, doo sureba ii deshoo-ka. ginkoo-de okane-o orosu*
> *Anata-wa takushii-o mitsukerarenai toki, doo sureba ii deshoo-ka.   basu-ni noru*
> *Anata-wa nihongo-no kotoba-ga wakaranai toki, doo sureba ii deshoo-ka.   jisho-o hiku*

Exchanging *meishi* is the first step in developing a business relationship with Japanese people. Be sure to have a generous supply of *meishi* ready when you know that you will be meeting with the Japanese. Have one side printed in English, the other in Japanese. When receiving a *meishi*, accept it with both hands, and read it over (even if you do not understand the words). Do not put it away until that person has left the room.

toogi suru
to discuss

tooi(i)
far

Toonan Ajia
Southeast Asia

toriireru(-ru)
to get and use

tsuzukeru (-ru)
to continue

wagasha
my company

wazawaza
taking so much trouble

yoo
like

yooi(na)
smoothly

yoroshii(i)
polite for *yoi*

DEPARTMENTS

bu
department

choosa-bu
business research

eigyoo-bu
sales

gijutsu-bu
engineering

2. -Kereba

Change the adjectives in the first sentence into the conditional form and combine the two sentences:

ex. *Sono tokei-wa takai desu. Tokei-ga kaemasen.*
➡*Sono tokei-ga takakereba kaemasen.*

Chuugokugo-wa muzukashii desu. Chuugokugo-ga benkyoo dekimasen.
Sono eiga-wa kowai desu. Sono eiga-o mitaku arimasen.
Karei-wa karai desu. Karei-o tabetai desu.
Soto-wa atsui desu. Oyogi-ni ikitai desu.

3. -Ra

Combine the two sentences into one sentence using the conditional verbs:

ex. *Okane-ga arimasu. Terebi-o kaimasu.*
➡*Okane-ga attara terebi-o kaimasu.*

Nihon-e ikimasu. Yamashita-san-ni aimasu.
En-ga takaku narimasu. Doru-ni ryoogae shimasu.
Rishi-ga takaku narimasu. Ginkoo-ni futsuu yokin shimasu.
Doru-o en-ni ryoogae shimasu. En-de kaimono dekimasu.
Koko-de machimasu. Iroirona hito-ni aeru deshoo.

4. Plain verb+deshoo

Change the given sentences into the plain verb + *deshoo* form:

Generally
speaking,
Japanese
companies do
not have legal or
labor depart-
ments.

> ex. *Ashita-wa ame-ga takusan furimasu.*
> ➡*Ashita-wa ame-ga takusan furu deshoo.*

> > *Kodomo-wa genki-ni narimashita kara,*
> > *ashita gakkoo-ni ikimasu.*
> > *Tonari-ni suwatte iru onnanoko-wa*
> > *chuugokugo-o hanashimasu.*
> > *Shujin-wa totemo isogashii node,*
> > *konban ichiji-ni kaerimasu.*
> > *Asatte Harada-san-wa Tookyoo-ni*
> > *kimasen.*
> > *Doyoobi-ni buchoo-wa gorufu-o*
> > *shimasen.*
> > *Konban sono purojekuto-o*
> > *katazukemasen.*

hooki-bu
legal

jinji-bu
personnel

kaigai-bu
international/
overseas

keiri-bu
accounting

kikaku-
shitsu
corporate
planning

koobai-bu
purchasing

koohoo-
shitsu
public affairs

roomu-bu
labor

seisan-
kanri-bu
production
control

senden-bu
advertising

shoohin-
kaihatsu-
shitsu
product
development

soomu-bu
general
affairs

zaimu-bu
finance

SHORT DIALOGUES

1. *ex.* doru, isoide iru

A: *Watashi-wa **doru**-o en-ni ryoogae shitai node, ginkoo-ni ikanakute-wa ikemasen.*

B: *Demo, kore kara **doru**-ga takaku naru-no dattara, kyoo **doru**-o en-ni ryoogae shinai hoo-ga ii desu yo.*

A: *Iie, kore kara en-ga takaku naru hazu desu. Ima no hoo-ga en-o yasuku kaemasu.*

B: *Sore dewa kyoo **doru**-o en-ni ryoogae shite hoo-ga ii desu, ne. Ima **isoide ittara** sugu ryoogae-ga dekimasu, yo.*

A: *Hai.*

   1. pondo, kono densha-ni noru
   2. doru, kono kami-ni ki'nyuu suru
   3. pondo, dekakeru
   4. doru, doru-o motte iru

2. *ex.* ashita, gorufu-ni, iku

A: ***Ashita gorufu-ni iku** tsumori desu-ka.*

B: ***Ikitai**-to omoimasu ga iroirona shigoto-o shinakute-wa ikemasen.*

A: *Kyoojuu-ni oeraremasu-ka.*

B: *Yatte mimashoo. Hirakawa-san-mo **ikimasu**-ka.*

A: *Ee, Hirakawa-san-mo **iku** deshoo.*

   1. ashita, tenisu-o, suru
   2. konban, ongakukai-ni, iku
   3. konban, sake-o, nomu

3. *ex.* eigyo, Kita Amerika

> *Buraun: Watashi-wa Ai-Bii-Emu-no Buraun
> desu. Meishi-o doozo.*
> *Hanabusa:Arigatoo gozaimasu. Aa, **eigyoo-**
> bu desu, ne.*
> *Buraun: Ee, soo desu. Kaisha-wa ima **Kita
> Amerika**-ni shinshutsu shite iru soo
> desu, ne.*
> *Hanabusa:Ima mada shinshutsu shite imasen
> ga, en-ga takaku nareba shinshutsu
> suru deshoo.*

1. kaigai, Yooroppa
2. koobai, Toonan Ajia
3. shoohin-kaihatsu-shitsu, Oosutoraria
4. zaimu, Amerika
5. seisan-kanri, Furansu

SELF-TEST

Translate the following sentences into Japanese:

1. The people from the accounting department will probably come to Mr. Yamada's farewell party.

2. If the sashimi is old, it is better not to eat it.

3. If that play is popular, I think we cannot buy a ticket.

4. If my daughter likes that toy, I will buy it.

5. The corporate planning department has reached a consensus, and it was decided that within three years (the company) will expand overseas.

Unscramble the following sentences:

6. jogingu nattara o desu suru tenki ni yotei.

7. deshoo ga shinshutsu en nattara e kaigai suru takaku.

8. tsumori wa ni o ni purojekuto desu resutoran kyoojuu katazuketara watashitachi iku.

9. ni booeki yoku deshoo gaikoku gaisha tsutomereba ni dekakeru.

10. ga hetanaraba watashi deshoo yameru wa supeingo.

LESSON TWENTY FOUR
O-IWAI SHIMASHOO

In this lesson you will learn:

- Verb phrases that show respect

- Verb phrases that convey humility

- How to state that a decision has been made

DIALOGUE

I

はなぶさ： とうぎを　つづけた　けっか　わがしゃは
あなたが　ごすいせん　くださった　システムを
つかう　ことに　きめました。

ジョンソン： ごじんりょく　いただきまして　ありがとう
ございます。　これ　からも　あなたの
かいしゃに　よい　せいひんを　ていきょう
する　ように　どりょく　する　つもり　で
おります。

はなぶさ： ありがとう　ございます。　けいやくしょの
なかに　しょうらい　かえる　かも　しれない
こうもくが　にさん　あります。　でも
とうぶん　だいじょうぶ　です。

ジョンソン： けいかを　みながら　やって　いきましょう。

はなぶさ： わがしゃに　とって　ただいな　とうし　ですが
おしはらいに　ついての　しんぱいは
ありません。

ジョンソン： それは　けっこうな　こと　です。

はなぶさ： これで　せいりつ　しましたね。

ジョンソン： こんばん　おしょくじに　ごしょうたい　させて
ください。　この　けいやくの　せいりつを
おいわい　しましょう。

はなぶさ： それは　いい　ですね。

ジョンソン： ちゅうかりょうりで　よろしい　ですか。

はなぶさ： はい　けっこう　です。

II

ジョンソン： かんぱい　しましょう。　りょうしゃの
はってんを　いわって。

みんな： かんぱい。

ジョンソン： わたしは　あさって　ニューヨークに
かえりますが　また　れんらく　させて
いただきます。

I

Hanabusa: *Toogi-o tsuzuketa-kekka, wagasha-wa anata-ga go-suisen kuda-satta shisutemu-o tsukau koto-ni kimemashita.*

Jonson: *Go-jinryoku itadaki-mashite, arigatoo gozai-masu. Kore kara-mo anata-no kaisha-ni yoi seihin-o teikyoo suru yoo-ni doryoku suru tsumori de orimasu.*

H: *Arigatoo gozaimasu. Keiyakusho-no naka-ni shoorai kaeru kamo shirenai koomoku-ga nisan arimasu. Demo toobun daijoobu desu.*

J: *Keika-o minagara yatte ikimashoo.*

H: *Wagasha-ni totte tadaina tooshi desu ga, o-shiharai-ni tsuite-no shinpai-wa arimasen.*

J: *Sore wa hshhaarnn kdn desu.*

H: *Kore-de seiritsu shimashita, ne.*

J: *Konban o-shokuji-ni go-shootai sasete kudasai. Kono keiyaku-no seiritsu-o o-iwai shimashoo.*

H: *Sore-wa ii desu, ne.*

I

Hanabusa: After continued discussion, our company has decided to use the computer system that you recommended.

Johnson: Thank you so much for working hard (to recommend my system). From now I plan to work hard to do a good job of supplying your company.

H: Thank you. There are some contract changes that may need to be made in the future, two or three parts, but for the time being it is all right.

J: Let's do those as we progress.

H: This is a very large investment for our company, but we have no worry concerning raising the funds.

J: That is fine.

H: That is all.

J: Please allow me to invite you (and your colleagues) to dinner this evening to celebrate the conclusion of our contract.

H: That is good.

Greetings are very important in that they set the tone for the entire meeting. Therefore, it is essential that both parties use very respectful, appropriate terms when they first gather together.

chokin savings	J: *Chuukaryoori-de yoroshii* *desu-ka.*	J: Would Chinese cuisine be good?
dakyoo **suru** to compromise	H: *Hai, kekkoo desu.*	H: Yes, that is fine.
	II	**II**
doryoku doing my best	J: *Kanpai shimashoo.* *Ryoosha-no hatten-o*	J: I'd like to propose a toast. Here's to the prosperity
hatten prosperity	*iwatte.*	of our two companies.
henkoo **suru** to change	Minna: *Kanpai.*	Everyone: Cheers.
hitsuyoo need	J: *Watashi-wa asatte Nyuu* *Yooku-ni kaerimasu ga,* *mata renraku sasete* *itadakimasu.*	J: I will return to New York the day after tomorrow, but I will keep in touch.

hodo
approximately

iwatte
here's to

jiki shoo
soo desu
too soon

jiki
time

jinryoku
doing your best

jooho suru
to concede

kaeru(-ru)
to change

kaiyaku
suru
to cancel

kanpai
cheers

GRAMMAR EXPLANATION

1. Go, o-__-ni naru

To show politeness and respect for another person,
use any of the following phrases:

> *(go) o-*<u>verb stem</u> + *ni narimasu*

ex. *Tanaka-sama-wa konpyuutaa shisutemu-*
*o **o-tsukai-ni natte** imasu.*
Mr. Tanaka is using the computer system.

*Doozo, **o-kake-ni natte** kudasai.*
Please take a seat (honorific).

Exceptions: *suru*   *nasatte*

For verbs paired with *suru*, use *go* or *o* + verb +
nasatte.

ex. ***Go-setsumei nasatte** kudasai.*
Please explain (honorific).

234

Keiyakusho-o **go-kaiyaku nasatte** *kudasai*.
Please cancel the contract (honorific).

Verbs like *iku, kuru,* and *taberu* are completely different words when speaking politely, and do not change into the *-ni naru* form (see p. 236, Exercise 1)

(see p. 236, Exercise 1)

> *o*-verb stem **kudasai**

-ni naru can be dropped from the *o*-verb-*ni natte kudasai* phrase.

> *ex.* **o-kake kudasai**
> **o-hairi kudasai**

2. O, go-_____shimasu, itashimasu

This verb phrase shows humility, and in very polite situations should be used to refer to one's self, group, or family.

> *o* or **go** verb stem +**shimasu** or *itashimasu*

> *ex. Watakushi-ga kyasshu kaado-o* **o-mochi shimasu**
> I hold the money card.

> *Haha-ga* **go-annai shimasu.**
> My mother will show you.

> *Chichi-ga anata-ni* **o-denwa itashimasu.**
> My father will telephone you.

The *o* verb stem-*ni naru kudasai* phrase and *o*-verb stem *kudasai* phrase show higher respect than *-te kudasai*.

Japanese people tend to take a problem solving approach to challenging situations instead of a conquering, win or lose approach. This stems from their being forced to cooperate with the harsh nature conditions existing in their islands. They have had to work with nature for thousands of years, and therefore look for ways to accommodate difficult circumstances.

235

keiyakusho
contract
document

keika
progress

-kekka
as a result of

kimeru(-ru)
to decide

koomoku
sections, parts

kooshin suru
to renew

kyoomi-ga aru
to be inter-
ested in

miokuru
to let go of

moshi moshi
hello
(telephone)

-ni totte
for

nisan
two or three

renraku
keep in touch

ryoosha
two companies

**seiritsu
suru**
to conclude

(o)shiharai
funds

shihon
capital

3. -Koto-ni kimeru

To say that one has made a decision, use the *-koto-ni kimeru* phrase. It is added to the plain form of verbs.

> *ex. Anata-ga go-suisen kudasatta kikai-o tsukau **koto-ni kimemashita**.*
> We have decided to use the machine that you did the favor of recommending to us.

> *Toobun-wa anata-no kaisha keiyakusho-o kooshin shinai **koto-ni kimemashita**.*
> For the time being, we have decided not to renew the contract with your company.

EXERCISES
1. Humble/honorific verbs

These verbs should be used in very formal situations:

	Humble	Honorific
kuru	mairimasu	irasshaimasu
iku	mairimasu	irasshaimasu
iru	orimasu	irasshaimasu
suru	itashimasu	nasaimasu
taberu	itadakimasu	meshiagarimasu

2. O-___-ni naru

Change the following sentences into the *o-verb-ni natte kudasai* form:

> *ex. Keiyakusho-o yomu*
> ➡*Keiyakusho-o o-yomi-ni natte kudasai.*

> tegami-o kaku   ryoori-o tsukuru
> kippu-o kau   ie-ni kaeru

> *jisho-o hiku*   *tooshi-ni tsuite kimeru*
> *atarashii konpyuutaa shisutemu-o tsukau*

3. O-verb stem + suru, itasu

Convert the following phrases into the *o*-verb stem *suru, itasu* form:

> *ex. yomu*
> ➡ *Gakusei: O-**yomi** shimashoo-ka.*
> *Sensei: Hai, **yonde** kudasai.*

karimasu	*matsu*	*motsu*
toru	*watasu*	*okuru*
harau	*yomu*	*toru*

4. -Koto-ni kimeru

Change the following sentence to reflect that a decision was made:

> *ex. Watashi-wa genkin go man en-o oroshimasu.*
> ➡ *Watashi-wa genkin go man en-o orosu koto-ni kimemashita.*

> *Watashi-wa en-o doru-ni ryoogae shimasen.*
> *Watashi-wa Buraun-san-ga kaitagatte ita saifu-o kare-ni agemasu.*
> *Yuube karita hon-o modoshimasu.*
> *Shigoto-no ato de Tanaka-san-no sukina resutoran-ni ikimasu.*
> *Kaigi chuu-ni suraido-o miseru.*
> *Kore kara jichoo-wa boonasu-o keisan shimasu.*
> *Kaisha-wa Kita Amerika-ni shinshutsu shimasu.*

-Kekka
Kekka is a suffix added to plain past verbs; it means "as a result of." *ex. Toogi shita-**kekka**, watashitachi-wa atarashii komyunikeeshon shisutemu-o suisen shimasu.* As a result of our discussions, we recommend the new communication system.

237

shikin
funds

shinpai
worry

shisan
assets

shoorai
future

**shoo shoo
o-machi
kudasai**
just a
moment (very
polite)

shootai suru
to invite

**shuusei
suru**
to correct

suisen suru
to recommend

tadai(na)
huge

teikyoo
supply/service

toobun
for the time
being

tooshi
investment

yoroshii(i)
good (polite)

yoyaku
reservation

yoyuu
afford

SHORT DIALOGUES

1. *ex.* seihin, motte kuru

   A: *O-jikan-o itadakimashite, arigatoo
   gozaimashita.*

   B: *Doo itashimashite. Wagasha-wa anata-no
   go-suisen kudasatta **seihin**-o kau koto-ni
   kimemashita.*

   A: *Go-jinryoku itadakimashite, arigatoo
   gozaimasu. Itsu anata-no kaisha-ni **seihin**-
   o o-mochi shimashoo-ka.*

   B: *Raishuu-no kayoobi-ni o **motte kite** kudasai.*

   A: *Hai, wakarimashita.*

   1. konpyuutaa, todokeru
   2. kikai, todokeru
   3. komyunikeeshon shisutemu, motte kuru
   4. seihin, todokeru

2. *ex.* koohii, seihin-o tsukau, jiki shoo soo desu

   A: *Doozo, o-kake-ni natte kudasai. **Koohii**-o
   ikaga desu-ka.*

   B: *Hai, arigatoo gozaimasu.*

   A: *Doozo, meshiagatte kudasai.*

   B: *Itadakimasu. Anata-no kaisha-wa wagasha-
   no **seihin-o tsukau** koto-ni narimashita-ka.*

   A: *Soo desu ne. Toogi-o tsuzuketa kekka, ima-
   wa **jiki shoo soo desu** node, miokuru koto-
   ni kimemashita.*

   B: *Wakarimashita. Dewa, mata renraku-o
   sasete itadakimasu. Shoorai nanika o-
   tetsudai dekiru koto-ga arimashitara,*

oshirase kudasai.

A: *Arigatoo gozaimasu.*

1. ocha, konpyuutaa-o tsukau, taihenna
jiki desu
2. koocha, kikai-o kau, mada kyoomi-ga
arimasen
3. koohi, seihin-o kau, mada yoyuu-ga
arimasen
4. koocha, shisutemu-o toriireru, mada
hitsuyoo arimasen

3. *ex.* denwa chuu desu, jippun

Sumisu: *Moshi moshi, Ai Bü Emu-no Sumisu desu.*
Hara: *Konnichi-wa.*
Sumisu: *Konnichi-wa. Tanaka-sama-wa
irasshaimasu-ka.*
Hara: *Shoo shoo o-machi kudasai.*
Sumisu: *Hai.*
Hara: *Moshi moshi. Sumimasen ga,
Tanaka-wa ima **denwa chuu desu**.*
Sumisu: *Sore dewa, **jippun** hodo shitara mata
denwa-o itashimashoo-ka.*
Hara: *Hai, onegai shimasu.*
Sumisu: *Jaa, mata.*

1. kaigi chuu de gozaimasu, ichijikan
2. orimasen demo sugu-ni mairimasu,
sanjippun
3. kaisha-ni orimasen, yonjippun
4. sukoshi isogashii desu demo sugu-ni
hima-ni naru deshoo, juugofun

SELF-TEST

Translate the following sentences into Japanese:

1. Our corporate planning department has reached a consensus, and we have decided to renew the contract.

2. Please use the computer (honorific).

3. Please buy a picture at that store (honorific).

4. My father will show you the post office (humble).

5. My older sister will call her boss (humble).

6. We have decided to go to Europe next month.

7. After continued discussion, my company has decided to expand overseas.

8. Please allow me to keep in touch.

9. I'd like to propose a toast.

10. Thank you for trying your best.

LESSON TWENTY FIVE
ATAMA-GA ITAI DESU

In this lesson you will learn:

- The parts of the body
- Expressing pain
- The -tame ni phrase
- The -reru, -rareru verb form

DIALOGUE

I

A: どう しましたか. いたそう ですね.

B: でんしゃの ドアに ゆびを はさまれて しまいました.
レントゲンを とる ために びょういんへ いかなければ
なりません.

A: ああ これは ひどい ですね. とても いたみますか.

B: すこし よく なりましたが レントゲンを とった
ほうが いい と おもいます. それに ともだちに
かぜを うつされて しまいました.

A: なにか わたしに できる ことが あったら おしえて
ください.

B: ありがとう ございます.

II

いしゃ: こっせつは して いない ので しんぱいは
ありません.

B: ああ よかった.

いしゃ: アスピリンを のんだら いたみは おさまる
でしょう. でも もし まだ いたかったら また
きて ください. しょほうせんを かきましょう.

B: ありがとう ございます.

いしゃ: アスピリンは ねつにも ききます. にさん にち
やすめば よく なる でしょう.

B: ありがとう ございます.

I

A: *Doo shimashita-ka.
Itasoo desu, ne.*

B: *Densha-no doa-ni yubi-o*

I

A: What's wrong? You look like
you are in pain.

B: The train door was shut

*hasamarete shimaimashita.
Rentogen-o toru tame-ni
byooin-e ikanakereba
narimasen.*

on my fingers. I have to
go to the hospital in order
to get an x-ray taken.

A: *Aa, kore-wa hidoi desu,
ne. Totemo itamimasu-ka.*

A: Oh, that's terrible. Does
it hurt a lot?

B: *Sukoshi yoku narimashita
ga, rentogen-o totta hoo-ga
ii-to omoimasu. Sore-ni
tomodachi-ni kaze-o
utsusarete shimaimashita.*

B: It is a little better, but I
think I should still get an
x-ray. Besides that, my
friend infected me with
her cold.

A: *Nanika watashi-ni dekiru
koto-ga attara oshiete
kudasai.*

A: If there is something I
can do, please let me
know.

B: *Arigatoo gozaimasu.*

B: Thank you.

II

II

Isha: *Kossetsu-wa shite
inai node, shinpai-wa
arimasen.*

Doctor: Nothing is broken, so
there is nothing to worry
about.

B: *Aa, yokatta.*

B: Oh, that's good.

I: *Asupirin-o nondara, itami-
wa osamaru deshoo, demo
moshi mada itakattara mata
kite kudasai. Shohoosen-o
kakimashoo.*

D: If you take asprin, it will
ease the pain, but if you
still have pain, please
come back. I can write a
prescription.

B: *Arigatoo gozaimasu.*

B: Thank you.

I: *Asupirin-wa netsu-ni-mo
kikimasu. Nisan nichi
yasumeba yoku naru
deshoo.*

D: The asprin will also help
your fever. You should be
better if you rest for two
or three days.

B: *Arigatoo gozaimasu.*

B: Thank you.

Very few private
doctors' offices
exist in Japan.
Most people
receive health
care at a
hospital,
irregardless of
the severity of
the illness.

hasamaru(-u)
to pinch

hidoi(i)
terrible

itami
pain

itamu(-u)
to feel pain

kiku(-u)
to have an
effect

kooun
lucky,
fortunate

kossetsu
broken

nyuuin suru
enter a
hospital

omimai
visit one in
the hospital

osaeru
to ease(object)

osamaru(-u)
to ease (no
object)

shinu(-u)
to die

sore-ni
besides that

tame-ni
in order to

*-te shimai-
mashita*
completely +
verb

GRAMMAR EXPLANATION

1. Expressing Pain

When a part of your body aches or hurts, the sentence to use is as follows:

Body part-*ga itai desu*.

*ex. Nodo-**ga itai desu**.*
I have a sore throat.

*Onaka-**ga itai desu**.*
I have a stomach ache.

2. Tame-ni

This phrase is used to describe why a certain action takes place. The sentence structure is:

Goal ***tame-ni*** what one does

Obj. + plain verb ***tame-ni*** object, verb

*ex. Genki-ni naru **tame-ni** kusuri-o nomimasu.*
Take medicine in order to get better.

*Nihongo-o benkyoo suru **tame-ni** Nihon-ni ikimasu.*
Go to Japan in order to study Japanese.

3. -Reru, -rareru

This verb form means that one has suffered as a result of another person's or thing's actions. To form this pattern, use the *nai* verb form. Drop the final *nai* and add *reru* for *-u* verbs and *rareru* for *-ru* verbs.

ex. yamenai	*yame**rareru***
yaranai	*yar**areru***
hasamanai	*hasam**areru***

Exceptions:	*shinai*	*s**areru***
	kuru	*kor**areru***

Sentence Structure:

> Sufferer+*wa* thing inflicting suffering-*ni reru, rareru* verb

ex. *Watashi-wa ame-**ni** fur**aremashita**.*
It rained on me.

*Honda-no kaisha-**ni** kaigi-o kyanseru*
*sur**emashita**.*
Honda cancelled the meeting on me.

EXERCISES
1. Memorize the body parts:

ears	*mimi*	*atama*	head
mouth	*kuchi*	*me*	eyes
neck	*kubi*	*hana*	nose
arm	*ude*	*ha*	tooth
stomach	*onaka*	*karada*	body
finger	*yubi*	*te*	hand
leg	*ashi*	*ashi*	foot

utsuru(-u),
utsusu(-u)
to infect

yasumu(-u)
to take a rest

**TYPES OF
ILLNESS**
arerugii
allergy

gan
cancer

haien
pneumonia

ikaiyoo
ulcer

kooketsuatsu
high blood
pressure

moochooen
appendicitis

netsu
fever

shinzoobyoo
heart
disease

teiketsuatsu
low blood
pressure

**DRUG-
STORE**
asupirin
aspirin

kazegusuri
cold medicine

megusuri
eye drops

*seki-no
kusuri*
cough
medicine
246

Using the vocabulary just learned, state that a specific part hurts:

_____-ga itai desu.

ex. **_Atama_**-ga itai desu.

2. -Tame-ni

Combine the given sentences using the *tame-ni* phrase:

ex. Itami-o osaetai desu. Desu kara, asupirin-o nomimasu.

➡ *Itami-o osaeru tame-ni asuprin-o nomimasu.*

> *Genki-ni naritai desu. Desu kara, shujutsu-o shimasu.*
>
> *Nihon-ni ikitai desu. Desu kara, arubaito-o shimasu.*
>
> *Kangofu-ni naritai desu. Desu kara, kagaku-o benkyoo shimasu.*
>
> *Kooza-o hirakitai desu. Desu kara, ginkoo-ni ikimasu.*
>
> *Hara-san-no tanjoobi-no paatii-no okurimono-o kaitai desu. Desu kara, genkin-o oroshimasu.*

3. -Reru, -rareru

Change the phrases into the -reru, -rareru form:

> *ex. Kodomo-ga kaze-o hikimashita.*
> ➡*Kodomo-ni kaze-o hikaremashita.*

*Toyota-no kaisha-ga keiyakusho-no
koomoku-o kaemashita.*
Buchoo-ga kaigai-o kyanseru shimashita.
*O-kyaku-san-ga keiyakusho-no
koomoku-o kaemashita.*
*Tomodachi-ga kuruma-no doa-de yubi-
o hasamimashita.*
*Chichi-ga watashi-no teiki yokin-kara
genkin-o hikidashimashita.*
Juugyooin-ga kyuu-ni yamemashita.
Isogashii toki-ni tomodachi-ga kimashita.
Haha-ga shinimashita.

SHORT DIALOGUES

1. *ex.* kodomotachi, kaze-o, utsu

   A: *Doo shimashita ka.*
   B: *Kinoo **kodomotachi**-ni **kaze-o utsusarete**
   shimaimashita.*
   A: *Aa, kore-wa hidoi desu, ne.*
   B: *Ee, sore-ni konban shujin-no kaisha-no hito-
   ni paatii-ni shootai sarete iru node,
   dekakenakute-wa ikemasen.*
   A: *Taihen desu, ne.*

   1. densha-no doa, ashi-o, hasamu
   2. tomodachi, kaze-o, utsusu
   3. kuruma-no doa, yubi-o, hasamu
   4. o-isha-san, chuusha-o, suru

chuusha
shot,
injection

do
degrees
(centigrade)

haisha-san
dentist

kangofu-san
nurse

*kenkoo
shindan*
physical
examination

kibun
feeling

hakike
nausea

(o)isha-(san)
doctor

itai
pain, hurt

rentogen
x-ray

shohoosen
prescription

shujutsu
operation

taion
body
temperature

2. *ex.* doitsugo, Doitsu

A: *Nani-o shite iru-no desu-ka.*

B: ___Doitsugo___*-o joozu-ni hanasu tame-ni
benkyoo shite imasu.*

A: *Aa, sore-wa ii desu, ne.* ___Doitsu___*-ni itta koto-
ga arimasu-ka.*

B: *Mada arimasen.*

A: *Jaa,* ___doitsugo___*-ga joozu-ni hanasu yoo-ni
nattara, soko-ni iku tsumori desu-ka.*

B: *Ee,* ___Doitsu___*-ni iku yotei desu.*

   1. furansugo, Furansu
   2. eigo, Oosutoraria
   3. chuugokugo, Chuugoku
   4. eigo, Igirisu

3. *ex.* fuku-shachoo, ikaiyoo

A: *Sakki hidoi koto-o kikimashita.*

B: *Nandesu-ka.*

A: ___Fuku-shachoo___*-wa hidoi* ___ikaiyoo___ *da soo
desu ne.*

B: *Shinjiraremasen, ne. Ima* ___fuku-shachoo___*-
wa byooin-ni iru-no desu-ka.*

A: *Ee, Yuube nyuuin shimashita.*

B: *Shujutsu-o suru-no desu-ka.*

A: *Ee, sugu-ni shujutsu-o suru soo desu, ne.*

B: *Jaa, isshoni omimai-ni ikimashoo.*

   1. senmu, gan

2. jichoo, shinzoobyoo
3. joomu, moochooen
4. kachoo, ikaiyoo

SELF-TEST

Unscramble the following sentences:

1. ni o toru tame byooin ni rentogen ikimasu.

2. naru ni genki shimasu ni o tame chuusha.

3. Toyota ni o kaisha kyanseru saremashita no kaigi.

4. doa no ashi shimaimashita o hasamarete ni basu.

5. ga itai node nomimasu kusuri o nodo.

Fill in the blanks with *wa, ga, de, o, ni, to, no, ka, ne,* or X:

6. Ude ___ totemo itai ___ desu. Desu kara, byooin ___ rentogen ___ torimasu.

7. Kusuri ___ kau ___ tame ___ yakkyoku ___ ikimasu.

8. Senshuu ___ tomodachi ___ kaze ___ utsusarete ___ shimaimashita.

9. Hara-san ___ kodomo ___ kaze ___ utsusarete ___ shimaimashita.

10. Yoku miru ___ tame ___ megane ___ kakemasu.

SELF-TEST ANSWERS

Lesson 1

1. Sumimasen, ima nanji desu-ka.
2. Paatii-wa rokuji kara juuichiji made desu.
3. Arigatoo gozaimasu.
4. Watashi-no denwa bangoo-wa ni go ichi no kyuu roku yon san desu.
5. Ima gozen juuniji-han desu.
6. Tookyoo-wa nanji desu-ka.
7. Tookyoo-wa ima asa desu.
8. Tookyoo-wa ima yoru desu.
9. Gogo sanji desu-ka.
10. Soo desu.

Lesson 2

1. Kinoo-wa getsuyoobi deshita.
2. Are-wa ikura desu-ka.
3. Ano shatsu-wa ikura desu-ka.
4. Kono wanpiisu-wa takai desu.
5. Ima sangatsu desu.
6. Kono kooto-o kudasai.
7. Are-wa ikura desu-ka.
8. Sono nekutai-wa yasui desu, ne.
9. Kyoo-wa nanyoobi desu-ka.
10. Sono booshi-o kudasai.

Lesson 3

1. Enpitsu <u>wa</u> kaban <u>no</u> naka <u>ni</u> arimasu.
2. Anata <u>no</u> hon <u>wa</u> teeburu <u>no</u> ue <u>ni</u> arimasu <u>ka</u>.
3. Michiko <u>san</u> <u>wa</u> kuruma <u>no</u> mae <u>ni</u> imasu.
4. Emiko <u>san</u> <u>wa</u> doko desu <u>ka</u>.
5. Isu <u>wa</u> teeburu <u>no</u> ushiro ni arimasu.
6. Jonson-san-no nooto-wa tsukue-no naka-ni arimasu.
7. Watashi-no pen-wa doko-ni arimasu-ka.
8. Kami-wa tsukue-no shita-ni arimasu.
9. Hara-san-no kutsu-wa doko-ni arimasu-ka.
10. Jonson-san-wa resutoran-ni imasu.

Lesson 4

1. Jonson <u>san</u> <u>wa</u> sushi <u>o</u> tabemashita.
2. Watashi <u>wa</u> mizu <u>o</u> nomimashita.
3. Michiko <u>san</u> <u>wa</u> Tookyoo ni kimashita.
4. Watashi <u>wa</u> nihongo <u>o</u> benkyoo shimasu.
5. Kinoo, Jonson <u>san</u> <u>wa</u> terebi <u>o</u>

mimashita <u>ka</u>.

6. Kyoo, watashi-wa eigo-o oshiemasu.

7. Kinoo, Michiko-san-wa Amerika-ni kimashita.

8. Sumisu-san-wa hashirimasu-ka.

9. Watashi-wa hon-o yomimashita.

10. Watashi-wa nihongo-o hanashimasu.

Lesson 5

1. Kochira-wa Michiko-san-no obaa-san desu.

2. Hajimemashite.

3. Doozo, yoroshiku.

4. Anata-no namae-wa nandesu-ka.

5. Kyoo kare-no otoo-san-wa eigo-o benkyoo shimasen.

6. Mitsumura-san-no imooto-san-wa sushi-o tabemasen.

7. Tanaka-san-no onii-san-wa hon-o yomimashita.

8. Watashi-no namae-wa Jonson desu.

9. Anata-no oba-san-no hon-wa tsukue-no naka-ni arimasen.

10. Kinoo, watashi-wa tomodachi-ni aimashita.

Lesson 6

1. Nemashoo.

2. Eigakan-ni ikimashoo.

3. Watashi-wa byooin-ni ikimasen deshita.

4. Anata-wa ocha-o nomimasen deshita-ka.

5. Watashi-wa aoi kuruma-o unten shimasen deshita.

6. Watashi-wa murasaki iro-no tsukue-o mimasu.

7. Anata-wa biyooin-ni ikimashita-ka.

8. Ano onnanohito-wa akai hon-o yomimasu.

9. Ano shiroi tatemono-wa ginkoo desu.

10. Kare-wa resutoran-ni imasu.

Lesson 7

1. Kuruma <u>wa</u> kiiro <u>kute</u> chiisai desu.

2. Akai budooshu <u>wa</u> arimasu <u>ka</u>.

3. Asoko <u>de</u> gohan <u>o</u> tabemashita.

4. Tanaka <u>san no</u> ie <u>de</u> yasashii hon <u>o</u> yomimashita.

5. Sumisu <u>san wa o</u> sashimi <u>ga</u> suki desu <u>ka</u>.

6. Sore-wa kirei-de takai desu.

7. Karashi-wa oishii desu-ka.

8. Akai budooshu-wa amari suki dewa arimasen deshita.

9. Gakkoo-de nihongo-o benkyoo shimasen deshita.

10. Tookyoo-ga daisuki desu.

Lesson 8

1. Oji san wa eigakan de eiga o mite imasu.
2. Onii san wa ginkoo de matte imasu.
3. Keigo san to Masaaki sanwa sakkaa o shite imasu.
4. Ame ga futte imasu.
5. Michiko san wa doko de ocha o nonde imasu ka.
6. Kanojo-wa akakute hayai kuruma-o unten shite imasu.
7. Kare-wa oishii ringo-o tabete imasu.
8. Watashi-wa nihongo-o naratte imasu.
9. Michiko-san-wa eigo-o benkyoo shite imasen.
10. Watashi-wa depaato-de iroirona hito-ni aimashita.

Lesson 9

1. Tenpura-o tabete kudasai.
2. Niji juugofun-ni uchi-ni kite kudasai.
3. Ginkoo-wa dochira desu-ka.
4. Kippu-o katte kudasai.
5. Nisen en tarimasen.
6. Obaa-san-wa o-genki desu-ka.
7. Goji sanjuukyuufun made matte kudasai.
8. Komakai okane-o motte imasu-ka.

9. Anata-wa mainichi shigoto-ni itte imasu-ka.
10. Kochira-ni kite kudasai.

Lesson 10

1. Maiasa X nihongo o benkyoo shite imasu.
2. Isshuukan ni san do resutoran de tabemasu.
3. Watashi wa ikkagetsukanni ikkai Kyooto ni ikimasu.
4. Senshuu no kinyoobi no tesuto wa muzukashikatta X desu.
5. Raishuu no mokuyoobi ni shigoto o hajimemasu.
6. Kinyoobi-wa yasumi dewa arimasen.
7. Isshuukan-ni ichi-do depaato-ni ikimasu.
8. Kyoo-wa juunigatsu itsuka desu.
9. Kinyoobi-ni muzukashii tesuto-o ukemashita.
10. Tanaka-san-to issho-ni hirugohan-o tabemashita.

Lesson 11

1. Raishuu-no mokuyoobi-ni Kyooto-ni ikitai desu.
2. Watashi-wa isshuukan-ni sankai nihongo-o benkyoo shitai desu.
3. Hayaku kite kudasai.
4. Kare-wa watashi-no senpai kamo shiremasen.

5. Tanaka-san-wa eigakan-ni ikanai kamo shiremasen.

6. Kyoo-wa amari samuku arimasen.

7. Ojii-san-wa genki dewa arimasen.

8. Anata-wa kurashikku-no ongakukai-ni ikimasen-ka.

9. Sono eiga-wa omoshiroku arimasen deshita.

10. Watashi-wa Fuji ginkoo-ni tsutometai desu.

Lesson 12

1. Nihon-to Oosutoraria dewa dochira no hoo-ga hiroi desu-ka.

2. Kono kissaten-wa totemo konde imasu ne.

3. Ano tatemono-ga ichiban takai desu.

4. Motto ookina seetaa-ga hoshii desu.

5. Hiragana yori-mo kantan desu.

6. Kono ningyoo wa hoka no ningyoo X yori mo takai desu.

7. Sono eiga to ano eiga wa dochira no hoo ga omoshiroi desu ka.

8. Kono saizu no hoo ga ookii X desu.

9. Watashi wa motto X ookina seetaa o kaitai desu.

10. Motto X akarui iro no mono ga arimasu ka.

Lesson 13

1. Mori-san-wa shinrigaku-no hon-o yonda-to omoimasu.

2. Kare-wa koogaku-o benkyoo shita-to omoimashita.

3. Watashi-no ushiro-ni suwatte iru onnanohito-wa gohan-o tabete imasu.

4. Hon-o yonde iru otokonohito-wa Jonson-san desu.

5. Kuruma-o unten shite iru onnanohito-wa Tookyoo-no kata desu.

6. Isshukan ni ichido X shinrigaku no kyooshitsu ni ikimasu.

7. Sushi o tabete iru X hito wa sensei ni naru to omoimasu.

8. Yamada-san no ushiro ni suwatte iru X hito wa Mori-san desu.

9. Megane o kakete iru X hito wa sensei desu.

10. Tanaka-san wa daigaku de iroirona supootsu o shita to omoimasu.

Lesson 14

1. Anata-wa Nihon-no zasshi-o yonda koto-ga arimasu-ka.

2. Anata-wa shashin-o totta koto-ga arimasu-ka.

3. Sono daibutsu-wa rippa desu.

4. Kio tsukete kudasai.

5. Akachan-wa aruite iru-no

desu.

6. Donna chizu desu-ka.

7. Kare-wa sukii-o shite iru-no desu.

8. Konna kamera-o tsukatta koto-ga arimasu-ka.

9. Kanojo-wa gakushi-o sotsugyoo shimashita.

10. Kanji-wa hiragana-yori-mo muzukashii desu.

Lesson 15

1. Daigaku ni ita toki rekishi o benkyoo shimashita.

2. Tanaka-san wa shigoto no ato de sake o nomitai to iimashita.

3. Ano hito wa jogingu o shinagara iyahoon o shite imasu.

4. Yamada-san wa zasshi ga zenzen nai to iimashita.

5. Hara-san wa tabako o suinagara hanashi-o suru-no desu.

6. Toyota ni tsutomete ita X toki X iroirona seihin o shookai shimashita.

7. Harada-san wa ⌈anata wa kono hon o yonda ka⌋-to kikimashita.

8. Yamada-san no tsukutta X gohan wa totemo X oishikatta desu.

9. Watashitachi ga kinoo X mita bideo wa sugokatta-n desu, X.

10. Hara-san wa anata ga katta seetaa wa kirei da to iimashita.

Lesson 16

1. Sono akachan-wa jibun-de arukemasu.

2. Obaa-san-wa eigo-ga hanasemasu.

3. Hara-san-wa tenisu-ga dekimasu.

4. Tenki-wa samuku natte imasu.

5. Yonin-de suwaremasu.

6. Natsu yasumi watashi-wa Sapporo-ni iku koto-ga dekimasu.

7. Tanaka-san-wa sukii-ga joozu-ni natte imasu.

8. Hitori-de uchi-ni koraremasu-ka.

9. Kekkon shiki-wa subarashikatta-to omoimasu.

10. Futari-wa kissaten-de o-bentoo-o tabeta no desu.

Lesson 17

1. Yuube, okurimono-o kawanakatta.

2. Raishuu kyooju-to hanasu yotei desu.

3. Jikan-ga nakatta-no desu.

4. Watashi-wa o-tera-ni ikitaku nai-to omoimasu.

5. Hara-sama-wa Honda-ni

tsutomete irasshaimasu-ka.

6. Kono shuumatsu sukii-o shitaku arimasen.

7. Watashi-wa Tookyoo-ni sunde orimasu.

8. Sono kuukoo-wa ookiku nai.

9. Nihon-no zasshi-wa Amerika-no zasshi-to chigaimasu.

10. Ashita, Oosutoraria-ni iku tsumori desu.

Lesson 18

1. Chichi-ga kono tokei-o kuremashita.

2. Otooto-ni tokei-o moraimashita.

3. Sensei-ga jisho-o kudasaimashita.

4. Sensei-ni pen-o itadakimashita.

5. Haha-wa Amerika-ni sunde orimasu.

6. Ojama shimashita.

7. Doozo, okamainaku.

8. Imooto-wa juuyon-sai desu.

9. Ani-wa Nihon-ni kitagatte iru-to omoimasu.

10. Morita sensei-wa chichi-no ie-ni irasshaimashita.

Lesson 19

1. Sensei-ga hanashi-o kaite kudasaimashita.

2. Watashi-wa Matsumoto-san-ni

yuubinkyoku-ni tsurete itte itadakimashita.

3. Watashi-wa Hara sensei-ni shoosetsu-o sashiagemashita.

4. Watashi-wa imooto-ni nihongo-no hon-o agemashita.

5. Morita-san-ni kono hagaki-o okutte hoshii desu.

6. Watashi <u>wa</u> haha <u>ni</u> bideo <u>o</u> agemashita.

7. Watashi <u>wa</u> sensei <u>ni</u> jibiki <u>o</u> sashiagemashita.

8. Chichi <u>ga</u> watashi <u>ni</u> hon <u>o</u> kaite <u>X</u> kuremashita.

9. Anata <u>ni</u> kore <u>o</u> mite <u>X</u> hoshii desu.

10. Kyoo <u>X</u> Mitsutake-san <u>wa</u> koko <u>ni</u> kuru <u>to</u> omoimasu.

Lesson 20

1. Ano kado de magaranaide kudasai.

2. Basu-wa sanji-ni koko-de tomaru hazu desu.

3. Anata-no (ga) tsukutta gohan-o tabete mo ii desu-ka.

4. Asatte, watashi-wa sukii-o suru tsumori desu.

5. Kono kado-o migi-ni magatte-wa ikemasen.

6. Kono koosaten-no temae-de yuu taan shite-mo ii desu-ka.

7. Densha-de Kyooto-ni itte-mo ii desu-ka.

8. Kyoo watashi-wa shigoto-o hachiji-ni oeru tsumori desu.

9. Untenshu-san, kochiragawa de tomaranaide kudasai.

10. Tookyoo-ni itte, tokei-o kaimasu.

Lesson 21

1. Kyoo-wa shinbun-o yondari sushi-o tsukuttari shite imasu.

2. Genkin-o hikidasu-no-wa, kono kyasshu kaado-o tsukawanakute-wa ikemasen.

3. Haha-no okurimono-o kawanakute-wa ikemasen.

4. Yonjuppeeji made yomanakute wa ikemasen.

5. En-o doru-ni ryoogae shite kudasai.

6. Morita-san-ga suki datta resutoran-ni itte mimashoo.

7. Shujin-no tsukutta gohan-o tabete mimashoo.

8. Akachan-wa tabetari, nemuttari shite imasu.

9. Atsuku narimashita kara mado-o akenakereba narimasen.

10. Kooza-o hirakanakereba narimasen.

Lesson 22

1. Sensei wa gakusei ni iroirona X hon o yomasemasu.

2. Kachoo wa juugyooin ni gorufu

ni ikasemasu.

3. Yamada-san ga aitai hito wa Ai Bi Emu ni tsutomete iru X soo desu.

4. Hara-san no hoshigatte X ita bideo wa omoshirosoo desu.

5. Yagi-san no musume san wa akarusoona X kodomo desu.

6. Hayaku kaerasete kudasai.

7. Kaichoo-wa kaigi chuu da soo desu.

8. Matasete kudasai.

9. Sore-wa takasoona kabin desu.

10. Shihainin-wa purojekuto-o kyoojuu-ni katazukeru soo desu.

Lesson 23

1. Tabun keiri bu-no hitotachi-wa Yamada-san-no soobetsukai-ni kuru deshoo.

2. O-sashimi-wa furukereba, tabenai hoo-ga ii-no desu.

3. Moshi sono geki-ga ninki-ga attara, kippu-wa kaenai-to omoimasu.

4. Musume-ga sono omocha-o sukinaraba, sore-o kaimasu.

5. Kikaku-shitsu-no gooi-o ete, sannen inai-ni kaigai-ni shinshutsu suru koto-ni natte imasu.

6. Tenki-ni nattara jogingu-o suru yotei desu.

7. En-ga takaku nattara, kaigai-e

shinshutsu suru deshoo.

8. Watashitachi-wa purojekuto-o kyoojuu-ni katazuketara, resutoran-ni iku tsumori desu.

9. Booeki gaisha-ni tsutomereba, yoku gaikoku-ni dekakeru deshoo.

10. Watashi-wa supeingo-ga hetanaraba, yameru deshoo.

Lesson 24

1. Kikaku-shitsu-no gooi-o ete, keiyakusho-o kooshin suru koto-ni kimemashita.

2. Konpyuutaa-o o-tsukai-ni natte kudasai.

3. Ano mise-de e-o o-kai-ni natte kudasai.

4. Chichi-ga yuubinkyoku-o go-annai shimasu.

5. Ane-ga buchoo-ni o-denwa itashimasu.

6. Raigetsu Yooroppa-ni iku koto-ni kimemashita.

7. Toogi-o tsuzuketa-kekka, wagasha-wa kaigai-ni shinshitsu suru koto-ni kimemashita.

8. Renraku sasete itadakimasu.

9. Kanpai shimashoo.

10. Go-jinryoku itadakimashite, arigatoo gozaimasu.

Lesson 25

1. Rentogen-o toru tame-ni byooin-ni ikimasu.

2. Genki-ni naru tame-ni chuusha-o shimasu.

3. Toyota-no kaisha-ni kaigi-o kyanseru saremashita.

4. Basu-no doa-ni ashi-o hasamarete shimaimashita.

5. Nodo-ga itai node, kusuri-o nomimasu.

6. Ude ga totemo itai X desu. Desu kara, byooin de rentogen o torimasu.

7. Kusuri o kau X tame ni yakkyoku ni ikimasu.

8. Senshuu X tomodachi ni kaze o utsusarete X shimaimashita.

9. Hara-san no kodomo ni kaze o utsusarete X shimaimashita.

10. Yoku miru X tame ni megane o kakemasu.

JAPANESE-ENGLISH INDEX

U

W

Y

ENGLISH-JAPANESE INDEX

HIPPOCRENE BEGINNER'S SERIES TITLES

Arabic For Beginners
204 pages · 5½ x 8¼ · ISBN 0-7818-0114-1 · NA · $9.95pb · (18)

Beginner's Albanian
150 pages · 5 x 7 · ISBN 0-7818-0816-2 · W · $14.95pb · (537)

Beginner's Armenian
209 pages · 8½ x 5½ · ISBN 0-7818-0723-9 · W · $14.95pb · (226)

Beginner's Assyrian
138 pages · 5½ x 8½ · ISBN 0-7818-0677-1 · W · $11.95pb · (763)

Beginner's Bulgarian
207 pages · 5½ x 8½ · ISBN 0-7818-0300-4 · W · $9.95pb · (76)

Beginner's Chinese
150 pages · 5½ x 8½ · ISBN 0-7818-0566-X · W · $14.95pb · (690)

Beginner's Czech
167 pages · 5½ x 8½ · ISBN 0-7818-0231-8 · W · $9.95pb · (74)

Beginner's Dutch
173 pages · 5½ x 8½ · ISBN 0-7818-0735-2 · W · $14.95pb · (248)

Beginner's Esperanto
342 pages · 5½ x 8½ · ISBN 0-7818-0230-X · W · $14.95pb · (51)

Beginner's Gaelic
224 pages · 5½ x 8½ · ISBN 0-7818-0726-3 · W · $14.95pb · (255)

Beginner's Hungarian
101 pages · 5½ x 7 · ISBN 0-7818-0209-1 · W · $7.95pb · (68)

Beginner's Irish
150 pages · 5 x 7 · ISBN 0-7818-0784-0 · W · $14.95pb · (320)

Beginner's Lithuanian
471 pages · 6 x 9 · ISBN 0-7818-0678-X · W · $19.95pb · (764)

Beginner's Maori
121 pages · 5½ x 8½ · ISBN 0-7818-0605-4 · NA · $8.95pb · (703)

Beginner's Persian
288 pages · 5½ x 8½ · ISBN 0-7818-0567-8 · NA · $14.95pb · (696)

Beginner's Polish
118 pages · 5½ x 8½ · ISBN 0-7818-0299-7 · W · $9.95pb · (82)

Beginner's Romanian
105 pages · 5½ x 8½ · ISBN 0-7818-0208-3 · W · $7.95pb · (79)

Beginner's Russian
131 pages · 5½ x 8½ · ISBN 0-7818-0232-6 · W · $9.95pb · (61)

Beginner's Sicilian
159 pages · 5½ x 8½ · ISBN 0-7818-0640-2 · W · $11.95pb · (716)

Beginner's Slovak
180 pages · 5 x 7 · ISBN 0-7818-0815-4 · W · $14.95pb · (534)

Beginner's Swahili
200 pages · 5½ x 8½ · ISBN 0-7818-0335-7 · W · $9.95pb · (52)

Beginner's Turkish
300 pages · 5 x 7½ · ISBN 0-7818-0679-8 · NA · $14.95pb · (765)

Beginner's Ukrainian
130 pages · 5½ x 8½ · ISBN 0-7818-0443-4 · W · $11.95pb · (88)

Beginner's Vietnamese
515 pages · 7 x 10 · ISDN 0-7010-0411-6 · W · $19.95pb · (253)

Beginner's Welsh
171 pages · 5½ x 8½ · ISBN 0-7818-0589-9 · W · $9.95pb · (712)

Hippocrene
CHILDREN'S
ILLUSTRATED
JAPANESE
DICTIONARY

ENGLISH · JAPANESE
JAPANESE · ENGLISH

Also from Hippocrene Books...

NEW!

Hippocrene Children's Illustrated Japanese Dictionary
English-Japanese/Japanese-English

94 pages · 8½ x 11 · $14.95hc · ISBN 0-7818-0817-0 · W · (31) · *July 2000*

The most recent addition to the Hippocrene Children's Illustrated Foreign Language Dictionaries, a series of dictionaries designed to make learning vocabulary in a foreign language at an early age easy and enjoyable!

- Designed to be a child's very first foreign language dictionary, for ages 5-10.
- 500 entries, each accompanied by a large illustration.
- The book design allows a young child to focus on each word and picture and make the connection between them.
- Each entry features the word in English and its foreign language equivalent, along with commonsense phonetic pronunciation.
- Entries include people, animals, colors, numbers and objects that children encounter and use every day.

"With their absorbent minds, infinite curiosities and excellent memories, children have enormous capacities to master many languages. All they need is exposure and encouragement. The beautiful images and clear presentation make this dictionary a wonderful tool for unlocking your child's multilingual potential."
Deborah Dumont, M.A., M.Ed.
Child Psychologist and Educational Consultant

Also available in:
Arabic, Czech, French, German, Irish, Italian, Polish, Russian, Scottish Gaelic, Spanish and Swedish.

Hippocrene Far East and Pacific Language Dictionaries and Learning Guides

Bogutu-English/English-Bogutu Concise Dictionary
4,700 entries · 98 pages · 5½ x 9 · $9.95pb · ISBN 0-7818-0660-7 · W · (747)

Cambodian-English/English-Cambodian Standard Dictionary
15,000 entries · 355 pages · 5½ x 8¼ · $16.95pb · ISBN 0-87052-818-1· W · (143)

Cantonese Basic Course
416 pages · 5½ x 8½ · $19.95pb · ISBN 0-7818-0289-X · W · (117)

Dictionary of 1,000 Chinese Proverbs
200 pages · 5½ x 8½ · $11.95pb · ISBN 0-7818-0682-8 · W · (773)

NEW!
Dictionary of 1,000 Chinese Idioms
170 pages · 6 x 9 · $14.95pb · ISBN 0-7818-0820-0 ·W · (91)

Chinese Handy Dictionary
2,000 entries · 120 pages · 5 x 7¾ · $8.95pb · ISBN 0-87052-050-4 · USA · (347)

English-Chinese Pinyin Dictionary
10,000 entries · 500 pages · 4 x 6 · $19.95pb · ISBN 0-7818-0427-2 · USA · (509)

Ilocano-English Dictionary and Phrasebook
7,000 entries · 269 pages · 5½ x 8½ · $14.95pb · ISBN 0-7818-0642-9 · W · (718)

Indonesian-English/English-Indonesian Practical Dictionary
17,000 entries · 289 pages · 4¼ x 7 · $11.95pb · ISBN 0-87052-810-6 · NA · (127)

Japanese-English/English-Japanese Dictionary and Phrasebook

Designed to help visitors to Japan communicate with local people in everyday situations, this book introduces the basics of Japanese grammar, followed by extensive phrasebook chapters, comprehensive vocabulary, and a Japanese-English/English-Japanese dictionary.

2,300 entries · 220 pages · 3¾ x 7 · $12.95pb · ISBN 0-7818-0814-6 · W · (205)

Japanese-English/English-Japanese Concise Dictionary, Romanized

8,000 entries · 235 pages · 4 x 6 · $11.95pb · ISBN 0-7818-0162-1 · W · (474)

Mastering Japanese

339 pages · 5½ x 8½ · $14.95pb · ISBN 0-87052-923-4 · USA · (523)
2 cassettes: ISBN 0-87052-983-8 · $12.95 · USA · (524)

Japanese Handy Dictionary

3,400 entries · 120 pages · 5 x 7 · $8.95pb · ISBN 0-87052-962-5 · W · (466)

Korean-English/English-Korean Practical Dictionary

8,500 entries · 365 pages · 4 x 7¼ · $14.95pb · ISBN 0-87052-092-X · Asia and NA · (399)

Korean-English/English-Korean Handy Dictionary

4,000 entries · 178 pages · 5 x 8 · $8.95pb · ISBN 0-7818-0082-X · (438)

Lao Basic Course

350 pages · 5 x 8 · $19.95pb · ISBN 0-7818-0410-8 · W · (470)

Malay-English/English-Malay Standard Dictionary

21,000 entries · 631 pages · 5 x 7¼ · $16.95pb · ISBN 0-7818-0103-6 · (428)

Pilipino-English/English-Pilipino Concise Dictionary
5,000 entries · 389 pages · 4 x 6 · $8.95pb · ISBN 0-87052-491-7 · W · (393)

Pilipino-English/English-Pilipino Dictionary and Phrasebook
2,200 entries · 186 pages · 3¾ x 7 · $11.95pb · ISBN 0-7818-0451-5 · W · (295)

Tagalog-English/English-Tagalog (Pilipino) Standard Dictionary
20,000 entries · 363 pages · 5½ x 8½ · $14.95pb · ISBN 0-7818-0657-7 · W · (5)

English-Telugu Pocket Dictionary
12,000 entries · 386 pages · 5 x 7⅓· $17.50hc · ISBN 0-7818-0747-6 · W · (952)

Thai-English/English-Thai Dictionary and Phrasebook
1,800 entries · 200 pages · 3¾ x 7 · $12.95pb · ISBN 0-7818-0774-3 · W · (330)

Vietnamese-English/English-Vietnamese Standard Dictionary
12,000 entries · 501 pages · 5 x 7 · $19.95pb · ISBN 0-87052-924-2 · W · (529)

All prices subject to change without prior notice. **To purchase Hippocrene Books** contact your local bookstore, call (718) 454-2366, or write to: HIPPOCRENE BOOKS, 171 Madison Avenue, New York, NY 10016. Please enclose check or money order, adding $5.00 shipping (UPS) for the first book and $.50 for each additional book.